THE LEADERSHIP WHEEL

THE LEADERSHIP WHEEL

*Five Steps for Achieving Individual
and Organizational Greatness*

C. Clinton Sidle

First published 2005 by
PALGRAVE MACMILLAN™
175 Fifth Avenue, New York, N.Y. 10010 and
Houndmills, Basingstoke, Hampshire, England RG21 6XS.
Companies and representatives throughout the world.

PALGRAVE MACMILLAN is the global academic imprint of the Palgrave Macmillan division of St. Martin's Press, LLC and of Palgrave Macmillan Ltd. Macmillan® is a registered trademark in the United States, United Kingdom and other countries. Palgrave is a registered trademark in the European Union and other countries.

ISBN 1–4039–6919–1 hardback

Library of Congress Cataloging-in-Publication Data

Sidle, C. Clinton
  The leadership wheel : five steps for achieving individual and organizational greatness / C. Clinton Sidle.
      p.   cm.
  Includes bibliographical references and index.
  ISBN 1–4039–6919–1 (alk. paper)
  1. Leadership.   2. Organizational effectiveness.   I. Title.
HD57.7.S498   2005
658.4'092—dc22[2005041644

A catalogue record for this book is available from the British Library.

Design by Letra Libre, Inc.

First edition: September, 2005
10 9 8 7 6 5 4 3 2 1

Printed in the United States of America

TO AUBRYN AND CONNOR

CONTENTS

LIST OF FIGURES

ACKNOWLEDGEMENTS

This book is the result of a lifelong journey of wanting to become a better person and to help create a better world. Many people have contributed to this journey as guides and teachers and this work would not have been possible without them. So I want to give thanks and acknowledge them here.

Harry Kisker for planting the seed as a young adult, and for being a true inspiration and a lifelong friend.

Sri S. N. Goenka for introducing me to meditation and a new view of freedom.

Aubryn and Connor Sidle for opening my heart and being the special beings I had hoped them to be.

Rodney Napier for his mentorship in working with groups, and for introducing me to the Native American Medicine Wheel.

Dan Tillemans for his friendship and counsel, and for reawakening me to the power of the outdoors.

Roxi Bahar Hewartson for being a loyal friend and long-term learning partner on my journey.

Chester Warzynksi for fully appreciating my journey and serving as a constant counsel, friend, and inspiration.

James Spotted Elk for being a rainbow brother and sharing his wisdom of Native American sacred ways.

Chogyam Trungpa Rinpoche for his profound vision for the world and creating enlightened society.

Peter Hurst for his friendship and patience in introducing me to Tibetan Buddhism.

Anne MacQuarrie for leading me to Shambhala training and Thinley Norbu Rinpoche.

Marlowe Brooks for her friendship and teaching me the ways of the wisdom energies of the Tibetan Mandala.

Esther Sullivan for her friendship and leading me to Khenchen Palden Sherab Rinpoche and Khenpo Tsewang Dongya Rinpoche.

Celia Barnes for her constant support and encouragement in writing this book.

Roy H. Park Jr. and his family for generously providing a wonderful practice field in the form of the Roy H. Park Leadership Fellows Program

Thinley Norbu Rinpoche for revealing the power of devotion in living the path of the heart.

Khenchen Palden Sherab Rinpoche and Khenpo Tsewang Dongyal Rinpoche for being my root teachers.

I also want to give a special thanks to my editors Paul Cash and Airié Stuart for their support and insight in bringing this book to fruition.

INTRODUCTION

The most exciting breakthrough of the 21st century will occur not because of technology, but because of an expanding concept of what it means to be human.

— John Naisbitt[1]

The premise of this book is that leadership is a particular way of approaching life, one that is an irrepressible outcome of being committed to a lifelong process of fulfilling human potential, not only for oneself but also for others. The book frames leadership as a vehicle for personal and organizational transformation in a way that redefines both leadership and the purposes of business. It begins with a look into the inner work of leaders, the work of personal development, and then turns to the outer work, the work of developing healthy relationships, teams, and organizations. In doing so, it reveals a unique, elegant, and powerful framework that serves both as a theoretical guide for understanding this process and as a practical guide for developing leaders who do well for themselves while doing good in the world.

Perhaps as never before, the challenges of our world today demand such a perspective on leadership. Globalization and advances in technology have combined to increase the pace of change, making the world more complex each day than it was the one before. And while the rise of modern capitalism has greatly expanded the material support for human life, the accelerated consumption of resources and the associated complexity and speed attending it threaten the health of the planet and the human spirit.

Environmentalist Paul Hawken points out that in the twentieth century alone we destroyed more of nature than in all of our prior history. In the name of growth and progress, we decimated forests, polluted lakes and the atmosphere, and lost *billions* of tons of fertile topsoil. If our current production system were rolled out to the rest of the world, our store of natural capital (water, minerals, trees, soil, air) would last only ten years. Most scientists also now agree that our carbon dioxide emissions are producing a global warming that is changing the climate, creating extended droughts, and melting polar ice caps that are thousands of years old.[2]

The social impact of our dominant economic system is just as striking. We produce more wealth than we can use in the developed world, create efficiencies that leave one-third of the world's population underemployed, and have built a society in which the top 1 percent earns more than the bottom 40 percent combined.[3] These trends are surely unsustainable because the forces for social and economic justice will eventually rise in resistance, as increasing terrorism and turmoil in the developing world show.

More insidious, however, is the impact on the human spirit. The powerful forces of modern capitalism are helping to shape a narrow society in which only material success seems to count. Social philosopher Charles Handy argues that "the system that was supposed to free us, is instead enslaving us to the economic imperative."[4] It turns us into workaholics, stealing time from family, friends, community, and higher human aspirations. It has made us confused about the purposes of life, and we chase success instead of meaning.

Too many of us have forgotten that there are environmental, social, psychological, and even spiritual limits to our current ways of doing business.

Perhaps the biggest challenge facing those who would lead today is a personal one. For our system to work, we need balanced, principled leadership. Yet self-interest often overpowers our leaders, and threatens the very efficacy of our system. Ironically, the very forces of self-interest that drive our system can also destroy it. Every year we witness executives and leaders derailed by greed, corruption, and collusion. Many of them reap millions before their fall, while misleading their investors and employees. Corporate boards, Wall Street analysts, and auditors have all at times been guilty of failing to fulfill their fiduciary responsibilities and giving in to temptation. It is human nature to be tempted, but as Abraham Lincoln once said, "If you want to test a man's character, give him power."

The combined effect of these challenges is that many of us, not just our leaders, have lost sight of wealth as a means to life and not life's goal. Too many of us have forgotten that there are environmental, social, psychological, and even spiritual limits to our current ways of doing business. We have become confused about what gives us spirit and meaning. We have been swept up in the momentum of a capitalism that narrowly links meaning with economic growth and financial success. The corporate scandals of the first few years of this century awakened us to these dangers, resulting in a wave of renewed ethical vigilance, but we are consistently challenged to find a more balanced way.

While modern capitalism has provided us with a great degree of comfort and freedom, it still leaves us with the questions of how long, for what purpose, and to what end. As playwright and Czech president Vaclav Havel admonished, "The salvation of this world lies nowhere else but in the human heart. . . . Without a global revolution of consciousness nothing will change for the better, and the catastrophe towards which this world is headed will be unavoidable."[5]

"For capitalism to be our servant rather than our master," as Charles Handy says, we need a fundamental shift in our perspective on the purpose of business.[6] No other social or economic system has proven superior to capitalism, but the way we practice it needs to be more sustainable. I believe that just as our capitalist system has led us here, it can also lead us out. We need a new brand of capitalism that treats people with fairness compassion, and respect, and the environment as a long-term asset.

There is no doubt that business drives economic and social change, and that business has the greatest chance to fundamentally address the imbalances just described. Advances in technology and changes in environmental, economic, and social policies will help, but they will not be sufficient. Business needs to drive the change to a new kind of capitalism by becoming more than just an instrument for profit. It needs to be called into the service of our higher needs, and made to provide for the environmental, social, and spiritual good of everyone just as it provides for material good.

While modern capitalism has provided us with a great degree of comfort and freedom, it still leaves us with the questions of how long, for what purpose, and to what end.

This is not revolutionary thinking. Adam Smith, the grandfather of modern economic theory, showed us over two centuries ago that while self-interest helps the general good by providing an "invisible hand"[7] to guide economic forces, it must be balanced with "sympathy"[8] or service to others if capitalism is to endure as a workable system of life. Self-interest is critical for aligning market forces, but it cannot be the only factor that drives business behavior. It must be restrained by a conscience, and by a desire to help cultivate the highest order of the community.

Likewise John Maynard Keynes, one of the most influential economists of the twentieth century, maintained that the economy's purpose is to generate the material basis for enabling society and its citizens to explore the higher dimensions of human existence.[9] Otherwise the system becomes imbalanced, and implodes from the weight of accumulated wealth and power in the hands of a few. Good business must promote good citizenship, and every act of commerce must be an act of service. We have fallen from this original vision, but the market system still can be made to balance self-interest with service.

In this book I argue that leadership is the key for making this shift. In their classic work on corporate culture and performance, Harvard professors John Kotter and James Heskett were among the first to show that the single most important factor in successful organizational change is competent leadership.[10] Leaders offer the highest leverage point for change because they are critical to establishing the strategic direction of the organization and creating and maintaining its culture. They set the tone through where they focus their attention, how they react in crises, and the example they provide for others. Just as important, this research shows that leaders of enduring companies are concerned about the welfare of all stakeholders and are personally involved in creating supportive, developmental climates for everyone.

. . . leadership is the key for making this shift.

The burning question, then, is how to produce such leaders. Although we have given leadership development a great deal of attention in recent years, we still lack a common framework for understanding what leadership is and how it is developed. As leadership guru James McGregor Burns put it, "Leadership is one of the most yet least understood phenomena on earth."[11] From Plato and Confucius to the litany of today's management authors, philosophers and theorists through the ages have struggled not only to define leadership but also to find a common perspective from which to study it.

The theories abound. Some say that personality characteristics determine leadership quality, and they focus their research on the traits of great people. Others take the situational perspective, arguing that the context creates the person. Still others follow contingency theory, saying that the most effective leaders adapt their style to the demands of the situation. There are also models of *transactional leadership* that view leadership as a reciprocal exchange between leaders and followers; *transformational leadership,* which suggests that a leader's role is to elevate followers to a higher moral level; *adaptive leadership,* which focuses on the leader's ability to learn and narrow the gap between the values people hold and the reality they face; and *servant leadership,* which encourages leading through serving others. There are even a Theory X, a Theory Y, and a Theory Z. And while some have claimed that leadership is something innate and available to only a few, others contend it can be learned and accessible by many.

. . . my personal search for . . . enlightened leadership has gone hand in hand with an interest in ancient cultures, traditions, and philosophical systems, to see what wisdom the old world may be able to offer the new.

Over the last decade, my personal search for a way to develop enlightened leadership has gone hand in hand with an interest in ancient cultures, traditions, and philosophical systems, to see what wisdom the old world may be able to offer the new. To paraphrase philosopher Alfred North Whitehead, the history of philosophical and spiritual thought consists of nothing more than a series of footnotes to the ancients.[12] In turning to the wisdom of the past, we might find clues for how to address some of the problems of the present.

Myths and philosophical views of ancient and indigenous traditions are often compelling in their simplicity and in their inherent wisdom. Centuries and continents often separated these cultures, yet they shared remarkable similarities in their basic views of human nature and the cosmos. Somehow they were able to identify, independently of one another, certain universal truths that cross boundaries of time and space. These truths are what Swiss psychologist Carl Jung called archetypal, and part of the collective human unconscious.[13] They are self-evident, pointing to the very essence of what it is to be human and to be engaged in human endeavor.

Yet some may argue that if the ancients knew so much and lived so wisely, we would be better off today than we are. But as University of Chicago psychologist Mihaly Csikszentmihalyi says, "To discard the hard-won information on how to live accumulated by our ancestors, or to expect to discover a viable set of goals all by oneself, is misguided hubris."[14] The age-old problem has not been with the idea but in the execution of it. We tend to ignore the lessons of the past, wanting to create new meaning of our own. So we restart the discovery process over and over again with each new generation.

It is true that these are things we need to work out on our own, but the ancients provide a well-worn path for those who wish to benefit from it. For me the question is: How can we assimilate the wisdom of the past for the sake

We'll look at leadership as a vehicle through which people can become fully human and transform organizations into movements of the human spirit.

of the future without losing the freedom and individuality that we have fought so hard to gain? This book shares the basics of what I've learned about this, and how leadership and leadership development provide an opportunity to capture this wisdom, pass it on from generation to generation, and create hope and momentum for the future.

As mentioned earlier, the premise of ancient philosophy, as well as of this book, is that the purpose of life is to grow toward human fulfillment. We'll look at leadership as a vehicle through which people can become fully human and transform organizations into movements of the human spirit. This kind of leadership is meant for everyone, not just the people at the top, and it develops from the inside out.

THE LEADERSHIP WHEEL

We'll begin by looking at ancient myths and philosophical traditions to help identify root motivations and inherent potential common to everyone. I then introduce an ancient, five-point paradigm I call the Leadership Wheel for understanding learning, change, and personal effectiveness that has proven its value and withstood the test of time for more than a thousand years. This simple, intuitive, and compelling paradigm serves not only the development of leadership, but also interpersonal relationships, teams, and organizations. It is based on the premise of human fulfillment, and draws on the basic goodness of human nature to address the imbalances of our time. In each chapter I provide time-tested exercises and practical applications that help actualize the potential pointed out by the Wheel.

I have used the Leadership Wheel and the exercises in all my work as a professional and a consultant in leadership, team, and organizational development over the last 15 years. From executives to academics, from middle managers to shop floor workers, I have presented the Wheel to thousands of people in well over a hundred organizations in both the private and public sectors. Although a unique framework, its authenticity and validity have never been challenged, and many participants in the programs I have developed based on the Wheel have called their experiences life-changing. The Leadership Wheel has never failed to inspire and motivate people to learn and grow as professionals and to create greater balance in their lives. Since 1998 I have also used it as the basis to design and deliver the Roy H. Park Leadership Fellows Program in the Johnson School of Management at Cornell University. This program is widely recognized as one of the premier leadership development programs in management education, and I have used the program as a practice field to develop and test many of the ideas contained in this book.

I begin in chapter 1 with a discussion of how we all possess an inherent urge to become, a hungry spirit, that can lead to destructive behaviors when turned exclusively toward self-interest. The discussion introduces the myth of the heroic journey as a metaphor for harnessing that urge and directing it toward human fulfillment and the greater good. With a variety of mythological, historical, and current leadership examples, I contend that the desire to embark on such a journey is inherent in each of us—it just needs to be fully awakened. I show that leadership begins as an inner journey and then manifests outwardly in actions that benefit the community. The chapter provides five examples of contemporary leaders from all walks of life who have embarked on this journey.

In chapter 2 I discuss how the ancients represented this becoming spirit in a paradigm with five archetypal aspects. This ancient paradigm maps the essence of the human mind, heart, and psyche. It reveals, with uncanny accuracy, a five-step process in the development of the ego, with each archetype having a wisdom aspect and a shadow aspect. The chapter also recasts this traditional paradigm into a modern framework for understanding and facilitating the development of leadership, learning, and change. This unique and highly integrated framework has powerful implications for how we think about what goes into the making of a leader.

Chapter 3 presents the Leadership Wheel (see figure I.1) as an action-learning model for guiding individual learning, change, and leadership development. It first shows that no other leadership framework offers a model for both leadership and leadership development, and shows how the Leadership Wheel is also a Learning Wheel. Then it draws parallels to and builds on modern management research. To illustrate and reinforce my main points, I bring in several contemporary examples of how leaders learn. I conclude by discussing different strategies for *how* to make a leader, and how that parallels *what* makes a leader. Leadership is a result, not a cause. It is an inside job.

Chapter 4 applies the action-learning framework of the Wheel to the development of teams. In contrast to many prevailing beliefs about teams, the

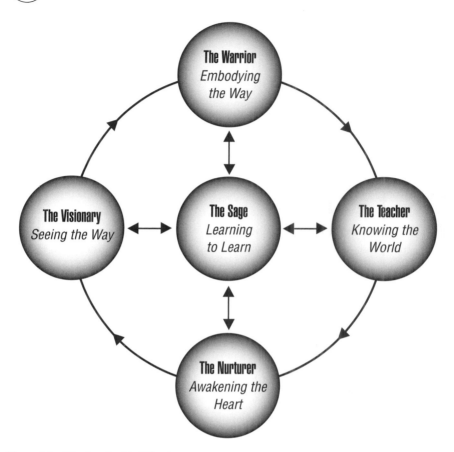

Figure I.1   The Leadership Wheel

Wheel explains how teams develop by consciously doing their task and reviewing their process as opposed to using separate process interventions. It
also shows how teams are important to individual as well as organizational
development, commitment, and performance, and how following the action-
learning framework leads to an enhanced team-learning culture. I illustrate
the main points with several examples and comparison with the current research of leading thinkers.

Chapter 5 applies the action-learning framework of the Wheel to organizational development and change at a systems level. I revisit the basic questions about the fundamental purposes of business, explore organizations as
purpose-seeking systems, and show how truly enduring organizations and
businesses are based on a cause that goes beyond simply making a profit. I
draw on and build upon key ideas of management author Russell Ackoff, who

describes organizations as purpose-seeking systems, as well as the work of Jim Collins and Jerry Porras about the core ideologies of truly enduring companies. The chapter provides 15 design principles associated with the 5 archetypes of the Wheel and shows how leaders can use them to help create meaning, facilitate successful change, and transform their organizations.

Chapter 6 draws on the ideas and the exercises of the preceding chapters and shows how to design and develop a leadership and organization program that results in more enlightened leadership and more socially responsible activity for the organization. I maintain that such a program must start with an individual developmental process that is structured, integrated, and sustained in a way that draws on inspiration from within the individual and that is supported by the system from without. With this established, I then show how to use real-life teams and change projects within the organization as action-learning vehicles for personal as well as team and organizational development.

THE HEROIC JOURNEY AND THE CREATION OF ENLIGHTENED SOCIETY

The world is too much with us; late and soon,
Getting and spending, we lay waste our powers:
Little we see in Nature that is ours;
We have given our hearts away, a sordid boon!

William Wordsworth

THE NATURE OF BEING HUMAN

To be human is to become. As human beings, we possess a hungry spirit and
an inherent need to find our place in the world and relevance for what we do.
This need to become is a process that Swiss psychologist Carl Jung saw as
the very essence of our evolutionary urge. It is a drive to complete ourselves,
to become more whole in a process he called individuation.

This urge to become can be traced to something in our psyche that says
we have fallen from grace or lost our original home, and that the only way back
is by making ourselves and our world whole. In Western tradition it is expressed in the story of Adam and Eve being expelled from the Garden of Eden
and striving to find a return home. In the East it is seen as the truth of suffering and the quest to overcome ignorance and return to our original nature. It

is also at the core of the creation stories throughout the world's indigenous cultures that often reveal a deep, elemental fear of being inadequate and not being enough.

Philosophical and spiritual traditions worldwide say that one of the few things we all possess equally is this deep sense of incompleteness that compels us to search for ever higher forms of understanding and wholeness. This root psychic force explains all our motivations in human endeavor and all our hopes and fears. It has launched wars, crusades, and nation states, as well as art, science, and religion.

Our cultures mold this evolutionary urge to become. In today's busy world, it is often shaped by the economic imperative and manifests itself in daily life as the pursuit of self-interest and the drive to achieve, to succeed, and to advance in our personal endeavors. In business, in sports, in all forms of competition, the driving motivation is to win, to improve, and to become better.

Likewise, the accumulation of wealth, power, and material goods, as well as the drive for position, prestige, and recognition, stem from a desire to become greater than what we fear ourselves to be. Our yearning for romantic connection has created whole industries to support this longing. Yet for many, having more and consuming more does not fill the void. We are still left with an existential angst.

This root psychic force explains all our motivations in human endeavor and all our hopes and fears.

The difficult truth is that this energy to become, this evolutionary life force of ours, when directed primarily toward self-interest, leads to a growing sense of emptiness and a gnawing lack of fulfillment. When we focus on ourselves, we lose the sense of belonging and the sense of connection to others. As a result, keeping up and expanding our personal enterprise easily turns into the paramount goal in our lives, often equating happiness with the consumption of the new and better and allowing speed and consumerism to hijack meaning—leaving us confused. Many of us fail to recognize the situation, and become increasingly stressed, hollow, or disconnected. To quote Shakespeare,

We are such stuff
As dreams are made on, and our little life
Is rounded with a sleep.[2]

In centuries past, the world was slower. People's energies were more grounded in a sense of identity that arose through connections with nature, family, and religion. As artisans, farmers, and merchants, people were connected to their work through personal ownership. Industrialization, technology, and increasing mobility, however, have since combined to rupture these traditional ties and erode the ground where the sense of identity, belonging, and relevance were customarily found. The market has replaced the church and the state as the primary regulator of change and put forth new ways of affirming ourselves through wealth, prestige, and security.

These changes have brought many extraordinary advances in civilization and human life. Yet they also take a toll on our mental and planetary health. Making money has been a tremendous driver of change, but it is *how* we make money that will count most in the future.

Our challenge today is to find ways to transform this energy of becoming from a preoccupation with personal achievement to an aspiration toward greater human fulfillment.

The irony is that the very energy that produces selfish behavior is the same as that which pursues noble causes. When we balance this energy with a pursuit of self-understanding and meaningful endeavor, we find relatedness, and develop a happier, healthier, and more fulfilled life. We see that one of the most satisfying things in life is to serve a purpose beyond ourselves. As Albert Schweitzer once said, "One thing I know: the only ones among you who will be really happy are those who will have sought and found how to serve."[3] The ancient Navaho knew this when they spoke of the need to be "selfish but social"[4]—to strive for success, but to do so cooperatively and for the benefit of the whole. Like Adam Smith, they found it important to succeed personally while doing well by all.

Our challenge today, then, is to find ways to transform this energy of becoming from a preoccupation with personal achievement to an aspiration toward greater human fulfillment.

OUR LEADERSHIP OPPORTUNITY

Leadership development is an opportunity to address this challenge—it can be made to serve self and help others to grow as human beings. Framed in this way, leadership development becomes a voyage of inner and outer discovery, and it is for everyone, not just the people at the top. It is a way of focusing humanity's evolutionary urge in ways that tap into our deepest human potential, and manifests itself as doing well for ourselves while doing good for our world.

This process starts with a look inward. University of Missouri professor Lee Bolman says that truly great leaders, leaders who have made lasting, positive contributions to the world, have a deeply held value system that is grounded in the belief in the basic goodness of human nature, which gives them the charisma, magic, and power to wield great influence.[5] They have led lives of personal inquiry that have enabled them to tap into deeply held beliefs that take them to the source of relevance, security, and identity and provide them with the clarity, commitment, and perseverance necessary to achieve the extraordinary. They have learned to express themselves authentically, according to their own deeply held beliefs, as opposed to trying to prove themselves against someone else's standard. Being consciously grounded in their own inner reality brings them happiness and a sense of abundance that enables them to turn outward, transcending self-interest, to care about, respect, and serve others in ways that inspire trust and confidence.

This process of first looking inward and then turning outward to care for and serve others is exemplified by extraordinary leaders of our time—men and women from many different walks of life. In this chapter and the ones that follow I provide brief portraits of leaders who have tapped their energy of becoming and turned it toward human fulfillment—doing well for themselves while doing good for the world. These high-profile examples draw attention to a type and style of leadership required to bring about positive and lasting change in our world. The message of these examples, however, is for everyone. It is about an attitude toward life and a way of living in the world. We each possess an inherent potential for making a difference, and that can manifest itself in many forms and from any place in organizational life.

$$\oplus$$

DAVID NEELEMAN, founder and CEO of JetBlue, is one excellent example. In the last 30 years there have been only two sustained airline start-ups; the first was Southwest in the 1970s, and the other is JetBlue. In the face of critics who scoffed at creating a low-cost airline out of New York City, Neeleman launched JetBlue in January of 2000 with a commitment to bringing humanity back to air travel. Offering low fares, friendly service, and a high quality product, JetBlue has since expanded to 30 cities operating 70 Airbus 320s, and become the largest carrier out of New York. JetBlue also boasts the lowest passenger-mile cost and a consistent record of profitability in an industry in which staggering losses are routine. Widely touted for outstanding customer service by industry magazines, JetBlue was the only start-up airline that did not reduce payroll in the aftermath of 9/11.

Low-key, humble, and caring, Neeleman thrives in one of the world's toughest businesses. His inimitable leadership style has brought him wide acclaim and earned him a reputation of unwavering commitment to people and customer service. Neeleman's first priority is take care of your people, because if you take care of your people, they will take care of your customers. "If you speak down to people, hold back information, and treat them like they are just employees, you will not be successful."[6] He grooms the people of JetBlue to be servant leaders by supporting others and helping them grow. "It is countless acts of kindness that happen on a day-to-day basis that create the heart and soul" of this company.[7] Modeling this philosophy and keeping it close to heart, he believes, leads to happy customers who come back regularly and spread the word.

Neeleman's leadership style is deeply rooted in a value system that emerged from his faith and his personal reflections in facing adversity. He suffers from attention deficit disorder—"there are positive things with it, creativity and other things. But there is a dark side that you know you are completely disorganized."[8] As a result, he did poorly in school, lacked self-confidence, and had doubts about whether he could make a living. A turning point for him was when, as a young Morman, he served as a missionary in the slums of Rio de Janeiro, where he spent days in religious study and spreading the word. He baptized two hundred converts. For the first time in his life he felt that he had accomplished something. He gained confidence, and when "I got back to University of Utah, I got straight As."[9] Intertwined with his faith, he also learned humility. "I spent most of my time with the poor and figured out they were the happiest people . . . they saw life in a proper perspective. I really became incapable of thinking I was better than anyone else. That suits me well at JetBlue."[10]

This value system has guided him in building a culture of commitment and service at JetBlue. When prospective staff are interviewed, for instance, they must buy into the company values of safety, caring, integrity, fun, and passion. He wants people who care. He recalls a story of a pilot applicant who called to complain to him about not getting a job. "I have fifteen thousand hours of flight time but didn't get the job." Neeleman asked the interviewer why, and she said, "I asked him, what else have you done besides just sitting and flying an airplane?" He didn't come up with one single example. "That's not someone we want in our company."[11]

For Neeleman, this commitment to service starts with the question, "Do you matter?"[12] He wants people to know how they can inspire others and make a difference. He challenges everyone to look inward to know who they are and what is important. For him, "the only way of achieving joy and happiness is serving other people."[13] Realizing this was a process for him—a lesson he learned to model over and over again in his career, whether it is rolling up his sleeves to help with loading bags, or limiting his salary to $200,000 so the company wealth can be shared with others. For Neeleman, as it is for each of us, this quest is a journey, an archetypal journey of personal learning and development.

THE HEROIC JOURNEY:
DISCOVERING THE INNER SIDE OF GREATNESS

The attempt to harness this evolutionary urge to become and find meaning is what comparative mythology scholar Joseph Campbell called the Heroic Journey. He saw this journey as a spontaneous production of the psyche and an archetypal process expressed in the myths and traditions throughout our ancient world cultures. It is a universal truth that portrays humanity's search for meaning in a tale of separation, initiation, transformation, and return.

In these myths the hero ventures forth into the unknown, faces miraculous tests and ordeals, wins mighty victories, and returns with the power to bestow boons upon others. Examples in Western culture include Odysseus' struggles on his return from Troy to release his family from bondage, and Percival in his 20-year quest for the Holy Grail to save King Arthur's kingdom. In the East we see King Gesar fighting the spirits of the four directions to pacify and unite his Tibetan kingdom, and Arjuna in the story of the Bhagavad Gita facing his doubts and fears before entering the battlefield to unite the land of India. On this journey, the hero embarks on a transformational experience that brings learning and change.

The attempt to harness this evolutionary urge to become and find meaning is what comparative mythology scholar Joseph Campbell called the Heroic Journey.

The Heroic Journey is very relevant to how we frame leadership and live our everyday lives. Leadership is about movement and change, and change begins at a personal level. The root meaning of leadership is "to go first." Every act of leadership is an act of courage. Thus a heroic person is anyone able to face the risks and challenges of change despite fears and uncertainties. For us, it is about mobilizing ourselves to tackle the challenges in our lives. Once we cross the threshold into change we leave our comfort zone and cross into unknown territory. Successfully meeting these challenges requires us to let go of old ways of doing things—relationships, perspectives, even identities—and enter new beginnings.

Heroic people are not always bigger than life—they are normal people like any of us who have struggled with the challenges of life. We all have faced change at some point, taking on the risk and facing the fears that often come with doing something new or different. For some of us, it is going off to college, getting married, traveling abroad, or quitting a job. For others, it is trying to resolve a conflict that we have been avoiding, or taking a stand on an issue we believe in. For still others, it is often just the simple acts of courage involved in facing the recurrent challenges of work and everyday life.

In today's world, this life-forming archetypal energy is often dominated by an outer quest to inflate the ego and fulfill self-interest such as the pursuit of wealth, power, or prestige. In the myths of our ancient traditions, however, the Heroic Journey turns this energy toward an inner quest to awaken the self and all human potential. It is the story in which we break away from our culturally induced projections, limitations, and habitual patterns, enter into the world of the unknown to rediscover lost parts of our selves, learn to experience life more fully, openly, and directly, and return to share what we have learned in order to make our communities better. It is an inward as well as an outward journey. Instead of fulfilling self-interest, the Heroic Journey serves self-discovery, the pursuit of wisdom, and the needs of humanity. To embark on the Journey, then, is to awaken from our slumber and dare to set out to achieve something extraordinary. We learn that even the most ordinary of circumstances can be transformed, when we see them through the light of who we might be.

Instead of fulfilling self-interest, the Heroic Journey serves self-discovery, the pursuit of wisdom, and the needs of humanity.

In addition to the mythological examples above, history is filled with examples of heroic leaders and of greatness achieved through a life examined. Political leaders, saints, and revolutionaries of all kinds have achieved the extraordinary by first knowing who they are and then applying their gifts to the benefit of others. Pericles, for example, was guided by the Greek philosophical tradition in overseeing one of the world's first experiments in democracy.

King Ashoka was bound by his Buddhist beliefs in his drive to spread peace and prosperity in ancient India, and Thomas Jefferson was guided by his ideals in writing the Declaration of Independence. Similarly, our extraordinary revolutionaries Gandhi, Martin Luther King, Jr., and Nelson Mandela derived the strength for their causes and the conviction of their beliefs through knowledge of themselves.

This pattern of an inner search resulting in an outer act of service, however, is not limited to the past or the political realm; it manifests in all walks of life—in the arts, in education, and in business. It is wired into our system if we take the opportunity to wake up to it.

$$\oplus$$

MICHAEL ABRASHOFF, former captain of the USS *Benfold,* a $1 billion guided missile destroyer, is an example of heroic leadership from the military that is as progressive as any in the business world. He sees his mission as no less than transforming the notoriously rigid management paradigm of the Navy. He is highly decorated, and is credited with making the *Benfold* the best ship in the Pacific fleet, winning the prestigious Spokane trophy for having the best combat readiness. When he took over, he inherited a dysfunctional ship and a sullen crew, one that typically performed at the bottom of the fleet. Under Abrashoff's leadership, however, within seven months the crew set new performance standards, finishing predeployment training in less than one-half of the previous record time. The *Benfold* also recorded a 100 percent retention rate for second tours compared to a typical 54 percent rate Navy-wide, and in 1998 returned almost one-third of its multi-million dollar maintenance and repair budget. And he did this without firing anyone—simply by tapping the potential that had never been recognized and creating an environment where people want to do well.

As in the case of Neeleman, leadership for him is about "understanding yourself first, then using that to create a superb organization."[14] Most leaders limit potential in others out of their own fear, insecurities, and ego needs. When they look deeply into themselves, to understand their inner world— the values, passions, and ideas that inspire commitment—"a transformation can take place."[15] No longer limited by fear, they give themselves over to their heartfelt cause. For Abrashoff this meant serving others by genuinely empowering them to reach their full potential. "I divide the world into believers and infidels. What the infidels don't understand—and they far outnumber the believers—is that innovative practices and true empowerment produce phenomenal results."[16]

Abrashoff believes leaders "don't just take command—they communicate purpose."[17] Leading others is not about training young people, many of whom come from bad situations; rather it is a matter of learning who they are and where they are coming from, then linking that to a purpose. In focusing on a purpose rather than chain of command, he shifted the ship's organizing principle from "obedience to performance. The highest boss is no longer the person with the most stripes but the sailor who does the work."[18] He learned to see and manage the ship from the eyes of the crew by listening to them and playing to their needs. This ability to connect with others was only made possible by first taking his own journey, and knowing what matters and what is to be served.

He tells the story of having difficulty meeting many of the youngest sailors because they spent so much time painting the ship. After asking them about the problem, he replaced the nuts and bolts made of ferrous metal with stainless steel bolts for $25,000. This saved thousands of future man-hours in painting with a paint job that is good for 30 years, and freed the sailors' time for more productive and rewarding activity. His sailors, in turn, responded by performing with devotion.

This theme of first knowing oneself also appears more and more in the management literature of today. Our foremost management gurus speak of the necessity of self-knowledge as the foundation for effective, enduring leadership, and for creating vibrant, sustainable organizations. Stephen Covey, Warren Bennis, George McGregor Burns, and Daniel Goleman, to name a few, each espouse a commitment to human fulfillment through first knowing self and then serving others as a primary premise for achieving extraordinary results.

Leadership is a journey of self-discovery, for breaking through old habits of thinking in order to achieve more than what seems possible, and to help oneself and others learn and find meaning in working together. Warren Bennis said that the central task of a leader is letting the self emerge "to free ourselves from habit, to resolve the paradoxes, to transcend conflicts, to become masters rather than slaves to our own lives."[19]

This process of self-discovery at first breaks the bounds of self-imposed limitations and then arouses a desire to make a difference in the lives of others. Leaders throughout organizational life are transforming their organizations into movements of the human spirit by first examining the self. They do so because they have tapped into their deepest sources of inspiration and motivation.

THE CHALLENGE OF THE HEROIC JOURNEY: STEPPING OUT OF THE COCOON

This challenge of waking the spirit to the possibilities of the Heroic Journey may not seem for everyone. Embarking on the journey is an act of courage, and we are often content to stay home and remain in our comfort zones. We enclose ourselves with the familiar and make ourselves numb to doubt, fear, and new possibilities. When challenged by problems at work or in our life circumstances, we feel burdened. So we blame the situation and others for our troubles, cast ourselves in the role of the victim, and deal with the troubles by retreating and avoiding—or worse, ignore them altogether by burying ourselves in endless activity and self-absorbed pursuits.

Every one of our failures to cope with a challenging life situation openly is a refusal to venture into the unknown and face a doubt or a fear, or to transcend our self-imposed limitations.

This is what Buddhist master Chogyam Trungpa Rinpoche calls "living in a cocoon."[20] Inside the cocoon we live with a scarcity mentality—we feel our lives do not provide us with enough, so we hold on to what we have and defend it tightly. We even hold on to ideas as if they are fixed and solid, and rarely open ourselves to new possibilities or get a breath of fresh air. Every one of our failures to cope with a challenging life situation openly is a refusal to venture into the unknown and face a doubt or a fear, or to transcend our self-imposed limitations. When we sell ourselves short like this, we restrict our consciousness, succumb to our doubts and fears, and allow our deepest desires and needs to go unmet. This unfulfilled energy often builds up and surfaces as anxiety or displays of anger.

The Heroic Journey is a call to everyone to wake up and make a difference. To be heroic is to stop the self-denial and answer the call to become and evolve into what it is to be fully human. This is not as far out of our reach as you might think. Rather, the Journey is often a more mundane process that begins right where you are, in the here and now of our everyday lives.

Unlike those who feel like victims in their lives, heroic people respond to the call to take on daily challenges as opportunities to learn and develop. You

To be heroic is to stop the self-denial and answer the call to become and evolve into what it is to be fully human. learn to live as a master of your circumstances. You break through the limits imposed by doubt and fear to achieve more than you believe possible. You venture outside your cocoon or comfort zone into the unknown aspects of your difficult circumstances, face the trials and uncertainties of dealing with your limitations, and challenge yourself and others to learn, develop, and grow. And you do this over and over again.

In this book I will show you how to inquire into the nature of yourself and your world, make yourself open and available to all your experiences, and constantly challenge yourself to break the mold of habitual pattern, learn from experience, and create new possibilities. This process, when repeated enough times, results in a personal growth that can reach extraordinary proportions. As American philosopher William James said, "Genius . . . means little more than the faculty of perceiving in an unhabitual way."[1] What before seemed unimaginable suddenly becomes an opportunity for greatness.

For many of us, the call of the Heroic Journey comes during a time of questioning or suffering, such as during a life transition or a personal crisis. In our work life it is often brought on by a lack of inspiration, a seemingly insurmountable challenge, or the loss of a job. Whatever the challenge, however, we face a choice. We can slip into a malaise and lackluster effort, or heed the call of the Heroic Journey and make it a chosen way of life. There is nothing more ennobling of the human spirit.

⊕

BEN ZANDER, the conductor of the Boston Philharmonic, is another example of one who rises to this challenge. Zander is world-renowned as a conductor, precocious composer, and gifted cellist since around the age of eight, and for transforming the performance of Beethoven's Fifth Symphony. But Zander sees himself as a teacher more than anything else, and has earned a reputation as a passionate and energetic motivational speaker in inspiring talented musicians and business leaders to see and achieve the possibilities in their lives. He has been on *60 Minutes* and has worked with many business leaders at organizations such as IBM, NASA, Shell Oil, and the World Economic Forum. His ideas are rooted in his partnership with Rosamund Zander, his wife and a practicing psychotherapist. Together they have woven a message that uses music as both a metaphor and a medium for understanding leadership.

For many years Zander, like most in his profession, practiced the role of conductor as dictator. It wasn't until he was 45 that he realized he was missing something. He was highly successful, but as is the case with so many at midlife, he was still unsatisfied. So along with Roz, Zander began to explore and was introduced to the teachings of philosopher Fernando Flores and to the experience of the Landmark Forum. Their message is perhaps best expressed by Flores as moving from the comfortable world of "What You Know You Know" to a richer, riskier world of "What You Don't Know You Don't Know"[22]—in other words, stepping out of the cocoon. Along with the support of Roz, the message helped Zander transform his role. He learned to emphasize the power of "seeing the possibilities as a means for transforming one's experience in the world,"[23] and to bring this message to his work. He discovered, for example, that "the conductor doesn't make a sound. The conductor's power depends on his ability to make other people powerful."[24] So he helps people break the self-imposed limitations of the cocoon and free themselves to a greater sense of possibility.

As performers, many musicians are entrapped by a "conversation in their head,"[25] a doubt telling them that they will miss a passage or that others can play it better—that same latent self-doubt that we all share about not being enough. As a leader, Zander works to silence that voice with the principle of "everyone gets an A."[26] At the beginning of a course or preparation for a performance, he gives everyone an A and then asks them to tell him what they will have learned in order to justify an extraordinary grade. He finds that this shifts their attitude and changes everything. The A helps draw out what is unique in people, and empowers them to be who they are without comparing themselves to others.

For Zander, then, as with Neeleman and Abrashoff, leadership comes from the inside out. A leader's job is to inspire a new way of being by breaking down boundaries, connecting to a sense of possibility, and believing that everyone can make a difference. That shift is freeing and enables limitless possibilities. He likes to say, "Never doubt the capacity of the people you lead to accomplish whatever you dream for them."[27] His dream at the moment is to "put a recording of Beethoven's Fifth in the hands of every man, woman, and child on earth. Beethoven intended the Fifth Symphony as an attack—on complacency, on the status quo, on the way people see things. He was shaking his fist at humanity."[28] Zander wants people to wake up to that spirit.

⊕

THE REWARD: DISCOVERING BASIC GOODNESS

In heeding the call of the Heroic Journey, the heroic person learns to harness this hungry energy of becoming, mount it, and ride as a master would a wild horse. Horses are mythical creatures, sacred in many ancient traditions, like Pegasus in ancient Greece and Windhorse in Tibetan Buddhist mythology. The horse evokes an image of something wild, raw, and powerful. In myths, the horse represents our hungry spirit and our longing to reconnect to our true and genuine nature that we ride to fulfill our deepest dreams and aspirations. Having mounted, we learn to ride our minds and hearts by overcoming our fear, doubt, and fixed ideas—of ourselves, our horse, and our situation.

You have trained hard on your journey, and . . . have touched your noble heart and see you are basically good, that you are enough.

As this applies to us, we see that we have trained hard on our journey, and our effort reveals what Chogyam Trungpa Rinpoche called our inherent "basic goodness."[29] We have touched our noble heart and see that we are basically good, that we are enough, and are filled with a confidence that requires no confirmation. We have broken away from our limitations, projections, and habitual patterns, and are free to see new possibilities and develop a sense of vision for what we are doing.

Grounded in our basic goodness, every situation becomes workable and fresh. And having awakened our self and our heart, we see the same inherent potential in everyone, and now desire to help them do the same. This is a natural process, it is trainable, and it is for everyone.

$$\oplus$$

TOM CHAPPELL, of Tom's of Maine, is a businessman who reaped the reward and shows how this process is trainable. He left the corporate world to found the company in the early 1970s along with his wife Kate. They wanted to build a socially and environmentally responsible business in natural personal care products, and began with an initial $5,000 loan and a natural toothpaste formula. Thirty-three years later, Tom's is nearly a $40 million business with more than 100 products. The company is widely acclaimed for its environmentally safe products and caring work environments, and has received numerous national and regional awards from the Council for Economic Priorities, CNBC, *Working Mother* magazine, and many others.

Chappell began with a determination to stick to his ideals of making personal care products—toothpaste, deodorant, shampoo—with natural ingredients only. By the mid-1980s he had built a $5 million company replete with MBAs and a mass-market appeal. Yet he was unhappy and his heart was no longer in it. He had hit a wall. He was drinking, judgmental, controlling, full of pride, and in his own words "a defensive know-it-all."[30] He was suffering from all the distractions mentioned above and the pitfalls of losing oneself in a busy world. Success had blinded him to his defects, and others in the organization started to emulate him. The work environment turned negative—full of political posturing, turf protecting, and defensive behavior. So he began to ask questions of himself. His questioning led him to Harvard Divinity School, where he enrolled for four years while continuing to be involved with the business from a distance.

At divinity school he learned about connecting to what he calls "goodness."[31] He learned about Plato's notion of the higher soul, and the Buddhist principle of the inherent goodness of human nature. But he was most profoundly influenced by Jewish philosopher Martin Buber, who saw that our relationships can be transformed by seeing others as a manifestation of the divine—the I-Thou—instead of as objects to be manipulated by the ego—the I-It. He found that to embrace our "goodness" in this way is to push self-interest aside and open up to others, and that self-knowledge is a path to finding meaning.

Chappell's experience at Harvard inspired a new management philosophy that turned toward serving others. He forged a leadership style that makes customers, employees, and suppliers just as important as profits. He rebuilt his business by stamping out a new mission, vision, and values for his company—and more important, for making these beliefs an integral part of life and work and Tom's. The people at Tom's created common values and now live them. The company incorporates respect and honor for everything that it does. It donates 10 percent of pretax revenues to local charities, and also encourages employees to give. His efforts have resulted in a new culture characterized by deep caring for employees, genuine participation in company business processes, and supportive relationships for everyone to live to full potential. According to Chappell, "It doesn't matter what business you are in, you can have a respectful attitude about society, nature, and people."[32]

As Chappell's example shows, the Heroic Journey is to learn first to see, and then to take our seat in, our intrinsic nature, our basic goodness. The journey awakens our minds and hearts and reveals a deeper meaning for what it is to be human. For some, this meaning is an inherent wisdom, for others it is deeply held values or beliefs, and for still others a purpose, a cause, or a vision based on human fulfillment. In all it is a set of guiding beliefs, passions, or assumptions about life that gives us an inner identity, meaning, and sense of relevance, and serves as the source of our strength.

You begin to trust yourself, and that trust dissolves the facade of self-interest. Your conviction about who you are frees you from doubt, and gives you the confidence and courage to remain true to your nature.

The ultimate ground for these virtues is our kind, gentle, and loving nature—our basic goodness. This nature is common to us all but our fear of being inadequate often holds us back from it. So we hide and protect ourselves through pursuits of self-interest to the point of becoming self-absorbed and neurotic.

Chogyam Trungpa Rinpoche said that discovering basic goodness gives birth to "authentic presence."[33]

In breaking through to your basic nature, you become more fulfilled, and all the games and delusions stop. You begin to trust yourself, and that trust dissolves the facade of self-interest. Your conviction about who you are frees you from doubt, and gives you the confidence and courage to remain true to your nature. This is confidence. not in the sense of knowing you can accomplish a certain task; rather, it is confidence in knowing that no matter what you face, the situation is workable. You already know who you are and there is nothing to lose. You know your strengths and weaknesses, align your actions with your beliefs, and become more real and authentic. The more authentic you become, the more genuine you are in your expressions, and the more others learn to relate to it and trust you.

Trusting yourself frees you to be more open to the views and concerns of others and to communicate sincerely and genuinely. You engage them as you would be engaged and wish for them what you have found. This is your field of power, your authentic presence, a range of genuineness so powerful that it radiates.

It is also the source of magic and personal authority that leaders need for making a difference. Each of the leaders profiled in this chapter has realized this, and it has given them the power and magic to do extraordinary things.

BESTOWING THE BOONS: CREATING ENLIGHTENED SOCIETY

The Heroic Journey begins as an inner process but gradually unfolds as an outward caring for the community. Once we have discovered our inherent wisdom, the final destiny of the Heroic Journey is to return to the world to bestow the boons upon others. In many myths, the culmination of the journey takes the form of creating what Chogyam Trungpa Rinpoche calls an "enlightened society."[34] The creation of enlightened society is reflected throughout our world traditions in tales of legendary kingdoms that served as sources of learning and culture and places of peace and prosperity like the ancient Himalayan kingdom of Shambhala, the lost city of Atlantis of Greek mythology, and Camelot of the Arthurian legends.

The creation of these societies represents the culmination of humanity's search for meaning and is a natural outcome of the Heroic Journey.

Throughout history we can find societies governed by wise and compassionate rulers, existing in harmony with the earth, where the boons of success were for the benefit of everyone. They were based on the highest human virtues of order, dignity, and human fulfillment, and they offered an important contrast to a world divided by greed and self-interest. In addition to the examples mentioned earlier, there is a long legacy of political reformers and religious groups worldwide who for centuries have founded alternative communities dedicated to self-understanding and greater human fulfillment. These include the Freemasons, whose roots go back to ancient Sumeria, the Pilgrims, Mennonites, and Quakers, and a long tradition of alternative communities in America.

A rich lineage of philosophical thought has also helped shape these societies. Plato's *Republic* was a tremendous influence on ancient Greece and on the shape of Western polity, as were the works of Confucius and Lao Tzu in ancient China and the philosophy of the Samurai tradition in Japan. This heritage continued in the West through Francis Bacon, who dreamed of a paradise of peace in a new Atlantis; Sir Thomas More, who coined the word "Utopia"; and Thomas Hobbes, who wrote of Leviathan, a society dedicated to human fulfillment. Later there was Rousseau and the social contract, and Marx, who found "man's use of man" degrading to the human spirit.

The message is that once awakened we have a natural urge to make this world a better place, but we must first take this journey. The creation of these societies represents the culmination of humanity's search for meaning and is a natural outcome of the Heroic Journey. In having discovered our inherent wisdom and basic goodness, we work together in solving the world's problems and creating a better place to live.

This evolutionary urge to seek and make a better world is also beginning to influence the shape and form of business. In looking at the history and evolution of commerce, futurists have identified a number of waves.[35] The first was the agricultural revolution and the freeing of humanity's bondage to the land. The second was the industrial revolution, in which humans reign supreme and commerce leads to many advances in the physical conditions of life but also undermines the health of our people and our planet. The third is a commerce based on balance and sustainability, and becoming more sensitive to life, cooperation, and the environment. We are just entering the third wave, and see it through increasing democratization of the workplace, growing sensitization to the needs of human capital, and expanding interest in socially responsible business and the "triple bottom line" of economic, social, and environmental sustainability. Concerns for our health and the health of the planet are forcing us to rework our notions of growth—particularly the notions that bigger is better and wealth means happiness.

There is yet a fourth wave that recent management authors suggest as an integration of all dimensions of life in service of the whole.[36] Robert Greenleaf, Peter Block, Peter Drucker, and Ken Blanchard speak to the need of business and business leaders to adopt a position of stewardship and service to the needs of the whole, to create organizations where the needs of total individual and society are served. For them, social transformation is the role of the leader in the post-industrial period.

As mentioned in the introduction, the most successful business organizations over time have been those that were able to adapt and learn. The most important ingredient for creating that ability is competent leadership dedicated to the needs and well-being of all stakeholders including stockholders, customers, employees, and surrounding communities. This suggests that the role of business and business leaders is evolving beyond the focus on the bottom line to being a vehicle for serving the fulfillment of human potential and sustaining the health of our society and planet. In transforming business, we transform the world.

$$\oplus$$

MAX DEPREE is a legendary example of a leader who is transforming business and creating a more enlightened society. DePree is an author and former chairman and CEO of Herman Miller, a furniture manufacturer, one of the most innovative and admired companies in America. DePree has won broad praise for his work and writings and has inspired many people to think differently about leadership and life.

Like others mentioned earlier, for DePree a leader's work begins with knowing who you are and understanding your beliefs about people. In knowing who you are first, you are then able to project that to others. In his mind, it is tough to follow somebody if he or she doesn't have a sense of him- or herself. DePree believes that knowing self is grounded in the conviction that we are all special and made in the image of God, and as we realize this in ourselves, we begin to see it in others as well. So every person possesses a legitimate place in the world and as leaders we need to work in a way that reflects that belief. If a person is in your work community, she or he is a legitimate part of that community and indispensable to the group. The fundamental message is that in order to build trust and effective relationships, we need to start with respect.

DePree says, "We had people who got to be as good as they could be because we were able to sort out their gifts and assign tasks according to those gifts."[37] Tasks are assigned in a way that gives that person hope. It wasn't just about results—it was about what kind of place people work in, what kind of relationships they have, and what effect work has on the families they go home to. Herman Miller is working on potential, the organization's and everyone else's, not just today's results.

His mentors include Dr. Carl Frost, an industrial psychologist who taught him a lot about participatory management: "He helped me understand to be abandoned to the strengths that others bring."[38] Another is David Hubbard, president of Fuller Theological Seminary: "He taught me that leaders don't inflict pain, they bear pain. And the primary purpose of power is not to use it, but to share it."[39] He also learned from his father, and from his brother who ran the company for seventeen years. Through all of it, he learned that the underlying theme is fulfilling a moral purpose. In addition to having good people and treating them right, they also tried to do the right thing.

DePree's beliefs are reflected in the culture and performance of Herman Miller, which has been listed among *Fortune* magazine's most admired companies in 16 out of 18 years. It also has been frequently recognized for its technological innovations and its practices in social responsibility.

Herman Miller describes itself as a company driven by values and people tied together for a common purpose. That purpose transcends the bottom line and is aimed at making meaningful contributions to all the people it serves. The stakeholders of the company, with all their truly diverse perspectives, ideas, and skills, are united in making a positive contribution to everyone's lives. They view their greatest asset to be their employee-owners, whom they encourage and support in taking charge of their careers and continuously improving themselves. They are both serious about business and serious about citizens, and manage their people not as controlled collections of human resources but as dynamic communities of free people. They are also serious about the environment, not because it makes business sense, but because it is the right thing to do for their communities and for the people who come afterward.

$$\oplus$$

The essential point in all these examples is that the desire to find a better world and leading from a place of basic goodness is inherent in all of us; it just needs to be awakened. Creating a more enlightened world represents the culmination of our search for meaning and possesses important messages for leadership and business. Since this urge is inherent in everyone, we can awaken it and make it a common goal. The current state of world affairs demands this change. As the dominant force in the world today, business is our most important leverage for making the change, and leadership is the fulcrum.

Since this urge is inherent in everyone, we can awaken it and make it a common goal.

Jung said that "The weal or woe of the future will be decided neither . . . by natural catastrophes nor by the danger of world wide epidemics, but simply and solely by the psychic changes in man."[40] Through the practice of a more enlightened leadership, we can learn to harness our evolutionary energy to become, and develop into agents of change for creating outer as well as inner prosperity. The will to lead in that direction is the needed psychic change that Jung was talking about, and it can be developed.

CONCLUSION

Depending on the choices we make, there are inner and outer, as well as individual and communal, aspects of the Heroic Journey. Those who choose it exclusively as an outer quest tend to pursue self-interest and often find themselves lost in imbalanced lives with destructive consequences to their health and the planet. Others who choose it primarily as an inner quest tend to pursue self-knowledge and often become monks and spiritual teachers. Still others, who choose an inner journey balanced with an outer one, tend to become highly effective people who serve as leaders and agents of positive change in the world, living lives balanced between individual achievement and personal contribution. The process of becoming effective in this way is trainable, with the grounding in the inner journey providing the strength and conviction for the outer. For those who choose this balanced course, the journey unfolds naturally from a quest serving the individual to one serving the community. Having awakened their inherent wisdom, leaders work to awaken the same possibilities in others, and strive to create a more Enlightened Society.

The metaphors of the Heroic Journey and the Enlightened Society provide the grand framework for exploring leadership. They provide us with insights into motivation for learning and change, connecting to personal authenticity, and defining what leaders do and how they engage the world. In the chapters that follow, we build on the Heroic Journey and explore in more detail the various aspects of this evolutionary urge to become. We will continue to draw upon the archetypal truths found in our world cultures, and upon an ancient paradigm that provides a method and a path for discovering a deeper understanding of ourselves, leadership, and change. That paradigm is also simple, elegant, and compelling.

○ EXERCISES ○

The following exercises, and the ones in chapters to come, are reflective pieces designed to help you personalize the material presented in the chapter. Taken as a whole, the exercises offer an integrated, pragmatic, and practical guide for developing enlightened leaders, teams, and organizations. Following the general flow of the book, they begin with a focus on the inner work of the self and then unfold to outer work with others, and they develop from managing self to managing others, teams, and systems. They are structured and guided, with examples and stories from my personal experience to help you get the most out of them. They are some of the very best activities that I have acquired through my work in leadership and change, and have proven to be very valuable tools for the businesses, schools, and agencies I have worked with over the years.

The two exercises in this chapter are designed to help increase your self-awareness and inspire a desire to change. The Lifeline activity will help you better understand the forces shaping your life, and provide insight into yourself and what is important to you. The Heroic Journey exercise will help you become aware of how you have faced change in the past and will provide insight and inspiration for taking on the leadership journey.

○ EXERCISE 1.1: KNOWING YOURSELF—THE LIFELINE[41]

Often the first step in knowing ourselves is to reflect on our personal history and acknowledge our life experience. Our attitudes, talents, and perspectives on life were developed over time from early in our lives. Our parents, family, and friends have played important parts in shaping our views. Personal achievements in school and work, and certain events such as the death of a close one and moving to a new place, have also played important roles. In this exercise, try to look deeply into the relationships, events and achievements that have shaped your life in order to gain greater insight into yourself.

Step 1: Take a piece of paper and three different colored pencils, and develop a three-part timeline of your life, as in figure 1.1 below, which is an abbreviated version of mine. You will plot the timeline on a two-dimensional chart, with the horizontal axis showing time and the vertical one showing positive and negative impact. The timeline extends from the earliest points in childhood to a point five years into the future.

   The first part, or line, on the timeline shows achievements through your life. These are events or situations surrounding major successes and failures, such as graduating from college, or the first job being a disaster. The second line records events that directly influenced your social and personal development. The focus of this line is on relationship issues that might include moving to a different house, loss of friends, or divorce of parents. The third line describes events that don't fall neatly into the relationship or achievement category but somehow had a profound impact on you. An inheritance, the death of a friend, a sudden insight, or a spiritual experience might fall into this category.

   In developing these timelines, go back as early as you can remember and come forward to the present. They represent trends and patterns. A series of positive or developmental experiences can be represented in an upward trend, a negative experience as a dip in a curve. Draw each line in a different color and note trends, spikes, and dips in the curve with an explanation of the experience.

Try to identify 10 to 15 items in each category. Use the following questions to help guide your reflection:

○ *Personal Achievements*
   1. What kind of student were you?
   2. What extracurricular activities have you participated in outside of school or work, and what role have these played in your life?
   3. What guided you in making choices about work, and how have you progressed? What are you good at or not so good at?
   4. What have been your successes and disappointments?

○ *Relationships and Social Life*
   1. Who was the most dominant parent(s) or adult(s) in your life and why?
   2. What was your relationship like with your siblings, and/or with friends at school? How did these relationships affect you?
   3. How were you in relationships: dominant, well-liked, shy, loner, rejected?
   4. When did dating begin and how has romance shaped your choices?

○ *Events*
   1. What events that don't neatly fall into relationships or achievement have shaped your life?
   2. Where have you experienced a loss such as the death of a close one, divorce, or moving and leaving home and friends behind?
   3. What events—such as an inheritance, a sudden insight, or a trip abroad—have helped you?
   4. Have religion, personal beliefs, or spiritual experiences helped shape your life?

Step 2: Although the building of a timeline is not necessarily a happy experience, it is one that provides valuable insight into the forces shaping your life, your talents, and your ability to lead. Often we have hidden patterns, things just below the surface of our consciousness that play an important role in shaping our lives. Chogyam Trungpa Rinpoche liked to say that we all have a

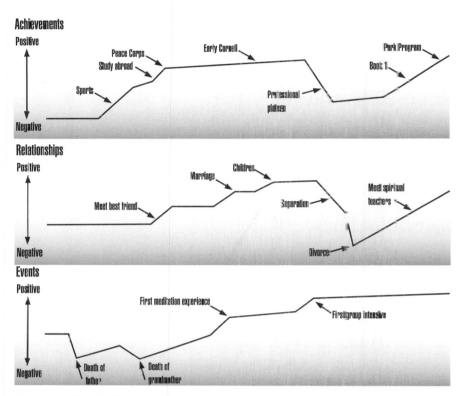

Figure 1.1   Sample Timeline

"thingy"[42]—a childhood wound that we are left to bear and resolve as an adult, and that keeps us in our cocoon. It is a basic insecurity, a feeling of not being enough, for which we often overcompensate in our actions. These typically include a sense of abandonment, a lack of confidence, or an insecurity about one's appearance, and they often play an important role in shaping our lives and our choices as an adult. The second part of this exercise is a reflection to help you deepen your understanding and insight into yourself, and to surface your "thingys."

1. What was the impact of each of these important relationships, achievements, and events in shaping your perspective and how you are in the world?
2. What are the patterns or evolutionary lines you see in your overall development? Where do you think you are headed?

3. What "thingy" might you have? How has it influenced your life? Are you able to let it go?

4. What does all this tell you about how you lead and what you want most and care about?

It is helpful to share your lifeline and insights with another person, someone who knows you well. Other people can ask questions to help you clarify your understanding, and point out patterns they see that you perhaps have not yet realized. Talking with another person also helps to surface the emotions of these experiences, so that you can develop a "sketch" of yourself that works at both an intellectual and a gut level. Getting in touch with that emotional energy is very important for motivating change.

○ EXERCISE 1.2: THE HEROIC JOURNEY

People often have difficulty thinking of themselves as ever having been heroic. But we all have faced change at some point, and by looking at how we faced the challenge of that change, we can begin to see what enabled us to adapt, grow, and learn from the experience. Some journeys never begin because the person never dares to leave the known world. Confronted with the unpredictable, our fears of failure and our self-doubt arise as obstacles in our path. By looking at where we have successfully met change in the past, we can gain insight into these obstacles and inspiration for overcoming them and undertaking the journey as a way of life.

Even when successful, however, we still face the challenge of the return, and how we work with the change in our homes and in our workplace. This return may be the most difficult part of the whole journey, because the change brought about by what we have learned may require changes at home. The change can reinvigorate the community, but sometimes heroic people are ignored and even shunned. They risk facing rejection by those who have not taken the journey themselves.

Step 1: Picking up from the Lifeline exercise, select a story in which you have been heroic in facing a challenge in your life. It is important that the experience you select had a significant impact on your life—that it be something through which you were personally inspired and changed. This could be the story of an adventure, or of a painful challenge such as overcoming alcoholism, or the loss of someone dear. With your story in mind, reflect on the following questions.

1. What precipitated this stage of the journey? Were you thrown into it, or did you heed the call?
2. What were the fears, insecurities, and demons you had to overcome to face the challenges of this experience?
3. What inner resources, strengths, or qualities did you draw on in helping you overcome these fears, insecurities, and demons?
4. What were your rewards and how did you change as a result of this experience? What were your emotional, psychological, or spiritual insights?
5. What happened to your old relationships when you returned, and did your changes have any impact on your community of family, friends, and colleagues?
6. What does this tell you about leadership, and the relationships and community you would like to create?

Here is an example from my personal history:

I was brought up in a blue-collar, Italian neighborhood in a small town. I went to college in my hometown, played sports, and lived a pretty narrow existence. By the time I was in my early twenties, I had barely traveled outside of the northeast. I thought myself unworldly, and a bit of a country boy compared to my classmates.

At this time, a number of my older college friends came back from the summer breaks having hitchhiked around Europe and telling of their adventures. I became fascinated with the idea and wanted to do the same. Eventually I managed to enroll in a one-year, French-speaking exchange program in Belgium. I spoke almost no French at the time so I decided to take a pre-program French language course in southern France. In making my plans, I decided that no matter where I went, I was going to hitchhike. So the day after landing at the airport in Luxemburg, I made a cardboard sign with "Paris" marked on it, walked to the side of the road, and stuck my thumb out. A young Portuguese man soon picked me up and drove me all the way to Paris. He spoke six languages, but no English, yet we had a great "conversation." He treated me to lunch, shared a bottle of wine, and we had a fun time together.

That first day was a great example of what the rest of my 16 months in Europe would be like. I traveled extensively, became fluent in French, and had many great adventures.

I was transformed by my experience. I saw that breaking through the fear of going off alone to live in a very strange place was very liberating. In learning a new language and absorbing a new culture, I felt free to experiment with myself and to try new things, as no one had any expectations of me. I learned about myself, about friendship, and about the world. It was a confidence builder that emboldened me to continue to experiment with my life. I also wanted others to know the rewards of that kind of experience. So later I sent my two brothers, and more recently my son, on similar adventures.

Step 2: In contrast to the heroic story you picked to reflect on in Step 1, now reflect on how you are now living. As we have seen, the challenge of the Heroic Journey is often daunting. So many of us shrink back into our cocoons, unable to face the risks and uncertainties of continuing the adventure we started. Reflect on the following questions and consider whether you are resting in your cocoon now or still on your heroic journey.

1. Do you have energy for your work and are you able to wake up Monday mornings ready to go?
2. Do you feel stress, anxiety, or boredom?
3. Are you clear about what things are most important to you in life and do you live them?
4. Do you know and use your gifts in a way that gives you meaning and adds value to the events of your life?
5. Do you feel when you go to sleep at night that this was a well-lived day?
6. Are there important decisions that you are procrastinating on or not making?

Share your story, insights, and reflections with a friend. Again, sharing helps to arouse the emotional and psychological energy necessary for change.

THE LEADERSHIP WHEEL
AND THE WISDOM
OF THE FIVE DIRECTIONS

Everyone knows that on any given day there are energies slumbering in him which the incitements of that day do not call forth. . . . Compared with what we ought to be, we are only half awake. The human individual usually lives far within his limits.

—William James[1]

THE ANCIENT PARADIGM

The shape of a circle has been an important symbol of unity and wholeness for cultures throughout the world from almost the beginning of time. The Mandala, or Medicine Wheel, the most sacred form of the unifying circle, has long been a universal image of the cosmos and the nature of existence. It appears in Tibetan, Hindu, African, Celtic, and Native American cultures, and in various forms of Christianity, Gnosticism, and other religions, as well as in mythology and alchemy.

The Wheel, as I call it here, generally consists of five primary energies or aspects of existence placed in the four cardinal directions of the compass with one in the center. Some of the earliest Wheels were laid out architecturally, such as Stonehenge in England or the Buddhist temple in Borobudur, Java. Others, such as the sand paintings of Tibet and of the Navaho of the Southwest, were drawn in the ground for rituals and initiation rites.

Carl Jung studied versions of the Wheel in Asian, African, and Native American cultures. He considered it a human archetype, a pattern occurring universally across cultures and representing the cosmos as well as the self. Since Jung, mythologists and anthropologists such as Joseph Campbell, Angeles Arriens, and Peter Gold have discovered remarkable similarities in the Wheel and its use to describe the social, cosmological, and spiritual realities of existence. They speak of the Wheel as a universal image representing wholeness and completeness, a map of the mind and of the sacred world. Each of the five directions symbolizes a part of the whole, a way of knowing, and an aspect of becoming. Traditional forms of this Wheel have served as a path to guide learning, change, and personal development for thousands of years. Heroic people of these cultures learn to journey along the Wheel to a place of greater wholeness, and to return to share boons of the journey with others.

Each of the five directions of the Wheel is an aspect of a cyclical energy of becoming that pervades the inner psychological and emotional world as well as the outer physical and phenomenal world. The directions provide a map of the mind and universe, and are applied to the elements of the earth, cycles of being, phases of the day, and the seasons. Often, the five directions are further divided into a spectrum of finer aspects, and linked to the twelve phases of the moon and the laws of the cosmos. In this way, the Wheel served as the basis for the cosmology of native peoples, explaining the hidden order that underlies the world.

Each of the five directions of the Wheel is an aspect of a cyclical energy of becoming that pervades the inner psychological and emotional world as well as the outer physical and phenomenal world.

The Wheel also has served as both the challenge and the guide for the Heroic Journey. The purpose of this journey always has been to become fully human, and in so doing, to become a teacher and leader of others. Heroic people learn to ride their hungry spirit toward personal awakening and serving the whole rather than just the self. They know that understanding themselves and their interdependence with the changing world is critical to personal fulfillment, and even survival.

As a guide to this journey, the Wheel works as a mirror to reflect on the place and value of all things, and as a path for harnessing the energy of becoming to develop our fullest potential. Each archetype offers a particular message for living in harmony with nature and with one another. As a whole, these five symbolize balance, perfection, and a guide for self-discovery and finding one's way in life.

The Wheel also has served as both the challenge and the guide for the Heroic Journey. . . . Heroic people learn to ride their hungry spirit toward personal awakening and serving the whole rather than just the self.

The ancient belief is that an individual is born with a preference for a single archetype and so enters the world imperfect, with little wisdom or understanding of the others. However, since the purpose in life is to venture beyond habitual preferences, to learn and grow toward wholeness, the heroic person is to make an effort to access the unique and complementary wisdoms found in each of the other four directions. Native peoples called this walking the sacred path to find the wisdom and balance necessary for acting in the most effective manner.

PARALLELS IN MODERN THOUGHT

Although no perfect parallels exist, similarities between the Wheel and the research literature of twentieth-century psychologists and management thinkers are unmistakable. There are clear parallels, for example, with the four Jungian personality types that form the basis for the Myers-Briggs Type Indicator. Jung developed these four root types from 20 years of clinical research with his patients. Seeking to validate them as archetypes, he explored other cultures and found similarities in the ancient traditions of Asia, the indigenous tribes in Africa, and the Navaho of the American Southwest. The Wheel also shows remarkable overlap with the dimensions of the Five Factor Model used in modern psychological research. This model is based on the work of psychologists Gordon Allport and H. S. Odbert and almost 70 years of subsequent research using language to describe personality traits.[2] The five factors are considered universal and have been validated in languages as diverse as German and Chinese. It is the framework most often used by academic researchers for understanding personality and leadership effectiveness over the last half century.

Likewise, management thought leaders of the last decade have also begun to arrive at models that parallel the Wheel in exciting ways. These include the five disciplines for achieving personal, team, and organizational effectiveness of Peter Senge, the five leadership challenges of James Kouzes and Barry Posner, and the four strategies for achieving personal greatness in the leadership diamond of Peter Koestenbaum. While there is no perfect fit among these various approaches, there is significant overlap and correlation. Just as remarkable are the parallels in learning and change, and the similarities between the journey around the Wheel, Jung's concept of individuation, Senge's discipline of personal mastery, and Koestenbaum's notion of achieving personal greatness. Each of these contemporary models offers a useful framework for personal growth and development, and points in an intriguing way to aspects of the same fundamental truths represented in the Wheel.

It is obvious that leading modern thinkers are rediscovering fundamental aspects of the wisdom that has guided indigenous cultures for thousands of years. The primary power of the Wheel is its utter simplicity and intuitive appeal as a device for bringing together what we know and pointing clearly to what we need to find.

THE WHEEL AS A DEVELOPMENTAL CYCLE

In essence, the five archetypes of the Wheel constitute a five-step cycle in the process of becoming, or development of the ego, and provide a vision for the totality of our being.

Most importantly, the Wheel serves as a framework for understanding how the energy of becoming naturally forms and moves toward knowledge, consciousness, and action. In essence, the five archetypes of the Wheel constitute a five-step cycle in the process of becoming, or development of the ego, and provide a vision for the totality of our being. They represent not only five phases of becoming, but also five ways of knowing, five kinds of intelligence, and five aspects of human nature. Each is a different aspect of universal truth representing certain expressions of our being, certain modes of how we become, know, and relate to our world. They are interdependent and interactive, and work together in an integrated cycle that culminates in understanding and action.

In many of these ancient traditions, especially in the East, each of these five archetypes has both a wisdom aspect and a shadow aspect. The inherent wisdom of the archetype becomes a shadow when it is used to validate the ego and serve self-interest. The archetype is distorted into neurosis by a "hanging-on" to particular views that manifest as strong attractions or aversions toward things of our world. This holding comes from a fear that arises out of our sense of incompleteness, and it stops us from venturing outside of our natural preferences. Instead we become stuck and rigid—sometimes even overplaying our view to the point that we turn an inherent strength into a weakness.

The shadow is transmuted into wisdom, however, as you let go of this solid sense of self, step through the fear, and dare to try to go beyond what you think you know. Instead of negating, limiting, or ignoring your fears, you turn them into vehicles for your own awakening. This is the process of the Heroic Journey.

Wisdom arises by letting go of your particular grip on the world and your habitual patterns of relating to it, and having the courage to cross the threshold of your fears and venture toward vaster perspectives.

In many of these ancient traditions, especially in the East, each of these five archetypes has both a wisdom aspect and a shadow aspect.

As you progress around the Wheel and open up to the wisdom of each archetype, you become more whole and complete. You learn more of your own undiscovered nature, connect to it, and a sense of wholeness and basic goodness arises.

The notion of the shadow has clear parallels in Jungian psychology and in the neurotic dimension of the Five Factor Model mentioned above. The wisdom and shadow aspects also have strong correlations with the leadership success and derailment studies of some of the foremost research and consulting organizations in leadership, most prominently the Center for Creative Leadership.[3] These researchers have studied success and derailment patterns of thousands of executives over the past few decades and provide a growing body of converging evidence of characteristics that lead to executive success and behaviors that derail progression in a career. As we will see, the success and derailment research mirrors the wisdom and shadow patterns of the Wheel.

THE FIVE ARCHETYPES

As a model for living, the message of the Wheel has been lost in many aspects of our dominant world cultures of today. Yet the Wheel still serves as a powerful and elegant framework for guiding us today. It helps us understand what leadership is, how individuals, teams, and organizations learn and how organizations can be made responsible to the whole.

Like the ancients, we are faced with constant change, and our success—even our survival—depends on our ability to keep pace with a rapidly changing world. The trials and tribulations of economic cycles, technological growth, competitive pressures, social upheaval, and environmental threats combine to make adversity as great as, and the rate of change faster than, ever in history. Leaders, teams, and organizations alike can enhance their capacity to adapt and change by learning to access and apply each direction of the Wheel. The challenges of today's world call for such a capacity, and many now believe that this capacity is the only true source of sustainable advantage.

. . . this same paradigm can be used to help create more enlightened leaders and more enlightened organizations.

More importantly, however, this same paradigm can be used to help create more enlightened leaders and more enlightened organizations. As a guide for learning and change, the Wheel engages people in a process to become fully human and transforms their organizations into vehicles for positive change. In moving around the Wheel, people learn about balance and wholeness, and about making their efforts sustainable and responsible to the whole. It is an elegant tool to help us develop balanced, principled leaders and make healthier relationships, teams, and communities.

In this chapter, I adapt the ancient Wheel as a model for leadership, and in subsequent chapters for individual, team, and organizational learning. In making this adaptation, I call it the Leadership Wheel and unpack the essential meaning of each direction to better fit today's cultural context. These adaptations are fully consistent with the original meaning and use of the directions.

I first describe each direction as a key aspect of human nature that shapes interpersonal effectiveness, and then present an example of how that quality manifests itself in some of our more visible leaders of today. The wisdom qualities are described in terms of learning routines that lead to personal growth, while the shadows are described as defensive routines that lead to derailment or stalling in learning and development. The wisdom arises from letting go of self and opening to other, while the shadow comes from holding on to the ego and serving self-interest. We all have preferences for certain archetypes but are enhanced by accessing the others. As we learn and grow, we remain true to our natural preferences but learn to incorporate the other directions.

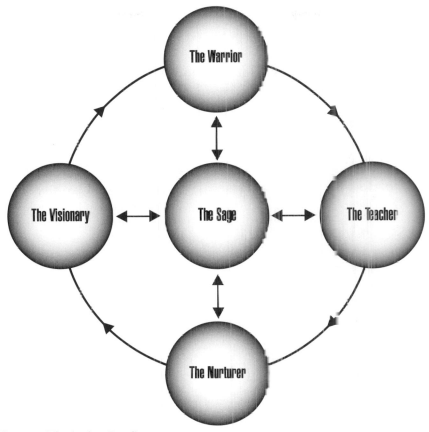

Figure 2.1 The Ancient Paradigm

EAST: THE WAY OF THE TEACHER—KNOWING THE WORLD

Luck is what happens when preparation meets opportunity.

—*Seneca*

The archetypal energy of becoming for the Teacher is about intellectual intelligence. It is the place of first illumination where our senses first recognize an object as it appears in our experience, like waking in the morning to the breaking dawn. It is where the mind is used to observe the world just as it is, coolly and objectively, without bias or projection from past experience, or hope or fear of the future. It is also the place of inquiry, where the intellect is used to grasp and analyze experience with a sharp and powerful logic and turn it into knowledge.

Teachers observe things just as they are, very precisely, accurately, and finely, and suffer few illusions. They sometimes appear unfriendly as their approach to the world is very rational, black and white, methodical, and structured. They are focused on the present, on the near, on the concrete, and on the reality of things. They are attentive to detail and like to ponder and analyze masses of data while attempting to bring order and understanding to reality.

The Teacher is about intellectual intelligence . . . where the mind is used to observe the world just as it is, coolly and objectively, without bias or projection from past experience, or hope or fear of the future.

It is tough to persuade Teachers to a different point of view, as they are conservative, quick to criticize, and difficult to influence without solid facts, figures, and data. Their sharp intellect frees them from doubt and inspires them to reach out to share their knowledge with others. Thus Teachers are known as the seeing ones, objective observers, knowledge holders, and immovable ones, as they see reality clearly and hold appearances as knowledge while remaining unmoved and untouched by them. They also help others see the world just as clearly.

In today's world, the Teacher represents the power to acquire technical, business, and industry knowledge necessary for informed decision making. As a Teacher you seek and analyze data to tell us where we are and how things are working. You like to work with the facts, immerse yourself in the details, and objectively and methodically question assumptions in order to see and understand reality clearly. To paraphrase Max DePree, your first responsibility as a leader is to define reality.[4] You are also smart, organized, and a quick study of the skills and competencies necessary for your job.

This is the leader as expert, where technical skill, rational thought, and acquired knowledge enable a clear view for taking action. *This is also the leader as teacher,* where, as knowledge holders, you feel a responsibility to share your knowledge with others. Seeing the world clearly, you are confident in your view and work to dispel the illusions of others. For this reason, as a Teacher, you also make a good coach and mentor.

LEARNING ROUTINES

Curiosity. Teachers inquire and investigate openly and honestly into the nature of reality. Their inherent curiosity and desire to understand drives them to acquire expertise and knowledge. They investigate assumptions and issues, seek data to prevent unforeseen circumstances, and help others improve their understanding of the world.

Logic. Teachers also are logical and rational in solving problems, evaluating opportunities, and providing the critical viewpoint and attention to detail necessary for grounding actions in reality. They are pragmatic when dealing with others and realistic in addressing problems.

Objectivity. Teachers remain coolly observant of the world, work openly with biases, and neutralize emotional reactions in order to help themselves and others see reality clearly and face it peacefully. They are also methodical, deliberate, and conscientious in their effort to see the world objectively and to anchor actions in truth and without projection.

$$\oplus$$

ORIT GADIESH, chairman of Bain & Company is an example of the powers of a Teacher at work. While only the world's eighteenth largest management consulting firm, Bain ranks second only to McKinsey and Boston Consulting Group for strategy consulting. Gadiesh joined Bain in 1977 as a Baker Scholar from Harvard and has been chairman since 1993, when she led a restructuring of Bain that led to its unparalleled success over the next decade.

Twice named as one of *Fortune* magazine's 50 most powerful women in business, Gadiesh is a widely acknowledged expert in solving management problems and developing corporate strategy. She measures success on getting results for her clients, and that begins with establishing a set of facts as the strategic point of departure. According to Gadiesh, "Information is the foundation to the right solution, one that must be practical and collectively obtained."[5] For a strategic solution to be successful, it must be workable, and that only happens if it is based on facts and not wishful thinking. Therefore she spends most of her time listening to clients, asking questions, analyzing data, and listening some more.

She and the people at Bain instill a diagnostic mentality. They are concerned with discovering the truth and developing solutions grounded in that truth. For a strategy to work, it must be supported at all levels of the organization, and that only happens if every level has been engaged in the fact-finding and analysis. "It means working with people at all levels, building a partnership that gives clients ownership, and sometimes telling them what they do not want to hear."[6]

In the search for new knowledge and solutions Gadiesh forces communication, development of shared knowledge, and the formation of a team. The success of this approach is grounded in her belief in abiding by the core values of the organization as the foundation for exploring new solutions together. She calls this the "true north" of the organization, and it forms the foundation for trust and mutual support necessary for organizations to move through change effectively. "Core competency is your knowledge, core value is your character," she says.[7] Thus true leaders are guardians of values as well as knowledge. Gadiesh emulates this belief by collecting data, acquiring knowledge, and making decisions in a way that develops trust, commitment, and partnership.

$$\oplus$$

The shadow of the Teachers arises out of a fear of being wrong or not knowing. When their view is thwarted by something outside their current range of understanding, they feel as if their idea, status, or self-concept is under attack. To compensate, they become overly attached to their view and try to make everything black and white, yes or no. They constantly want to be right and stubbornly fixate on their ideas, so they become uptight and righteous. They stay in their cocoon to further analyze and fragment, fail to see the big picture, and fall victim to analysis paralysis. They also resist ambiguity, turn things into shoulds and shouldn'ts, and respond to threats of their understanding by becoming overly critical and defensive. When all else fails, they become annoyed, even angry. The less intellectual they view as weak, muddled, and emotional. We have all seen some version of these tendencies at work. This is the shadow of the Teacher.

DEFENSIVE ROUTINES

Fixation. The energy of becoming for Teacher types compels them to define themselves and their self-worth through their intellect, so they want to turn everything into black or white, right or wrong. When this goes too far, they solidify their ideas and stubbornly fixate on their views.

Righteousness. Teachers can become self-righteous when challenged and inflexible and rigid in the face of change. They can become so stuck in their view that they become argumentative and overly critical of others. To protect themselves, they can become uptight and defensive, and even lash out in anger when their ideas are threatened.

Analysis Paralysis. Shadow Teachers are so enamored with problem solving that they suffer from analysis paralysis. When pressed for results, they may seek unnecessary data and detail, just work harder at what they do, and become so wrapped up in the analysis that they fail to see the big picture or place their work in the appropriate context.

For Teachers, the shadow is transmuted into wisdom by letting go of their anxiety and relaxing in their objectivity. The *wisdom activity* of the Teacher is an *absolute clarity* that *pacifies* the struggle to understand with peaceful, objective, and insightful observations and knowledge. Anger arising out of a previously thwarted fixation is transformed into a sharp, precise clarity, revealing the fluid nature of the world and reality. As a result, incredible memory and intellectual skills develop. The clear observations and knowledge of the Teacher remove doubt of reality and put everyone on firm ground and at ease. In the purified form, Teachers have cleared away the deceptions of self-interest in an uncompromising way. This makes them able to cut through doubt, fear, and emotion to reveal their basic goodness.

Teachers are unshakeable because, for them, reality is always the ultimate starting point and the foundation where the journey begins. Just as mirrors reflect reality, they are impartial and untouched by the images. There is no stickiness, no clinging, aversion, or indifference to experience, just a fascination with knowledge and the details. It is, as Chogyam Trungpa Rinpoche says, like water flowing over a flat surface, leaving nothing unexplored or hidden while remaining completely transparent, reflective, and fluid, a mirror for self and others.[8]

The element associated with The Teacher is water, in the sense that Teachers see reality undistorted as in the crystal-like clarity of an undisturbed pool. The color is dark blue as the sky before dawn. The time of day is dawn as in the first light, and the time of season is spring as in planting of the first seed.

SOUTH: THE WAY OF THE NURTURER—AWAKENING THE HEART

Effective leaders are alike in one crucial way: they have a high degree of emotional intelligence.

—*Daniel Goleman*[9]

The archetype of the Nurturer is one of emotional intelligence. It is the place where our first contact with the world through the Teacher is enriched and deepened through a feeling and emotional reaction, as in the spreading of warmth from the midday sun. It is the place of feeling, emotion, and encouraging the heart that creates a sense of confidence, wealth, and abundance that is generously shared with others. It is also the place of unconditional love, trust, and compassion, and of wholesome values for producing strong relationships, families, and communities.

> The Nurturer . . . is the place where our first contact with the world through the Teacher is enriched and deepened through a feeling and emotional reaction . . .

Nurturers see everyone as equal, so they are communal and concerned with making relationships work. They serve and care for others as the mother who looks upon all beings as her own children. Their support and encouragement helps others to extend out into the world to learn with a sense of safety, and without fear or inhibition. Nurturers believe that when individuals feel valued and trust each other, they will be more motivated and willing to make sacrifices for the community. Nurturers are known as the ones born from the jewel, because their sense of richness is so great they extend it to all.

In a modern context, the Nurturer represents the power to be emotionally in touch with self and others, and to build strong relationships. As a Nurturer, you are socially skilled, and make a good listener, communicator, and networker. You are also a good collaborator, committed to producing strong teams and cultures and fostering learning, commitment, and synergy among others. You also care how people treat one another. As such, you provide the moral and ethical compass of the organization, because you feel that how things get done is just as important as what gets done. You are open and trusting, and believe in the basic goodness of everyone, which allows you to freely serve and give your support to others. *This is leader as servant,* as in Servant Leader, the notion espoused by Robert Greenleaf.

As a leader, your authority comes from others knowing that you care and are supportive of their efforts and development. Warren Bennis says, for example, that people don't care how much the leader knows, they want to know how much the leader cares.[10] When such sentiments are broadly shared, they create a greater sense of community and organizational culture. Peter Senge refers to this as "communities of commitment,"[11] where people with shared bonds and mutual support align their energies and talent in working toward what they could not achieve on their own.

LEARNING ROUTINES

Empathy. Leadership research overwhelmingly shows that the ability to relate and work well with others is critical to success. Effective relationships are based on empathy and the ability to listen well and put oneself in the shoes of another. Empathy is an honest openness to the frames of reference of others and it enables a genuine dialogue and thinking together about problems and new ideas. This builds the trust upon which relationships, teams, and cultures develop in a learning organization.

Values-Guided. A strong sense of values also builds trust. Values are the set of first principles by which an individual, a team, or an organization stands. They are the moral and ethical code that leads us to regard some goals or ends as more important than others, and are built on fundamental beliefs in basic goodness and human fulfillment. When these ethical values are clarified and shared with others in the organization, they become a powerful force for guiding decisions and learning how to work together.

Resilience. Finally, being grounded in their emotional well-being provides Nurturers a resilience and a source of strength that frees them from doubt, liberates them from self-interest, and opens them to care for, support, and serve others. This provides them with a sense of worth and resourcefulness that enables them to bounce back from adversity and makes them feel that every situation is workable.

⊕

MIKE KRZYZEWSKI, coach of the Duke Blue Devils basketball team, is a great example of the powers of the Nurturer. Coach K has made his program the most admired in the nation, with three national championships and eight

Final Four appearances since 1986. He has also won five National Coach of the Year awards.

Coach K says he does not coach winning the game; rather, he coaches a winning culture. For him, it is not just teaching basketball; it is about values, honesty, and the integrity of your work. It is about developing emotional bonds, trusting relationships, and collective responsibility in the pursuit of mutual goals. Above all, it is about transcending self-interest and individual differences to support one another in serving a greater cause.

As an example of his team orientation, he tells the story of one early season where two freshmen were late for the team bus. No one knew where they were, no one called, and every other member of the team was on time. Eventually the players came and Coach K was ready to unload on them, but after hearing that they overslept, he wondered why other members of the team had not checked up on them. So rather than reprimand the latecomers on the spot, he talked to the team as a whole about what it means to be a team. "If one of us is late," he told them, "then we are all late."[12] Soon after, he set up a buddy system where everyone looked out for one another so no one was ever late.

Krzyzewski coaches teamwork, mutual respect, and caring for one another. It's not simply about offense and defense and winning the game. It is about people working together as one, to do what it takes to fulfill everyone's potential. He has done that by getting players to take ownership of the team along with the coach and to play like they are not afraid of failing. And he has succeeded not only as a coach, but also as an important and positive and lasting influence on the lives of his players.

⊕

The shadow of the Nurturer arises out of a fear of not being or having enough, and it manifests itself in an insatiable need to hold on, proclaim, and aggrandize the sense of self. Here, the attachment to feeling and emotion is turned inward to the point of over identifying with the self and results in indulgent pride, defensiveness, and even arrogance. Other-feeling turns into self-feeling. So, whereas shadow Teachers are hung up on their *ideas of things,* shadow Nurturers are hung up on their *idea of themselves.* They take themselves too seriously, becoming prideful and overly sensitive to criticism and the suggestions of others. Worse, they manipulate their external world in order to prove themselves superior over and over again, without ever looking inward. They also become so attached to harmony in their relationships that they avoid conflict at almost any cost. This makes authentic relationships with them difficult, as everything is skewed toward supporting and protecting their emotional sense of self.

DEFENSIVE ROUTINES

Oversensitivity. Nurturers' need for acceptance and harmony can be so great that they become oversensitive to criticism and avoid conflict altogether. Nurturers want to please and are afraid to fail in the eyes of others, so at times they will take every criticism personally, feel guilty about differences, and try to make amends without challenging the issues. To protect themselves and others, they will become unassertive, withhold information, fail to challenge ideas they might not agree with, and agree to things they don't really mean.

Dependence. Nurturers also tend to become dependent on others for support or advocacy and fail to act independently or speak for themselves. They seek harmony so much that they become reactive to the expectations of family, colleagues, and other people's agendas. This arises out of their dependence on others for feeling acceptance, love, and belonging, so they fill themselves with a busyness for others.

Pride. In extreme cases, Nurturers protect their feelings by distancing themselves and becoming aloof. Often they appear to be arrogant as their fear of losing the emotional support of others becomes so great that they try to prove themselves over and over again. Operating out of a sense of poverty instead of a sense of abundance, they become absorbed in looking good and proving themselves in the eyes of others.

This shadow tendency of the Nurturer is transmuted into wisdom by moving from a self-centered feeling to a feeling of equality with others. The *wisdom activity* of Nurturers is *equanimity,* and that equanimity allows them to relax and feel an *enriching* depth, expansiveness, and abundance of all life. Connecting with a friend or engaging others on a team in a worthy endeavor allows them to forget themselves and reminds them of what is most important. So instead of being focused on self, their feelings and emotions are widened to focus on relationships and encompassing a feeling of solidarity, unity, and equality with all.

In the purified form, Nurturers have awakened to their basic goodness, and that gives them confidence and the emotional resilience to tackle life's difficult problems. They have moved from a place of poverty to one of abundance, and from a place of pride to one of confidence, enabling them to reach out and enrich, nurture, and serve others in their world. Nurturers are not wimps, however—when their values systems are violated they react with the ferocity of a mother protecting her young.

The element of the Nurturer is the earth, as in providing ground and fertility. The color is yellow as in the sun. The time of day is noon as in warmth of the midday, and season is summer as in rapid growth and flourishing of the coming harvest.

WEST: THE WAY OF THE VISIONARY—SEEING THE WAY

All men dream, but not equally. Those who dream by night in the dusty recesses of their minds awake to find it was vanity, but the dreamers of the day are dangerous men, for they may act their dreams with open eyes, to make it possible.

—*T. E. Lawrence*[13]

The Visionary gathers the sensing and feeling impressions of the first two directions to form a conceptual understanding of the experience, as in harvesting the fruit of labor at the end of the growing season. It is the place of intuitive intelligence, where the sensory input from the world is collected, assimilated, and transformed into deep insight and broad understanding that inspires a commitment and passion for moving forward. It is one level up in abstraction from the powers of the Teacher and Nurturer.

The Visionary . . . is the place of intuitive intelligence, where the sensory input from the world is collected, assimilated, and transformed into deep insight and broad understanding . . .

Visionaries are able to step back to see the whole and the interrelationships of all things while also discerning the uniqueness of every individual and situation in a way that reveals their natural beauties, innate qualities, and possibilities. This enables them to gain perspective and to be creative in making new combinations. It also helps them make sense and meaning out of experience, and gain insight into the possibilities and purposes for self and life.

Visionaries know their purpose and what provides meaning, so they look upon the world with hope and opportunity. Their sense of purpose sparks a passion that mobilizes inner resources and inspires them to move toward desired ends. Thus the direction of the Visionary is also the place of vision and commitment for attaining the highest goals in life. Visionaries are known as the meditative ones, as in taking stock to reap the lessons of experience. They are also known as the ones of infinite light for their ability to tap into the unlimited potential and expanse of the human mind and heart.

As a Visionary in today's world, you are creative and a strategic thinker. You love ideas, think out of the box, and develop new approaches and ways of doing things. You see clearly despite complexity, synthesize quickly, and are able to make judgment calls based on gut feelings. Your ability to see the big picture helps you see new opportunities and possibilities. This enables you to form a clear sense of purpose and vision for the future that guides your actions. You are motivated to learn and achieve, and you have an energy for work that goes beyond simply chasing money, security, or promotion. You are also a good communicator, because you communicate through inspiration—you magnetize others and draw them in. Your vision serves to uplift aspirations, foster commitment, and galvanize the passion of all toward the overarching goal. *This is leader as visionary and architect.*

LEARNING ROUTINES

Judgment. Visionaries are able to challenge the existing thinking and zero in on ideas and issues that have the most promise. They are able to take stock of a situation, connect the dots, and make judgment calls on effective courses of action. They are comfortable with ambiguity and able to define an issue and make a decision without complete information.

Perspective. Visionaries also conceptualize broadly, take a systemic perspective of the world, and understand how things work together. They see issues and problems from multiple perspectives, recognize interdependencies, and understand the possibilities and broad implications of potential actions.

Creativity. All this enables Visionaries to be creative and to synthesize new concepts and mental models. Even if not inherently creative themselves, great leaders develop processes and environments that encourage fresh perspectives, nurture breakthrough thinking, and identify directions and purposes that capture the imagination, ingenuity, and commitment of others.

⊕

JOHN CHAMBERS, CEO of Cisco Systems, is a good example of a Visionary. Chambers is considered one of the most dynamic and innovative chief executives in the country. Since taking the helm of Cisco in 1993, he has built an Internet networking powerhouse from a relatively small $600 million company to one that briefly topped $500 billion before the Internet crash in late 2000. It was an unprecedented rate of growth. He has been called "The Best Boss of the Year," "CEO of the Year," and "CEO of the 21st Century" in a number of business magazines.

Although Cisco lost some of its luster in the market crash, and some of the past success in retrospect seems inevitable, Chambers has nonetheless left an indelible mark on the company and the industry. His vision was to build the country's most influential company—"not just successful financially, but successful in changing so many aspects of our lives and developing a supportive culture."[14] He believes the key to this success is that the people of Cisco believe in themselves and in that vision. In an interview with author Glenn Rifkin, Chambers described how he wants Cisco to do for networking what Microsoft did for PCs and IBM did for mainframes. He believes networking to be the fourth evolution of computers behind mainframes, minicomputers, and personal computers and that Cisco is going to lead the way.[15]

To get there, he places maximum focus on developing a culture, modeled after the old Hewlett-Packard, that fosters value-centered management, teamwork, and respect for people. He wants to make Cisco a place where people want to come and do good work.[16] Even in the face of layoffs in the spring of 2001, Chambers and Cisco modeled this aspiration by offering six months' pay to affected workers, and a furlough to others with partial pay if they worked for a charitable organization supported by Cisco.[17] He found it especially important in tough times to treat everyone with sensitivity, dignity, and understanding.

Finally, Chambers even has a vision for his top people. "If you take my top 100 managers," he said in an interview, "I know what motivates all of them and what is important to them, and we align their goals with company goals."[18] Chambers, then, not only has vision for his industry and his company, but also for his culture and his people.

$$\oplus$$

The shadow side of Visionaries arises out of a fear of emptiness or loss of purpose in life. They overcompensate by becoming attached to the pursuit of meaning and fanning the flames of becoming to the point of arousing a constant desire to pursue, attract, and possess the next best idea, thing, or possibility. They validate their sense of self by pursuing things outside themselves, and falling into a habitual pattern of compulsively chasing dreams, objects, and passions to the point of addiction. As a result they suffer from an inattention to detail and lack of follow-through, allowing all their distractions to suck the space out of every moment and leaving no time for their reflective or discriminatory faculties to function. Failure to break out of their grasping and possessive quality objectifies and depersonalizes experience, making authentic relationships with them difficult.

DEFENSIVE ROUTINES

Scattered. A Visionary's need to constantly find new possibilities and seek deeper meaning in experience can lead to a scattering of focus and inattention to detail. Visionaries are constantly distracted, and caught in a web of ideas. This can lead them to skip over detail, fail to penetrate below the surface of things, and leave a trail of inattentiveness and lack of follow-through.

Overcommitment. For a Visionary, the fear of losing out on possibilities can make every opportunity seem interesting and worthwhile—making it difficult to focus on and prioritize what is most important. They find everything so important that they constantly take on additional challenges and pursuits, leaving too little time and energy to properly attend to multiple activities.

Compulsiveness. Finally, the constant seeking of the new can become almost an addiction. The result for the Visionary is to depersonalize experience and become compulsive in the search for the new. To borrow a quote from Reinhold Niebuhr that is now the motto for Alcoholics Anonymous, the challenge of the Visionary is to "Grant me the serenity to accept the things I cannot change, the courage to change the things I can, and the wisdom to know the difference."

These shadow tendencies of Visionaries are transmuted into wisdom by letting go of indiscriminate grasping, and reopening themselves to their power of discriminating awareness. The *wisdom activity* of the Visionary is *a discriminating vision* that is *magnetizing*, as in the sense of drawing self and others into what is most important. Visionaries let go by stepping back, and assimilating a situation before moving on to the next thing. This allows them to reconnect with what is most important and to prioritize their actions accordingly. Grounded in a vision, a sense of purpose, or a cause, the self-interest of the Visionaries falls away, and their passion is transformed into compassion. They venture to understand other things, not as objects to possess, but rather with a genuine sense of openness and understanding of the natural promise of all things.

In the purified form, the discriminating mind of the Visionary cuts through the myriad of concepts and emotions to discern, envision, and draw everyone into new and deeper states of understanding. Native Americans nurture the energy of the Visionary through the vision quest ceremony, in which people are isolated for periods of time and deprived of sustenance in order to stress the body and cut through habitual patterns so that they can connect to an inner vision. This vision enables them to relax in their being and to be intimate, to communicate well, and to connect genuinely and authentically with others.

The element of the Visionary is fire as in passion. The color is red as in the setting sun. The time of day is dusk as in time for reflection and contemplation in preparation for the next cycle, and season is fall as in harvesting the crops and reaping the lessons of experience.

NORTH: THE WAY OF THE WARRIOR— EMBODYING THE WAY

Knowing is not enough, we must apply; willing is not enough, we must do.

—*Johann Wolfgang von Goethe*[19]

The Warrior is the archetype of action intelligence. Warriors absorb the formative and conditioning force of the previous directions, and take conscious, volitional action for achieving a desired result, as in bringing closure to the day or the end of a cycle. As such, they represent the ability to actualize plans, internalize the lessons, and close the gap between knowing and doing.

Warriors possess the will and determination to get things done as they
know they should be done, even in the face of risk and

*The Warrior is the
archetype of action
intelligence . . . they
represent the ability
to actualize plans,
internalize the
lessons, and close the
gap between
knowing and doing.*

obstacles. Thus they are courageous, strong, and self-sacrificing, as heroic people are in being independent, self-starting and tenacious in facing adversity or taking a stand for the good of the whole. Warriors are task-oriented, tough-minded, and decisive individuals who take charge and go after a problem. They possess drive and ambition, are willing to learn through trial and error, and often rise to positions of influence

Warriors seek power, not for personal gain, but for making things function more effectively. In taking full control and responsibility, they strive to create safety and freedom for themselves and others. They are fully present. They face the full truth of reality and are willing to act based on that truth. As such, they are masters of themselves, stand firm by their truths, and align actions with words. Models of integrity and fully authentic, they act with their whole being and leave nothing out. Warriors are known as the all-accomplishing ones, victorious over self and the situation.

In today's business world, as a Warrior you represent the power to focus on the task, take action, challenge the process, and model the way for others in achieving results. You execute, follow through, take control to make things better, and persevere to make it happen. You see the gap between the current reality and the desired future, and are disciplined and courageous in closing the gap between the two.

You are also able to make and remake yourself by exercising free will and taking risks to narrow the gap between who you are and who you want to be. You strive to lead as a whole person, and provide the example for others to follow. You model, demonstrate, and embody the visions you espouse for yourself and your organization. This gives you integrity and demands trust. This also makes you authentic and gives you the magic and personal power and authority for making things happen. *This is leader by example.*

Warriors stay on task and stand by their beliefs, and they encourage, challenge, and empower others to do the same. This is also leader as sacred warrior, meaning that, as in the ancient traditions, a Warrior transcends the need for personal achievement to protect and selflessly serve the whole community.

LEARNING ROUTINES

Courage. Warriors are driven, learn by doing, and experiment in trying new things to move forward. Often this places them in tough situations and forces them to make difficult decisions, but they have courage to take risks and make those tough choices. They do what is right despite personal risk or discomfort, and challenge others to do likewise.

Integrity. Warriors also possess integrity and understand that what they do is far more important than what they say. They walk the talk and match word with deed. They inspire trust, commitment, and confidence in serving as living models of the principles for which they stand, and this quality gives them the personal power to establish an environment of uncompromising integrity.

Discipline. Finally, Warriors are disciplined in staying on task and serving their beliefs. This discipline comes from a certain internal strength and perseverance that comes from consciously connecting to what is truly important to them. They take action based on values and principles rather than impulse or desire, and make decisions in a reasoned, comprehensive, and integrated fashion.

$$\oplus$$

AARON FEUERSTEIN, CEO of Malden Mills, is a remarkable example of the powers of the Warrior. Malden Mills, makers of Polartec synthetic sportswear fabric, is a small company located in Methuen, Massachusetts. On the evening of December 11, 1995, a fire burned most of Malden Mills to the ground, leaving 3,000 people out of work.

In the parking lot during the fire, employees heard Feuerstein say, "This is not the end."[20] Rather than lose his employees and devastate the economy of the small town, Feuerstein spent millions of his own money to keep all 3,000 employees on the payroll for three months while he rebuilt the company. Where he could have taken tens of millions in insurance settlements or sold the company to rivals and walked away, instead he invested millions of his own money to save the livelihoods of his employees and the economy of his small town.

In stark contrast to other executives of our time, Aaron Feuerstein lived up to his words and took care of his people. The outpouring of employee and public support were so great as a result of his actions that shipments from the new plant were double within a few weeks after reopening from what had been before the fire. Malden Mills is still not out of trouble, however, as more recently the company has refused to follow the industry trend of exporting jobs overseas and struggles to remain solvent while it searches for ways to protect and keep jobs at home.

Aaron Feuerstein rises at 5:30 A.M. to study passages of the scriptures and Shakespeare. "Too many people depend on me," he says. "I have to be worthy."[21] He works at being good, and he did "what was merely the decent thing to do."[22] For him, the workers are the most valuable asset of Malden Mills, and he has a responsibility to them as well as to the community. More importantly, however, he has the courage to stand by his convictions even in the face of personal risk. He models the way and does what most people might do if given the time to reflect and act on their priorities. His actions were not an accident; they are the result of his dedication and hard work at being clear on what is most important to him and acting accordingly.

$$\oplus$$

The shadow of the Warrior arises out of fear of being left behind, of not being adequate, or of losing control. Warriors can become so attached to accomplishing goals that they constantly compare their results to the achievements of others, and become compulsively ambitious and competitive. They try to save the day by taking actions that will prove and substantiate them—becoming hyperactive, overly aggressive, and competitive. Their achievements become their personal triumphs and identity, yet they are haunted by an anxiety that they are still not doing enough. They remain in their cocoon by holding on to a sense of distrust of their own abilities while constantly doing things to prove otherwise. They become busybodies, doing for the sake of doing, and as a result, they often charge off in the wrong direction. Their suspicion of what others have or are about to take also makes them irritated and controlling, and causes them to validate themselves by putting others down.

DEFENSIVE ROUTINES

Busyness. The identity of shadow Warriors is wrapped up in their ability to get things done, but at times they can place so much emphasis on results that they lack focus on priorities and are seemingly rudderless in the actions that they take. They do for the sake of doing, afraid to stop and reflect for fear of losing time or momentum.

Intimidation. A Warrior's need to achieve and get results can be so great that it leads to an intimidating and insensitive style. In extreme cases, a fear of being left behind or paranoia of someone getting the better of them leads Warriors to bulldoze and to validate themselves through putting others down. Having lost or having never gained a true bearing on what is important, they see everything as win or lose and become jealous or envious of accomplishments not of their own making.

Micromanagement. Warriors' need to be in charge can lead them to be over-controlling. This tendency can make them unwilling to delegate, insist on doing things their way, and micromanage the efforts of others. They approach leadership in a top-down management style, and make it a habit to intrude on the work of others by wandering around, peering over shoulders, and telling everyone the proper way to do things.

This shadow tendency is transmuted into wisdom through letting go of the paranoia to reveal a keenness for action that is without ego or need to self-proclaim through accomplishment. The *wisdom activity* of the Warrior is *all-accomplishing action* in the sense that it draws on the formative powers of the first three directions to willfully *subjugate* and cut through obstacles of self-interest. By tapping into those powers, the Warrior overpowers the ego to enable a balanced and selfless action that is rooted in a deeper consciousness.

In the purified form, Warriors embody a momentum toward maturity, where the full and balanced development of all sides of the Wheel grounds them in an inner wisdom, and enables them to act fearlessly and with confidence. The need to pursue personal accomplishment falls away and is transformed into an all-accomplishing wisdom that is focused on the total functioning of the being. The enlightened Warrior draws on all the intelligences and makes the body an instrument of the spirit. This is doing without the doer, selfless action that springs from inner wisdom and the dissolution of self-interest. This intelligence brings a genuineness and freedom of expression that makes them authentic and real for others. Free from fear and inhibition, empowered to function completely, the enlightened Warrior works selflessly and tirelessly to make things more efficient, and to guide the self and others to full maturity.

The element of The Warrior is air and wind as in movement. The color is dark green as in a moonlit night. The time of day is night as in completion, and the season is winter as in cool, pure, unbiased, and selfless action.

CENTER: THE WAY OF THE SAGE—LEARNING TO LEARN

The basic difference between an ordinary man and a warrior is that a warrior takes everything as a challenge, while an ordinary man takes everything either as a blessing or as a curse.

—Don Juan, Yaqui Master[23]

The archetype of the Sage is about spiritual intelligence, and it is both the first and last step in the five-step cycle of becoming. It is the place of consciousness where wisdom develops, and the latent, driving, and governing urge to individuate and realize the potential for higher states of understanding and being awakens. It is one step up from the awareness of the Teacher—it is awareness of awareness, thinking of thinking, and a consciousness that sparks further consciousness. This ground of awareness makes Sages calm, serene, open, and easygoing. It also serves to awaken the inherent potential of all other directions.

. . . the Sage is about spiritual intelligence . . . where wisdom develops, and where the latent, driving and governing urge to individuate and realize the potential for higher states of understanding and being resides.

In its highest awakened state, the intelligence of the Sage is both the sum total and the origin of the other four directions. It is the sum total in the sense that the highest awakened state of the Sage is a place of balance, not in a rigid sense, but in a dynamic, agile sense where the equilibrium of life is achieved by invoking the powers of the other directions as required by the situation. It is also the origin because it is the unfolding of consciousness from the center that awakens the other qualities and promotes their development. It is a place of optimism and self-mastery where the predisposition to reflect and become fully conscious makes Sages feel empowered to develop and make a difference with their lives. Sages possess a positive attitude and view every experience as an opportunity to learn and grow.

This positive attitude also makes them want to reach out to do the same for others. They awaken others to their journey and their path. This is different from the sharing of wisdom of the Teacher. It is as poet Kahlil Gibran said: "If he is indeed wise, he does not bid you enter the house of his wisdom, but rather leads you to the threshold of your own mind."[24] As such, the Sage is also known as the illuminator and the radiant one.

As a Sage in today's world, you are a continuous learner, and are agile and able to constantly adapt to the shifting demands of a situation. You seek to be fully aware, take responsibility for your life, and realize your fullest potential. You have a desire not only to learn but also to learn how to learn, and to take charge in being able to grow. That desire is driven by a positive attitude that makes every situation seem workable, and allows Sages to derive the most out of every circumstance. This makes you balanced and able to adjust, even thrive, in a variety of contexts. *This is leader as learner.*

Peter Block says that "leaders confront themselves and others with their own freedom,"[25] meaning that a leader's first responsibility is to inspire optimism and a desire to learn and become masters of their journey. The awareness of the Sage lights this desire within, and moves people to take dominion over life. *This is also the leader as victor and master* over self and circumstance, as a monarch in taking seat as lord of the realm. The Sage's awareness is the root for all your learning and is where your leadership journey both begins and ends.

LEARNING ROUTINES

Awareness. The energy of becoming of the Sage is directed toward awakening all one's inherent powers and creating a holistic and balanced approach to personal development. Awareness comes from observation and reflection, and is essential to self-knowledge and the root to self-improvement. It allows us to be open and candid and provides the ground for being flexible and responsive.

Optimism. This awareness gives insight into personal strengths and weaknesses, and provides the impetus to want to make change, take charge of life, and make a difference. Sages see the opportunities life provides, and are moved to become fully empowered and responsible for taking control of their destiny. They live their lives as masters rather than as victims of circumstance, and feel empowered to turn any situation into an opportunity for personal growth and achievement.

Agility. Sages learn how to learn and work to become fully free and conscious, seeking challenges and reaching beyond their comfort zones to learn, grow, and develop. They draw on all the powers of the other directions in their learning, to seek data, work with others, find purpose, and act in service of their growth and development. This makes them balanced and agile, able to adapt, learn, and grow to meet the changing demands of the situation.

⊕

COLIN POWELL displays the powers of the Sage. The child of a humble immigrant family in the Bronx, Powell has bootstrapped himself in his extraordinary career to both professional success and personal contribution. His strong values, hard work, and high standards quickly raised him to prominence—first as a White House fellow in the Nixon administration, then as Chairman of the Joint Chiefs of Staff under Bush the elder and Clinton, and finally as Secretary of State under George W. Bush. He has served four presidents, been decorated widely as a military and civilian hero, and is broadly respected by Americans of all stripes and colors. Although at times criticized for his role in the choices of the Bush administration in foreign affairs, Powell was still considered a voice of reason among his often more strident fellow cabinet members.

Powell is noted for his self-effacing style and apparent ease in dealing with crisis and power, but perhaps most importantly his leadership is distinguished through the use of what he calls "optimism as a force multiplier."[26] For him, optimism is not based on our external reality; rather, it is determined by how we regulate our inner world. It is an attitude toward life that encourages us to continue where pessimists would give up. He follows three maxims: "It ain't as bad as you think, it can be done, and don't take counsel of your fears or naysayers."[27]

Optimism is the power to spur bold action and extraordinary results by taking responsibility for the hand that you are dealt, and feeling fully empowered to make a difference. It is not an unbounded optimism; rather, it is a disciplined optimism. For Colin Powell, good leaders ground their optimism in an awareness and knowledge of themselves and the situation, and are able to learn from their experience and make adjustments. This optimism becomes a "force multiplier"[28] when the seemingly impossible is achieved and motivates people to even greater standards in the future. His career in the military and as a public servant has been a model for setting and creating a positive and productive tone for others.

$$\oplus$$

The shadow of the Sage arises out of a fear of powerlessness over life. The shadow can make Sages feel victimized and withdraw from taking responsibility for their lives. So they want to hang out and not be bothered, which leads to a habitual pattern of leaving the details of life unattended to, uncared for, and neglected. Sages can shrink from reality and lose focus on who they are and who is doing the experiencing. They can even lose the sense of their own being. They stay in their cocoon and become complacent, constantly ignoring important signals or feedback in their lives to change, grow, and develop. Nothing excites or moves them. They are numb, and as a result, they also numb the qualities of the other four directions.

DEFENSIVE ROUTINES

Complacency. Shadow Sages fall into a habitual comfort zone, and they like staying there. They are somewhat like Bill Murray in the movie *Groundhog Day,* where the pattern repeats over and over again without the main character getting the message to change or become more conscious. Inattention to the details of life leads them to become careless, to drift through daily experience without direction, motivation, or development.

Victim Mentality. As a result of this complacency and self-delusion, the shadow Sages feel like victims rather than masters of circumstance. They believe their security and happiness grow out life's conditions rather than their own choices, so they remove themselves from the explanation of their problems. Thus they feel victimized, and blame others and the circumstances when things go wrong.

Self-Delusion. They also shrink from reality and numb themselves into an unconscious coziness. They become self-absorbed and feedback bounces off them. They are swallowed up by their routine, and stubbornly shut out anything that threatens them. Instead of learning, they simply cope with what is given to them and become pessimistic, unmotivated, and stuck.

This shadow tendency is transmuted into wisdom by waking up and letting go of doubt, sloth, and stupor, and venturing out into the world. The *wisdom activity* of the Sage is *a vast alert awareness,* or consciousness, and it is *all-encompassing* in the sense that it awakens all the directions and all aspects of being. Thus the key to letting go for the Sage is to reawaken to the inherent power of awareness.

Awareness is the dawn of wisdom, and the central coordinating quality that transforms the confusion of dullness into higher states of consciousness. Simply taking time to pay attention and reflect on things activates a sense of reality becoming more workable. This reflection empowers Sages to begin to go forth out of their slumber. As such, they emerge as the ruler, sovereign, or lord of experience, feeling empowered to attack and defend all quarters of the land.

In the purified form, the Sage is the place of primordial space, empty, vast, and devoid of inherent existence, yet imbued with and not separate from an all-pervading sense of love and compassion, our basic goodness. This is the essential nature of being fully human, the space that is revealed after peeling back all the layers of self-delusion, and the ground that exists before the obscurations of self-interest appear. We don't change—our true self just begins to shine through.

The element of the Sage is the sky as in spacious awareness, and the color is white as in the integration of all other colors of the rainbow.

FOLLOWING THE PATH OF THE WHEEL

. . . the Wheel was an integrated path to knowledge and spiritual awakening that begins and ends with the governing hand of the Sage, progressing through a five-step cycle to higher and higher states of consciousness.

Having taken this introductory tour, we can see how ancient cultures used the five directions of the Heroic Journey to awaken themselves to their world and their own full potential. For these cultures, the Wheel was an integrated path to knowledge and spiritual awakening—it begins and ends with the governing hand of the Sage and progresses through a five-step cycle to higher and higher states of consciousness. This cycle could take place in an instant, as in acting quickly in response to input from the world on a daily basis, or it could unfold gradually over a lifetime, as in a quest for completeness and maturity by learning the wisdoms of all directions.

The Teacher provides the intellectual ground by taking in information objectively and giving a sense of reality. The Nurturer adds emotional depth to that experience by reacting to the input with a feeling of pleasure, pain, or indifference. The Visionary assimilates this data and forms an intuitive perception around its meaning that arouses an inner desire for change. Finally, the Warrior, having been conditioned by the previous aspects, takes appropriate action to close the gap between idea and reality.

Although all five archetypal energies of becoming are always active and interactive, people dwell in different places and have certain preferences toward one or more of the directions. This natural preference shapes their view of the world and forms the basis of their personal style. According to indigenous traditions, when we are born we come into this world through a single direction. That direction is our original gift and the place where we naturally feel most comfortable. This place is our comfort zone, or cocoon. It forms our perspective, shapes our personality, and determines our particular style of becoming, knowing, and relating. It is a lens through which we filter our input and project our perspectives, a process that inevitably renders our understanding of the world incomplete. The purpose of life, however, is to create greater balance and understanding by venturing out and journeying around the Wheel to learn the qualities of all the directions.

. . . the more this cycle is repeated, the more the basic goodness and authentic presence of Heroic people are revealed . . .

When applied to leadership, you are presented with a choice of either holding on or letting go at each step along the way. The more you hold on to a particular archetypal point of view, the more you distort it and make it the ground for serving self-interest and neurotic behavior. Teachers who hold too tightly to the powers of their intellect, for instance, can fixate and become rigid in their view. This holding, as mentioned, stems from a latent and natural fear of personal inadequacy or insubstantiality that is associated with each direction. On the other hand, the more Heroic persons let go and open to this energy, the more they transmute the fear and make it the ground for wisdom. An open Teacher sees ideas and reality just as they are without feeling any need to defend them.

Similarly, the more this cycle is repeated, the more the basic goodness and authentic presence of Heroic people are revealed, and the more moved you are to let go of self-interest and serve greater causes. For most Heroic

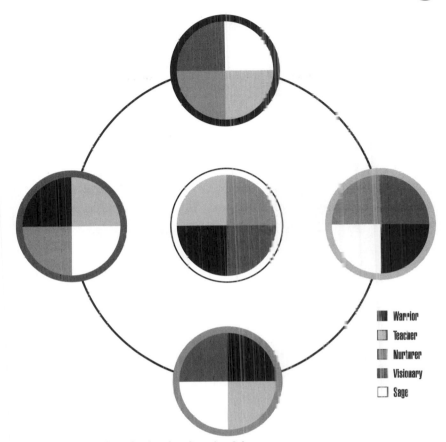

Warrior
Teacher
Nurturer
Visionary
Sage

Figure 2.2 The Wheel: Each Direction Contains Others

people, experiencing basic goodness remains a goal that, once tasted, arouses a yearning for more. With repeated tastes, the emerging breadth and depth of understanding begin to change and transform your behaviors and attitudes. You relax in who you are and what you have to offer and become more authentic. You know yourself and what is important, and this empowers you to be that in the world.

As you grow and progress along the path, you do so from your natural place or preference on the Wheel. As a Warrior, you do not become a Teacher, Nurturer, or Visionary, for example; rather, you learn to develop the wisdom aspects of the other directions to become a fully integrated and enlightened Warrior. Thus basic goodness and authentic presence can be realized from any direction.

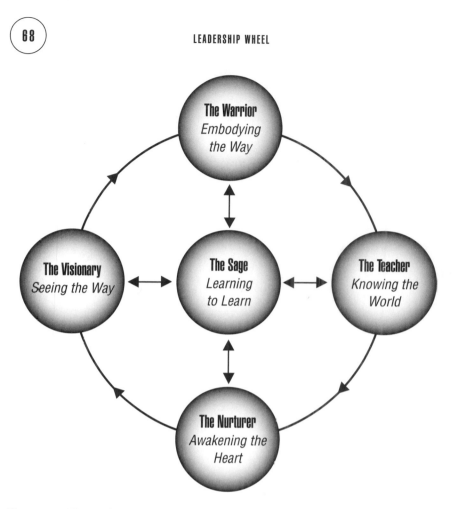

Figure 2.3   The Leadership Wheel

THE WHEEL AS A MODEL FOR LEADERSHIP

As a model for leadership, the first essential message of the Wheel is one of balance, adaptation, and learning. Each direction offers a unique and important intelligence, and taken together they move the individual toward wholeness. Often we make the mistake of thinking that intelligence equates to the intellect or IQ, but the Wheel shows that it takes emotional, intuitive, action, and even spiritual intelligences to be complete.

These five intelligences of the Wheel overlap and are interdependent. They reinforce and build on one another in a cyclical process that continually fosters learning and development. The Sage provides the awareness, the Teacher the intellect, the Nurturer the support, the Visionary the purpose, and the Warrior the action for learning and change to occur. Figure 2.3 shows how each direction is necessary for effective leadership, and none is sufficient alone.

The message is that leaders must learn and adapt their style to the needs of the situation. Charles Darwin once said that it is not the strongest, fastest, or smartest species that survive, it is the most adaptive. Thus a person too dominant in one area may succeed in the short run, but will not be able to learn, change, and adapt over time. Each example of leadership discussed previously is a balanced leader with strengths in multiple directions. Colin Powell is as much a Teacher and Nurturer as a Sage, and Gadiesh as much a Warrior and Nurturer as a Teacher. The same can be said for the other three.

For leaders to aspire to greatness or even sustain their leadership role in the face of changing conditions, they must strive for balance.

For leaders to aspire to greatness or even sustain their leadership role in the face of changing conditions, they must strive for balance. That balance can be achieved through complementing one's skills by working through others or through developing one's own capabilities. Strong Visionaries, for example, may seek the advice of Teachers to balance their focus on the future with the realities of the current situation; or they could also learn to master the details of the current reality as a way of balancing out their skill set. Either way, enduring leaders are able to develop balance and to succeed in diverse and dynamic environments.

Research has proven that this kind of agility is essential to long-term success. The Wheel provides a framework for developing this ability by giving us a means to assess strengths and weaknesses and make adjustments in working toward the ideal. In doing so, we become more balanced and learn to access, master, and apply each direction based on the demands of the situation.

As an aid to personal growth, the root patterns of the Wheel can be extended into a set of leadership skills. The learning routines are the inherent psychological preferences people of that archetype have for working and relating to their world, while the defensive routines are the shadow tendencies that can cause people trouble when they hold on to and overplay those psychological preferences. In contrast, leadership skills are the learned behaviors that research has proven to be important to personal effectiveness and leadership success. They manifest naturally from one's preferences, but they can also be developed to overcome the shadow tendencies and extend us beyond our natural preferences.

A Nurturer, for example, can learn to be more decisive and action-oriented, and a Visionary more attentive to detail. People grow by learning competencies outside their archetype. The learning routines, then, are psychological preferences that remain relatively stable, and the skills are learned behaviors that can be developed to enhance, counter, and step beyond those preferences.

Many organizations have developed these notions into leadership competency models that they use to drive corporate culture through the process of selecting, training, and promoting their leaders. The inherent danger is that many of these models are biased and tend to reinforce an existing culture that may not be suited to the long-term learning and strategic needs of the organization. Aggressive Warrior-Teacher competencies, for example, are often overemphasized to the detriment of the cooperative and innovative tendencies of the Nurturer-Visionary. As a result, the organization's ability to learn and change is compromised. The benefit of using the Wheel as a leadership model, in contrast, is that it is holistic and based on the premise of learning and human fulfillment. As such, it offers a powerful tool for developing more enlightened leaders and sustainable organizations.

Table 2.1 summarizes the five directions of the Wheel as a model for leadership. Each direction represents a basic intelligence, or way of being, that translates into a particular style of leadership. These styles have basic learning routines that promote personal development and reflect the tendencies of people of that archetype. They also have shadow, defensive routines that can stall or even derail learning and growth. The leadership skills are those behaviors that can be learned to strengthen a style, access another, or overcome the shadow.

To create balance in traveling around the Wheel, we have to peel back and let go of the layers of self-interest.

An essential message of the Wheel to emphasize is the one of basic goodness and enlightened activity. To create balance in traveling around the Wheel, we have to peel back and let go of the layers of self-interest. In doing so, we redirect our energy of becoming and open ourselves to others, and that results in enlightened work and a desire to contribute to the greater good.

Management author Jim Collins calls this Level 5 leadership. Collins says, "Level 5 leaders channel their ego away from themselves and toward the greater goal."[29] The leadership examples previously discussed are people who have opened their hearts and are dedicated in their own way to making this world a better place. Whether it is Powell through serving a public purpose, Gadiesh through her values-driven approach and philanthropy,

TABLE 2.1: THE LEADERSHIP WHEEL SUMMARY

Teacher: Knowing the World (intellectual intelligence). The influence of leaders rests in part on their expertise and their intellectual grasp of their profession and industry. Their technical skill, rational thought, and objective minds enable them to see reality clearly and objectively. This is leader as expert.

Learning Routines	*Defensive Routines*
Curiosity	Fixation
Logic	Righteousness
Objectivity	Analysis paralysis

Leadership Skills	
Business and technical acumen	Organizational skill
Analytical ability	Attention to detail
Technology skills	Process engineering

Nurturer: Awakening the Heart (emotional intelligence). Effective leaders are able to recognize and manage the feelings and emotions of self and others. This makes them good at relationships. They care about people and working collaboratively toward common ends. They are socially skilled, good listeners, communicators, networkers, and team players. This is leader as servant and people person.

Learning Routines	*Defensive Routines*
Empathy	Oversensitivity
Values-guided	Dependence
Resilience	Pride

Leadership Skills	
Listening	Collaboration
Interpersonal relationships	Networking
Interpersonal communication	Service orientation

Visionary: Seeing the Way (intuitive intelligence). Leaders are able to see the big picture and think strategically and systematically in a way that helps them see the opportunities and the possibilities. They also have a clear purpose and vision for what they are doing and the purpose that guides their actions. That vision serves to uplift aspirations, foster commitment, and galvanize others. This is leader as visionary.

Learning Routines	*Defensive Routines*
Judgment	Scattered
Perspective	Overcommitment
Creativity	Compulsiveness

Leadership Skills	
Strategic thinking	Systems thinking
Working through systems	Change management
Vision development	Purposefulness

Warrior: Embodying the Way (action intelligence). Leaders are task and result oriented, and able to get things done. They actualize plans, take control of a situation, challenge the process, and take risks and experiment to make things happen. More importantly, they walk the talk, model the way, and align their actions with their words and deeds. This is leader by example.

Learning Routines	*Defensive Routines*
Courage	Busyness
Integrity	Intimidation
Discipline	Micromanagement

Leadership Skills	
Follow-through	Taking charge
Achieving results	Assuming responsibility
Setting the example	Decisiveness

Sage: Learning to Learn (spiritual intelligence). Effective leaders know themselves and what they have to offer. They are learners, know themselves, and are open, candid, and humble in their striving to grow and develop. They feel empowered to make a difference and make the most out of any experience. This makes them agile and able to adapt to changing situations. This is leader as learner.

Learning Routines	*Defensive Routines*
Awareness	Complacency

Optimism	Victim mentality
Agility	Self-delusion
Leadership Skills	
Self-knowledge	Learning from experience
Self-development	Balance
Reflection	Patience

Krzyzewski through team learning, Chambers through a vision for a new way of doing business, or Feuerstein through a commitment to community, each has done well for him- or herself while doing good for the world. To experience the Wheel is to experience basic goodness and to become fully human.

With courage, openness, and commitment, we all learn to expand our realities and see the depths of our potential. And as we grow, we all learn to ride our energy of becoming to move toward human fulfillment and make this world a better place.

⊕

WENDY KOPP, founder of Teach for America, is another good example of a balanced and agile leader, dedicated to creating a better world. From her senior dorm room at Princeton University, Kopp launched a plan for a volunteer teacher corps based on her senior thesis. She was convinced that a teaching corps of bright, ambitious college graduates from all backgrounds across the country could help reduce the disparities in American education and give every child in this country an equal opportunity to succeed. "The idea wasn't to create this little non-profit organization," she recalls. "It was to create a movement of some of our most talented leaders."[30]

Wendy Kopp started with just a vision and a passion for addressing educational inequality. Over a decade later, Teach for America is a group of about 2,600 corps members that annually reaches out to 200,000 students nationwide, and 60 percent of the 7,500 corps alumni has chosen to continue in the field of education.

To achieve this kind of success, Kopp traveled a very steep learning curve. First, as a naïve 21-year-old, she had the courage and perseverance to raise funds from some very senior and skeptical potential donors. Sending up to a hundred letters a week to top executives and handpicked CEOs, she was relentless in pursuing her dream and was eventually rewarded with $2.5 million in her first year—including a $500,000 grant from Ross Perot.

The early years were tough, however, as a young group of idealistic social entrepreneurs soon discovered that their franchise had quickly outgrown their ability to manage the operation. Early training conferences, logistical support, and subsequent fundraising efforts proved shaky, often leaving in doubt the very future of the cause. Taking advice from board members, consultants, and funders alike, Kopp learned how to right the effort and become a balanced, agile leader. She learned how to build a team based on values that empowers its members and fosters a culture supportive of their mission. She also learned how to reorganize and restructure the operation to meet the overwhelming organizational challenges of a young, rapidly growing enterprise. Finally, she consciously paid attention to her own learning and to the development of her staff and her volunteers, pulling in advisors from her increasingly large network of supporters to help grow a new generation of leaders. She started with the dream of a Visionary and tenacity of a Warrior, but also learned to be Nurturer, Teacher, and Sage. Kopp traveled the Wheel to become a balanced, agile leader, dedicated to human fulfillment.

$$\oplus$$

Contrast Wendy Kopp's story with those of the failed CEOs of our time. Where Wendy Kopp is driven by a cause, the others lost sight of any business purpose other than the imperatives of economic growth and accumulation of wealth. They were overwhelmed by the forces of self-interest—driven to insider trading, tax evasion, aggressive accounting, and building bloated organizations—and became icons of corporate greed. As mentioned several times before, the system only works if self-interest is balanced with other-interest, or service to others.

SUMMARY

The Wheel offers five ways of becoming, five kinds of intelligence, and five aspects of human nature for those undertaking the Heroic Journey. It is a challenging yet rewarding five-step journey of self-discovery that culminates in Heroic people returning to take their seat as enlightened rulers of themselves and of their world. In conquering all sides of the self, they are moved to help others to do the same. The essential message of the Wheel, then, is one of learning and balance in striving toward human fulfillment, and provides many important insights into the behavioral, psycho-emotional, and spiritual aspects of human existence.

The fundamental challenge for leadership today is to rediscover the journey of self-discovery as well as "the return" to share the boons of that process with society. Yet the path of the journey is like traveling on a razor's edge. To realize the wisdom of each direction, we must first become vulnerable and open ourselves to experience its particular potential. The learning routines of each direction have an opening-up or other-oriented quality. In contrast, the defensive routines have a holding-on or self-oriented quality. To let go of self-interest and open up to others is to learn how to inherit the innate wisdoms. The result is greatness and human fulfillment. To hold on to habits based in self-interest is to serve the self out of fear and to distort the inherent wisdom of the direction. The result is smallness and derailment. Success comes from letting go of self-interest and opening up to others, while derailment comes from holding on and serving self. The razor's edge is the fear we face in the transition, and the highest leverage point for personal change.

Overall, this perspective makes the practice of leadership synonymous with the practice of being fully human. Yet most often the study of leadership focuses on the behavioral aspects and not the fundamental aspects of being, which may explain why we are left with so many unanswered questions. It is difficult to discuss leadership in any depth without ultimately raising questions of spirituality. The experience of leadership, like the experience of life, is a continuum from the behavioral to the psycho-emotional to the spiritual. In this book I use the spiritual aspects to frame and understand leadership, but the focus will remain primarily on the behavioral and psycho-emotional. The spiritual path ultimately needs to rest in the hands of the journeyer.

○ EXERCISES ○

○ EXERCISE 2.1: SURFACING THE SHADOW

Understanding shadow is a subtle challenge. According to Jung, shadows are manifestations of hidden, unexplored, or unresolved parts of ourselves that we don't want to deal with.[31] We are often blind to them; but they are important to reveal because they obscure a view of a portion of ourselves that can derail us from learning, change, and becoming more effective.

We all have these tendencies, and they usually stem from a feeling of fear, insecurity, or inadequacy. As discussed, a shadow often arises from overplaying our hand, as with an overdeveloped strength that becomes a weakness. Shadows also arise out of overcompensating for something we feel we lack. Personal drive can turn into workaholism, confidence into arrogance, or conscientiousness into compulsiveness. Likewise the need to achieve turns into overcompetitiveness, the need to be right into rigidity, or the need to feel liked into pride, and so on.

We can't change what we don't see. The more self-aware we become, the more we disempower the hold of the shadow. This exercise is meant to help you see what you will need to deal with to move ahead.

Step 1: Take a few minutes to reflect on the following questions. Take your time and write your responses down on a pad of paper. Often the process of writing surfaces things that would not otherwise arise out of simple reflection.

These questions are designed to be thought-provoking for surfacing our shadows. If they seem difficult, remember: You are trying to see something that does not want to be seen, as its power stems from remaining in the unconscious. This is a first step in becoming the leader of your own thought processes.

1. Do people give me feedback that is inconsistent with my view, and that might be pointing to a blind spot?
2. Where might I be stuck and not open to feedback or learning from another's point of view?
3. What fear might I be covering up when I react emotionally to situations?
4. Where do I get in trouble in my relationships?
5. What strengths do I turn into weaknesses in certain situations?
6. What needs might I be holding on to and overcompensating for?
7. What beliefs or fears are generating these qualities?
8. How might my shadows cost or potentially derail me?
9. How can I transmute my shadow into wisdom—where must I let go?

In reflecting on these questions myself, I remembered that I used to receive feedback that people did not trust me. To me this was inconceivable, because I believed I would do almost anything for a friend in true need. "A friend in need is a friend indeed," I believed, and I was always true to that. So I had a hard time accepting such feedback. I was always there when people really needed me, yet the issue kept coming up. So I began to question what was going on.

I realized that the only time I was ever truly present for someone was when that person was in trouble. I also realized that this was when I was at my best, but for most people this foul weather friendship was not enough.

An acquaintance once shared this with me: "Friendship is like a garden, you need to nurture it for it to flourish." Yet most of the time I was too absorbed in one of my "projects" to pay attention. I wouldn't make time, because I was often trying to prove myself through other venues, especially through professional accomplishment. There was no balance. Upon reflection, it was clear that the root cause was my own poverty mentality, and the sense of not being enough. Holding on to this set of fears was costing me in my relationships.

I know my strengths include being tremendously creative, spontaneous, and fun-loving, but rather than invest these qualities in friendships, I used them to achieve and promote myself in the eyes of other people. Even with the very people I was closest to—rather than *relate* to them, I was trying impress them. I was shaping my image rather than attending to people. These are shadow Warrior and shadow Visionary tendencies. So I committed to letting go of the need to achieve as my central focus, and to balance my life with spending more quality time with those who matter most.

Step 2: Consider sharing your reflections with a dear friend. Close friends can be very helpful in providing further insight into places where we become stuck. Sharing and verbalizing our thoughts also helps to increase our sense of ownership of the underlying issues and our ability to dissolve them.

○ EXERCISE 2.2: PERSONAL EMPOWERMENT— FROM VICTIM TO VICTOR

Possessing the positive attitude and optimism of the Sage is perhaps the most important ingredient for becoming an effective leader. Without a positive attitude and a sense of feeling personally empowered to make a difference, personal change and leadership development never leave the launching pad. It is the source from which learning and developmental change spring. Inspirational author Charles Swindoll says the following about attitude:

The longer I live, the more I realize the impact of attitude on life. Attitude . . . is more important than facts. It is more important than the past, than education, than money, than circumstances, than failures, than successes, than what other people think or say or do. It is more important than appearance, giftedness, or skill. . . . The remarkable thing is, we have a choice every day regarding the attitude we will embrace for that day. We cannot change our past. . . . We cannot change the inevitable. The only thing we can do is play on the one string we have and that is our attitude. . . . I am convinced that life is 10% what happens to me and 90% how I react to it. And so it is with you. . . . we are in charge of our Attitudes.[32]

Often however, many of us fall into the trap of a victim's mentality. A victim feels disempowered by circumstance and dependent on others for direction, time, and resources. Victims remove themselves from the explanation of their problems and thus disempower themselves from doing anything about them. They tend to believe that their security and happiness grow out of life's conditions and other people's approval—boss, colleagues, or spouse—rather than their own. So when things go wrong, they tend to blame others or the circumstances. They feel oppressed or even angry, look for reasons why any suggested change won't work, and wait for others to take the lead. "No one ever tells me what is going on," "I just do what I'm told," "They don't know what they're doing," and "It's not my job" are common clichés of the victim. Such an attitude derails any potential for change or personal development.

In contrast, consider the attitude of the victor. A victor sees the glass as half full as opposed to half empty, and feels like a master of circumstance instead of a victim of it. Victors believe that they succeed and learn because they place themselves in the position of being the creators of their own reality. They see within themselves that they have a choice and the wherewithal to learn from every experience and make a positive difference in their lives, regardless of the circumstances. This view is based on a deep-rooted belief that their safety, worth, and freedom lie in their hands. A situation does not determine their reactions; rather, they see that they have a choice to respond in a way that is consistent with their values, their purposes, and the world they are trying to create.

The key difference between a victor and a victim is that victors are aware of this freedom to choose while victims are not.

Step 1: Think about an unsatisfactory situation you have been in or are going through—an ineffective team meeting, a harsh conversation, or a frustrating event. Answer the following questions from a victim's point of view (play the victim's role completely):

1. What was the problem?
2. Who was to blame?
3. What did you want to happen (that didn't)?
4. How did you disempower yourself?
5. What were the costs of acting this way?
6. How does being a victim feel?

Step 2: Now answer the following questions relative to the same story with a victor's point of view:

1. What challenge did you face?
2. What response did you choose?
3. How did you empower yourself?
4. What principles guided your actions?
5. What are the benefits of acting this way?
6. How does being a victor feel?

The situation I remembered in answering these questions is one in which I thought my job was in jeopardy. I felt paranoid, with reason, sure that a few colleagues wanted me to lose my job. I didn't understand why. It came at a time when I thought I was doing well and hitting home runs, but others were displeased and wanted a change. A circle of gossip and innuendo was circulating that I only came to know through friends. I felt victimized, became defensive, and started to act out in kind. I shared my feeling with mutual friends, but my words got to my critics and circulated back to me again, making matters worse. I felt powerless and began to spin on the thought of losing my job.

Eventually, I consulted with close colleagues who were savvy enough to advise me in such a situation. They told me to stop feeling the victim and become proactive in changing the situation. I sought coaching on how to approach the upper levels of management with my version of the story in a way that was not blaming or attributive, and would not put them on the defensive. I also prepared to, and finally did, approach my critics with my perspective. I gave them facts that supported my view; then instead of accusing them, I asked them for their perspective and advice in resurrecting the situation. It worked.

The issue boiled down to differences in philosophical approach. Prior to realizing that, however, both my detractors and I filled the void made by those differences with inaccurate assumptions and negativity. In discussing them, we were able to dispel the erroneous assumptions, apologize to each other for the gossip, and make adjustments for moving forward. These adjustments improved our relationships, and made me and the others more effective in working together and delivering our programs.

I learned not to allow myself to spin in negativity, and that every situation is workable if I take a positive, proactive attitude.

Step 3: Reflect on the difference between the two scenarios of steps 1 and 2 (victim vs. victor perspective) and ask yourself about how and where you might live your life differently if you were a victor more often. Leaders find ways to take themselves off the victim's hook and open to the world of greater possibility. That requires a commitment to making a change, and that commitment starts with asking yourself the following questions on how much you want to become a leader.

Rate yourself on a scale of one to five, with five being the highest:

1. How empowered will you choose to be over your own experience in becoming a leader?
2. How willing are you to risk failure and learn from it if it happens?
3. How able are you to know when and how to ask help from others?
4. How willing are you to engage challenging situations instead of avoiding them?
5. How invested do you plan to be in everyone else's experience and not just your own?

I wrote my responses to these questions in my journal, and I return to them whenever I am challenged and feeling victimized. It helps me keep my head in the right place. Leadership development is a difficult challenge, and we need to constantly renew our commitment. So it is important to remind yourself of your responses to these questions by periodically returning to them.

○ EXERCISE 2.3: THE LEADERSHIP WHEEL ASSESSMENT

This set of questions is designed to help assess your current access to each of the directions of the Wheel. Although this is designed as a self-assessment, it also can be given to others for their perspective on where you stand relative to each direction. Having others also complete the assessment can provide powerful additional feedback and insight.

Step 1: Using a total of ten points for each of the five-item sets below, divide the points in any way you wish between the five choices, assigning more points to the characteristics you feel are more like you or the individual being scored, and less, or even zero, to the others. Be sure to use ten points for each of the five-item sets. This assessment is adapted from the work of my colleagues Rodney Napier, Patrick Sanaghan, and Julie Roberts.

1. ____ would rather generate and build on ideas than implement them

2. ____ chooses to be more thoughtful than spontaneous

3. ____ prefers to implement ideas rather than discuss them

4. ____ tends to value feeling and process over ideas

5. ____ is open and flexible to new directions

6. ____ is seen as a divergent thinker who seeks new connections

7. ____ is analytical and attentive to detail

8. ____ is recognized as result- and action-oriented

9. ____ is inclusive and seeks the input of others

10. ____ is considered agile and able to adapt to changing circumstances

11. ____ is a natural caretaker and nurturer of people

12. ____ is a far-sighted visionary and big picture person

13. ____ is well-organized and methodical

14. ____ naturally takes charge of a situation

15. ____ has composure in stressful situations

1. ____ is perceived as creative and an explorer of ideas

2. ____ is seen as an objective and clear thinker

3. ____ is able to get things done

4. ____ major focus is on relationship and interaction with people

5. ____ is patient and allows events to unfold

6. ____ is able to quickly prioritize and see what is most important

7. ____ is seen as rational and logical

8. ____ is decisive in moving things along

9. ____ is known as a natural networker, collaborator, and team player

10. ____ is self-aware and knows strengths and weaknesses

11. ____ is known for loyalty and dedication to people

12. ____ is future-oriented in addressing issues

13. ____ is a critical evaluator of people and ideas

14. ____ is known for being tenacious and persevering

15. ____ is focused on learning and personal development

16. ___ naturally seeks information and data

16. ___ is pragmatic when dealing with others

17. ___ is emotionally resilient and naturally trusting of others

17. — is driven by personal values and impact on people on the issues

18. ___ sees clearly despite complexity

18. ___ is recognized as quite intuitive and insightful

19. ___ is seen as one who stands by their beliefs and walks the talk

19. ___ likes to get on with the task at hand

20. ___ is known as calm and even tempered

20. ___ is seen as comfortable in different situations

21. ___ is seen as knowledgeable and competent

21. ___ is realistic in solving problems and addressing issues

22. ___ is seen as courageous and willing to take risks

22. ___ is competitive and seeks challenges

23. ___ is seen as warm and friendly

23. ___ spends time supporting and helping others

24. ___ is personally open and candid with others

24. ___ is optimistic and able to make the most out of situations

25. ___ is inspirational and passionate about ideas and possibilities

25. ___ is a strategic and systems thinker

Step 2: Referring to the answers above, add together the two scores next to each question with the same number (questions 1 through 25) and place the total next to the corresponding number below. Then add the numbers down each column and place the total score in the spaces provided.

Teacher	Nurturer	Visionary	Warrior	Sage
2. _____	4. _____	1. _____	3. _____	5. _____
7. _____	9. _____	6. _____	8. _____	10. _____
13. _____	11. _____	12. _____	14. _____	15. _____
16. _____	17. _____	18. _____	19. _____	20. _____
21. _____	23. _____	25. _____	22. _____	24. _____
Total _____	_____	_____	_____	_____

Score Range:
0–10 Very little access to this style
11–20 Can use this style if need to
21–30 Natural preference for this style
30+ May overuse this style

Step 3: Reflect on your responses with the following questions in mind:

1. What are your natural strengths and preferences?
2. What styles might you need to access more to create more balance?
3. Where are you subject to defensive patterns that get you into trouble?
4. What insights does this provide on your ability to lead in different circumstances?

After doing the self-assessment, it is often useful to ask another person who knows you well to also do one for you. Discussing the similarities and differences in response can be useful in revealing hidden strengths and blind spots. It also helps to deepen awareness, self-understanding, and the impact we have on others.

3

DISCOVERING LEADERSHIP

AWAKENING THE POWER WITHIN

A human being is part of the whole called by us "Universe," a part limited in time and space. He experiences himself, his thoughts and feelings, as something separated from the rest, a kind of optical delusion of his consciousness. This delusion is a kind of prison for us, restricting us to our personal desires and to affection for a few persons nearest to us. Our task must be to free ourselves from this prison by widening our circle of compassion to embrace all living creatures and the whole of nature in its beauty.

—Albert Einstein[1]

One of the age-old questions of leadership is whether leaders are born or made. The mounting evidence shows that the answer to this question is both. Some people are born as natural leaders, others grow into it and still others are drawn out and transformed by life circumstances. Rudolph Giuliani, when asked about his calm resolve during the 9/11 crisis, said that his father "taught" him to quiet himself and take charge when everything was chaotic.[2] The emphasis here is on "taught," and the role of learning in bringing forth leadership qualities.

Saying leaders are only born, not made, is like saying that people cannot learn, develop, or mature as human beings. Developing leadership qualities is about learning from experience and making the most of the opportunities presented in life. It is about growing up and becoming a full adult.

Center for Creative Leadership researchers McCall, Lombardo, and Morrison, along with others such as Professor Richard Boyatzis at Case

The fundamental question . . . is not whether leaders are born or made; rather, it is how to instill or arouse the necessary desire to learn and grow.

Western Reserve, provide clear evidence that leadership can be developed. They show that people who develop as leaders "have an extraordinary tenacity in extracting something worthwhile from their experience and in seeking experiences rich in opportunities for growth."[3] They have an urge to learn. For some, this urge comes naturally, while for others it is awakened and shaped by life events. The fundamental question, then, is not whether leaders are born or made; rather, it is how to instill or arouse the necessary desire to learn and grow.

For an answer to this question, we return to the Heroic Journey to see what compels a venturing forth to explore what it is to be fully human. According to the ancients, all things of the universe have spirit but it is only human beings who have a becoming spirit, a hungry spirit that yearns to be complete. Jung said this is our inherent human tendency to seek wholeness. When our becoming energy is turned exclusively toward self-interest, it dulls us, distorts our growth, and cuts us off from the greater harmony of life and existence. We remain incomplete and our learning remains incomplete. To achieve wholeness, we must learn to balance this energy by letting go of ourselves, and opening up to find broader relationships with our world.

The Wheel serves as a guide for such growth. It reminds us to channel our energy of becoming toward balance and wholeness by awakening to the power of each direction and experiencing the harmony of all things. We are each a living Wheel, and possess an inherent desire to awaken to all our gifts, and not be limited to just our beginning gift or natural preference. To Native Americans, we achieve this by "Giving Way,"[4] meaning letting go of ourselves through opening up and venturing out to learn the different gifts and perspectives of each direction and every experience. This is the Heroic Journey and the search for personal meaning.

This process begins with the question "Who am I?" According to Native American wisdom keeper Hyemeyohsts Storm, pursuing this question, this mystery of life, lights the Fire of Self, the Great Medicine Fire of the People.[5] The Fire of Self is deep within us and, once awakened, arouses a desire to learn and grow to become fully human and to seek the same for others. It gives us a passion for life, learning, and growth. As the poet William Butler Yeats once said, "Education is not the filling of the pail, rather it is the lighting of the fire within." So it is with developing leaders. We use the journey around the Wheel to light this fire to learn and awaken the power within.

THE WHEEL AS A MODEL FOR ACTION-LEARNING

In addition to being a model for leadership, the Wheel serves as a model for action-learning. It is both a Leadership Wheel and a Learning Wheel. As a model for learning, the five directions of the Wheel become a dynamic five-step process for personal development. This process can transpire in an instant, as in the hundreds of adjustments and decisions we make from moment to moment based on the input of daily experience; or it can unfold as part of a longer personal developmental process that may take months, or even years. Each direction or step is interdependent with the others, and represents a different aspect of learning, change, and growth. No one way of knowing and being is sufficient on its own. It is a cycle that can start or end at any point, but is presented here, as in the previous chapter, in a linear fashion for the sake of clarity. Completing and repeating the cycle results not only in changes in behavior but also in a gradual upward spiral that transforms outlook, and even consciousness.

This process begins with the question "Who am I?"

Here again, each direction presents both an opportunity and a hazard. We learn by opening up and letting go, and we derail by holding on to one or a few of the directions and subjecting ourselves to their shadow.

THE TEACHER: KNOWING THE WORLD

The action-learning process often begins with the Teacher. The intelligence of the Teacher is about intellectual recognition of experience and the ability to seek, observe, and rationally reflect on the facts, data, and consequences of experience. It asks the question "What do I know?" It is the ability to take in data, analyze it without judgment, and determine whether experience is real based on the evidence. It is also about acquiring the technical and intellectual knowledge necessary for learning and change, and being structured and orderly in pursuit of that knowledge.

When you are learning a new leadership skill—such as conflict resolution, for example—this intelligence emerges as your desire to acquire the facts necessary to understand the conflict and gain the technical knowledge for dealing with it. It is your ability to assess conflicts and resolve them objectively, as well as your ability to absorb and evaluate feedback without bias or defensiveness.

THE NURTURER: AWAKENING THE HEART

The Nurturer is the intelligence that expresses itself through our immediate emotional reaction to the intellectual stimulus of the Teacher. It is the ability to be open to the messages of our heart, and to recognize the mood and the impact of reality on oneself and others. It asks the question, "How do I feel?" Our feelings and emotional reactions are often overlooked in the learning process; but they tell us what behaviors are good or bad, and help us become aware of what inspires and gives us heart. Anger, anxiety, fear, denial, procrastination, and defensiveness are frequent obstacles to learning and change, and offer clues to areas we might address.

The Nurturer recognizes these feelings of self and others, and tries to work with equanimity in taking them into account. This sensibility is essential to building effective relationships, and enables us to learn through them. In conflict resolution, this intelligence is your ability to be aware of your own emotional responses to the conflict, to empathize with those of others, and to work with those emotions consciously in reaching resolution. So instead of shrinking in fear or erupting in anger when dealing with difficult issues, you learn to be aware of them, check your impulses, acknowledge their source, and consciously work with them. In receiving constructive feedback, this intelligence is what makes it possible for you to understand your feelings without spinning in hurt and self-doubt. It also opens you to learning from the point of view of others.

THE VISIONARY: SEEING THE WAY

The third step is the Visionary, the intuitive intelligence that conceptualizes and generalizes information from the Teacher and Nurturer into a meaningful plan. It asks the question "What is my purpose?" The intuitive insight of the Visionary differentiates and sorts through the objective and emotional data aroused in the first two directions and completes the process of perception. It does this by seeing the possibilities, identifying what is most important, and conceptualizing how things should be in moving forward.

This conceptual view and understanding provides meaning and inspiration, and arouses the commitment necessary to move people into action. In our conflict resolution example, this intelligence expresses itself as your ability to identify areas of mutual interest, to see the possible options for resolution, and to develop a plan of action that inspires the commitment of all concerned. In assimilating personal feedback, this intelligence is at the core of our ability to interpret the objective and subjective data received and choose a course of action that is personally meaningful.

THE WARRIOR: EMBODYING THE WAY

The learning cycle culminates with the Warrior. The intelligence of the Warrior takes in the thoughts, feelings, and perceptions of the previous directions and expresses them in words, deeds, and actions. It is concerned with deploying self as a whole person. It asks the question "How do I act?" Having identified what needs to be done, Warriors act on that information by deploying themselves in a way that aligns their actions with their intention. This is a challenging step in the learning process, as there is often a gap between knowing and doing. This gap drives the learning process, and closing it internalizes the learning.

In keeping with the ancient Greek notion of teleology, Warriors constantly examine and adjust their conduct in light of their intentions, goals, and purposes. This process requires the discipline and courage to step out of one's comfort zone and experiment with new approaches. In our conflict resolution example, this is your ability to execute and follow through on the plan developed through the first three steps in the learning process. Often this requires having the courage to feel awkward and to persevere in trying a new way. In dealing with conflict or providing constructive feedback, this may mean being conscious of the plan for delivery while also overcoming habitual patterns of aggression or fears of rejection that have been barriers to dealing with the conflict constructively in the past.

THE SAGE: LEARNING TO LEARN

In one sense, the learning process always both begins and ends with the Sage. The core intelligence of the Sage lives the all-pervading question of "Who am I?" It is the reflective power of awareness that lights the Fire of Self and leads to the creation of greater levels of consciousness. Research by the McKinsey Society for Organizational Learning shows how raising the level of consciousness in an organization leads to higher levels of performance and quality of experience, both individually and collectively.[6] To learn conflict resolution, for instance, you need first to arouse the commitment to learn, and then become a conscious participant in the learning process. You also need to know to draw on the other directions in the learning process—to seek data, understand emotional impact, develop a plan, and take action. Awareness drives this process by helping us see areas of need and why they are important to address.

Each direction of the Leadership Wheel represents a different and distinct step and style in the learning process.

Such awareness arises in our daily lives through reflecting on the input from each of the other directions. The primordial energy of the Sage is at the core of that process. It draws our attention to how we take in and react to new information and feelings, whether or not we take time to develop new models of understanding based on that information, and how well or poorly we incorporate that understanding into our actions. As such, the power of the Sage is a reflective, conscious awareness that helps increase the capacity to think, feel, act, and learn. It is thinking about our thinking and learning. And as we become more conscious, we gain confidence to repeat the cycle and take more responsibility for our lives and our ability to learn.

Figure 3.1 summarizes the Learning Wheel process. Each direction of the Leadership Wheel represents a different and distinct step and style in the learning process. The Teachers and Nurturers take in factual and emotional information, the Visionary conceptualizes that information and generalizes it into meaningful plans, and the Warrior experiments and puts it into action. If we are learning a particular skill, for example, we want to know what the facts are, how those facts impact self and others, what the plans are for moving forward, and how to implement them. The first half of this cycle, then, involves becoming aware of experience, and the second half involves forming, inspiring, and acting on plans.

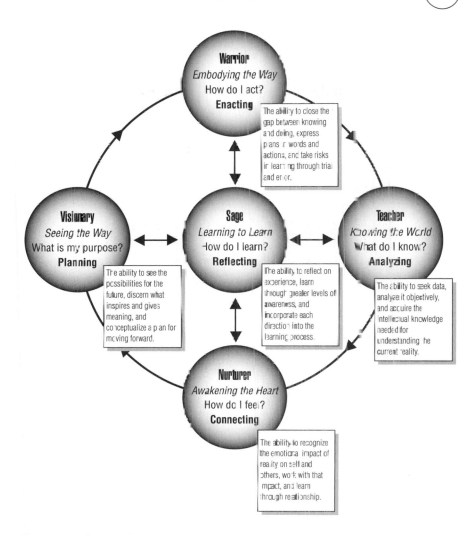

Warrior
Embodying the Way
How do I act?
Enacting

The ability to close the gap between knowing and doing, express plans in words and actions, and take risks in learning through trial and error.

Visionary
Seeing the Way
What is my purpose?
Planning

The ability to see the possibilities for the future, discern what inspires and gives meaning, and conceptualize a plan for moving forward.

Sage
Learning to Learn
How do I learn?
Reflecting

The ability to reflect on experience, learn through greater levels of awareness, and incorporate each direction into the learning process.

Teacher
Knowing the World
What do I know?
Analyzing

The ability to seek data, analyze it objectively, and acquire the intellectual knowledge needed for understanding the current reality.

Nurturer
Awakening the Heart
How do I feel?
Connecting

The ability to recognize the emotional impact of reality on self and others, work with that impact, and learn through relationship.

Figure 3.1   The Learning Wheel

As this learning cycle is repeated, it becomes an upward spiral of ever-increasing mastery and expansion of learning and consciousness. The ancients called this "Turning the Wheel," and each turning results in deeper understanding, further inquiry, and higher realization. This upward cycle is the spiral of experience and maps the process for learning how to learn from experience. Aldous Huxley said that "experience is not what happens to you, it is what you do with it that happens to you." The Sage awakens the desire to learn, turns the wheel, and governs the process. The Sage reflects on each step of the process to reap the lessons of experience and inspire ever higher levels of consciousness.

In reflecting on this cycle, it is important to keep in mind that each individual has a preferred learning style. Some people prefer learning through the intellect of the Teacher, others through the feeling response of the Nurturer or the insight of the Visionary, and still others the action orientation of the Warrior. Whatever the preferred style, however, the message of the Wheel is to create a balance in the learning process itself. A Teacher's learning process may be dominated by the intellect, for instance, but that person still needs to consciously find ways to incorporate the learning qualities of the other directions. The technical expertise and business knowledge of the Teacher may help people rise to the top, but balancing that expertise and knowledge with wisdom developed in other areas is what will keep them there. Similarly, a Warrior's tendency to learn by doing can be misguided by not having enough objective and emotional data, or by not having an appropriate plan of action. No one way can do without the rest.

A preferred style also can be overused and derail the learning process through the defensive routines.

A preferred style also can be overused and derail the learning process through the defensive routines outlined in chapter 2. Teachers, for instance, derail when they lose their objectivity and hold on and defend their view of the situation, their approach, or their capabilities. Likewise, shadow Nurturers lose their equanimity and become clingy, sentimental, and overly sensitive. Each direction faces the hazard of its defensive routines and the risk of stalling or even derailing the learning process.

Finally, it is important to point out that *the directions of the Wheel are not only the path of the learning process, they are also the result of that process.* As we move through the learning steps, we also awaken to the natural learning qualities and wisdom of each direction. In progressing along the path of developing any particular skill, we become more balanced by incorporating into that skill the style of each direction in our learning. A natural Warrior, for instance, in learning conflict resolution skills, will also develop the qualities of each of the other directions to become a more balanced human being. Thus, in traveling around the Wheel, as we learn a new skill we also learn to become more complete, more balanced, and more agile.

THE ANCIENT PARADIGM REVISITED:
THE ROLE OF OPENNESS IN TURNING THE WHEEL

According to the ancients, the key to traveling around the Wheel and developing this balance is openness. Openness comes from the practice of awareness and compassion and together they make up the two foundational practices necessary for traveling around the Wheel. They help us access the archetypes and transmute the negative energy of the shadow into wisdom. Awareness is represented in the East-West axis of the Wheel and shapes how we know the world. It reflects the combined powers of the Teacher and the Visionary in helping us see, discern, and make sense of our experience. Compassion is the North-South axis and shows us how we engage the world. It reflects the wisdom powers of the Nurturer and the Warrior merging to determine how we relate to and engage others in compassionate action.

Openness comes from the practice of awareness and compassion and together they make up the two foundational practices necessary for traveling around the Wheel.

In Native American tradition, awareness and compassion are known as the "Giving Way" mentioned earlier. In Eastern traditions, awareness and compassion are known as *Prajna* and *Karuna,* respectively. Together, they are said to be like the two edges of a sword that cuts and slices away the ego, and opens us fully to our experience. Awareness enables us to cut through obscurations and habitual patterns to see our intrinsic human nature, while compassion awakens our hearts and enables us to reach beyond self-interest to help and serve others.

These two are fundamental to our learning and constitute the basis from which all our faculties grow. They suspend the sense of self, open us to other views, and allow us to access the powers of each direction. Research by emotional intelligence guru Daniel Goleman supports these ancient notions, showing that meditation on awareness and compassion activates the parts of the brain that open us to our experience and overcome destructive emotions.[7]

Awareness and compassion meet in the center of the Wheel—the place of the Sage—that represents both the ground of these practices and their fruition. In other words, they are the practices of the path as well as the two inseparable aspects of the desired result—basic goodness. They are essential aspects of the Sage but also inherent in each of the other directions and key to every level of the upward cycle.

Awareness enables us to access our experience and influence our behavior. It helps us see our tendencies, strengths, weaknesses, and habitual patterns so we can work consciously with them. This is why the reflective process of the Sage is so important to each step and direction of the learning process. It brings awareness into the developmental process in a way that drives the process. To learn and grow, you must stay alert or risk missing critical details of your life—opportunities for change, insights into yourself, or evidence of changes in your relationships with others. It is through the mundane and the familiar that you discover the true depths of who you are. To become fully aware requires us to suspend our hold on self, and open to the world.

Compassion is almost inseparable from awareness. Like awareness, its very nature requires you to suspend preoccupation with yourself and open to others. It helps you let go and make yourself more vulnerable to your experience. Yet compassion also arises naturally from awareness. The more aware you are, the more you open your heart, and the closer you come to a sympathetic sense of others. In awakening to your deeper self, you awaken to being part of all of life. You learn to empathize with others and take seriously their realities, their inner lives, their emotions, and their external circumstances. As Albert Schweitzer said, "I am life which wills to live, in the midst of life which wills to live."[8] Thus, the more aware we are, the more compassion we feel because it is the stuff of which we are made. It arises naturally out of moderating our sense of self.

This is not to say that we need to become bleeding hearts to be effective leaders. Rather, it is simply to say that we need to practice openness to learn and grow to full maturity. Openness is inherent in the wisdom activities that transmute the shadow into wisdom for each direction. The objectivity of the Teacher, the equanimity of the Nurturer, the discriminating awareness of the Visionary, the all-accomplishing action of the Warrior, and the all-encompassing awareness of the Sage have their root in selflessness, and serve as an antidote to the shadow. There is an awareness and a compassionate aspect to each, and both are fundamental to peeling back the layers of self-interest.

Openness is also inherent in the learning routines. These routines call on us to suspend our sense of self in order to fully understand the situation. When we hold on to self we cut ourselves off from these wisdoms and distort our reality through projection. They are essential to how we learn as well as how we collaborate with others. In inviting feedback, for instance, we build awareness, and in working with others we develop empathy and compassion.

THE WHEEL AND TODAY'S
THINKING ON LEARNING AND CHANGE

ACTION LEARNING

The teachings embedded in the Wheel parallel much of today's management thinking on action learning and change. There are many similarities, for instance, to the action-learning model developed by Professor David Kolb of Case Western University and its many variations. Kolb's interest lay in exploring the processes associated with making sense of concrete experiences and the different styles of learning involved. He describes action learning as a four-step process that includes concrete experience, observation and reflection, formation of abstract concepts, and testing in new situations. Kolb says that we learn by taking action on something new, observing the results, and reflecting on the lessons to develop a revised plan for action. This process is repeated in an upward spiral as the lessons are mastered and applied to a widening spectrum of experience. His model is now widely used in adult education, lifelong learning, and leadership development programs.[9]

The teachings embedded in the Wheel parallel much of today's management thinking on action learning and change.

More recently, Otto Sharmer introduced another variation on this concept to include a greater focus on learning from the future. The Kolb learning cycle is based on reflections of learning from the past. In new business environments leaders must learn to seize opportunities as they arise. This suggests a different kind of cycle that enables learning as prospects emerge. This style of learning is much more *on the spot* and calls for the ability to tune in to signals of a reality that has not yet fully manifested itself. He describes a five step sequence of seeing (Teacher), sensing (Nurturer), envisioning (Visionary), enacting (Warrior), and "presencing" (Sage). The key is "presencing," meaning the ability to be aware and take hold of the future as it emerges.[10] The essence of "presencing" is awareness. It is the ability to sense more subtle experiences and see the whole as it emerges in its parts. The enabling condition for this awareness, however, he says, is love. Love not in an emotional sense, but in the ability to connect empathically and compassionately with others. Only through such a suspension of the self are we able to fully open and learn *on the spot.* The parallels to openness, and the practice of awareness and compassion, are clear.

SINGLE AND DOUBLE LOOP LEARNING

The Wheel also has parallels with Harvard professor Chris Argyris's theory of single loop and double loop learning. Many of the best contemporary thinkers in this field are indebted to Argyris for his contributions to understanding organizational learning and deepening our understanding of action learning.

Single loop learning . . . focuses on . . . mastering the technique . . . without questioning whether it is the right thing to do.

Single loop learning is incremental in nature, and involves the "detection and correction of error."[11] It assumes that our assumptions are valid and that the underlying goals, plans, values, and belief systems driving our actions are not drawn into question. It focuses on becoming more competent, efficient, and capable in the execution of a preset plan and process, and on mastering the technique for doing so without questioning whether it is the right thing to do. Following our conflict resolution example, single loop methods focus on learning and going through the steps of conflict resolution while taking for granted the basic assumptions, values, or conflicting goals that may underlie the conflict. As Argyris says, it "focuses on the technique and making the technique more efficient."[12]

In contrast, double loop learning is more adaptive, and goes beyond technique to ask why the problem exists in the first place. It reframes the conflict resolution example by openly questioning and modifying the assumptions, goals, and values underlying the conflict—and it does so to develop a higher level of understanding. Reflection is a key element of this process, as learning in this model comes through a willingness to reveal and confront one's assumptions while inviting others to do the same.[13]

Double loop learning is learning from experience through publicly testing the beliefs and frames of reference that guide our actions at each step in the cycle. Whereas single loop is technical, double loop is adaptive; and where single loop focuses on doing things right, double loop focuses on doing the right things. Double loop is both more adventurous and more creative than single loop because it goes beyond simply acquiring ideas and techniques. It also requires the practice of openness in order to shift the frames of reference and expand the level of consciousness.

Stories by management authors Barbara Mackoff and Gary Wenet on the inner work of leaders provide examples of how different executives, whose

*Double loop
learning is learning
from experience
through publicly
testing the beliefs
and frames of
reference that guide
our actions at each
step in the cycle.*

dominant learning styles match different directions on the Wheel, learn through reframing and double loop learning.[14]

A *Teacher* reframes by examining and reflecting on the objective messages of experience. Elaine Rosen, President of UNUM Insurance of America, embodies this learning style in how she observes and appraises her behavior. She says that one of the most important things she has learned as a leader is to see herself as others see her, so she constantly seeks feedback from others to expand her frame of reference. She uses the data from that feedback to objectively assess herself, adjust her mental models, and adapt her process. "I have learned to watch myself every minute of the day."[15] She also does the same for others: "I tell my people what I observe and why that makes them more or less effective."

In contrast, a *Nurturer* reframes by examining and reflecting on the more subjective measures of experience. Dr. Harold Shapiro, former president of Michigan and Princeton universities, explains that it is important to learn by attempting to understand the views of others—regardless of whether we believe they are right or wrong. He is aware of mood and uses it to understand himself and others. In successfully dealing with student protests over the years—many of which appeared naïve, mistaken, or outrageous—he found that "what really matters is for me to care enough to ask if there is something here I should be understanding."[16] So he pushes aside his judgments and tries to work with equanimity in understanding the deeper meaning and determining an appropriate response.

A *Visionary* is guided by an inner knowing that helps assimilate, conceptualize, and reframe experience. Tim Girvin is president of Tim Girvin Design, a marketing company that has designed logos for well-known products and generated titles for more than 200 films. Girvin is a 25-year student of Zen and reframes through the Zen-inspired focus on meditation and searching for the *ch'i*, or spirit, of an object in his learning process. This process helps him discern and get to the essence of things in creating design strategies for his clients. "My function," he says, "is to get as close as I can to the center point of the organization, discover all there is to know, and find that central point—that spark, that central idea—and ignite it."[17]

Warriors learn through trial and error in taking action. They operate out of personal beliefs and persevere in the face of challenges. Once Warriors have a vision or a conviction for the right direction, they pick themselves up when something goes wrong, reflect on the situation, reframe the experience, and try again in a different way. They evaluate their conduct and results in terms of their purpose and reframe to narrow the gap in a way that allows them to act as a whole person.

The late Fred Rogers, founder of the children's television program *Mister Rogers' Neighborhood,* overcame many obstacles and early failed attempts to bring his program to television. People did not take him seriously and thought him a little corny. His essential message—"Dare to be yourself"—is the conviction that anchors both the message of his program and his leadership style. He dared to be himself as he experimented with different media and worked to find an appropriate fit. But he never wavered from his message. He fought through ridicule and satire to put his message into action, and eventually became one of the most trusted figures in children's programming, with the longest-running program in public television history.[18]

Finally, *Sages* learn by constantly reframing how they learn how to learn. David Giuliani, CEO of Optiva Corporation, maker of the Sonicare toothbrush, learns from his experience by asking a litany of questions to help him reframe: What? So what? and Now what? Giuliani explains, "I have always liked to watch myself work and see what the cutting edge is for me, and put my efforts into the parts of myself that I really want to burnish and grow. I keep myself almost like a little piece of sculpture, always being worked on. Some parts, I let dry, other parts, I keep my hand on and try to shape myself into what I want to be. It's a long, gradual process."[19] It is a habit of mind as if having a third eye—an awareness—for watching and mirroring oneself in self-appraisal.

TRIPLE LOOP LEARNING

More recently, several management authors have talked about triple loop learning. Triple loop learning is transformational in nature, and investigates the context and nature of learning itself. Management consultant and author Fred Koffman says it is transformational because it questions our notions of what is real and who we are, and it calls into question why we are predisposed to view the world in a particular way.[20] It is about learning to be conscious of how we let go and change our mental models for how we do things.

Ultimately, triple loop work draws into question our personal identity. Like the Sage, it poses the question of "Who am I?" It asks why you behave and think the way you do, and inquires into hidden habits of how your lan-

Triple loop learning is transformational in nature, and . . . ultimately . . . poses the question of "Who am I?"

guage, assumptions, thinking, reactions, and mental models affect how you learn. In short, it draws into question how you view yourself. Also like the Sage, it is about learning how to learn from experience or learning how to double loop learn. At each step of the process, we open by reflecting, questioning, and surfacing the assumptions, belief systems, and mental models that shape our ideas, motivations, perspectives, and actions.

⊕

PAUL WIEAND's experience as a corporate CEO is a good example of triple loop learning. Wieand went on a quest for success and was derailed by his own ambition. He became one of the banking industry's youngest-ever CEOs, but his world collapsed under the weight of his own self-interest. As a result, he went on a search for the meaning of leadership and now helps others on their journey at the institute he founded, The Center for Advanced Emotional Intelligence (AEI).

At age 37, Wieand had become the CEO of Independence Bancorp. He was on top of the world with "money, power, success: I had everything I wanted."[21] But he had bullied his way to the top, and the resentment he stirred up forced others to plot secretly against him. His board dismissed him, and he sank into depression.

Without his position, he says, "I didn't know who I was I lost my identity."[22] He used the trauma of this setback to spur himself into rediscovering himself as a leader. He went to graduate school with a mission to seek answers and understand. He found that leaders need to learn and to be true to their authentic selves; otherwise, they become subject to the destructive powers of ambition and cut themselves off from constructive criticism. "In a time when change is the only constant," he writes, "a leader's self-concept can't remain fixed. They must be willing to listen and learn from feedback."[23] Otherwise their identity solidifies and they become intolerant and push their strengths to the point of becoming weaknesses.

Wieand learned to ask: "Who am I and why am I here?"[24] Asking this question over and over again reveals a secret fear of being inadequate or unworthy that drives ambition and the need to succeed—sometimes to the point of obsession. The process helped him see how successful people can begin to define themselves by their job—a position—rather than by who they really are inside. He observes, "If you idealize your role, you fool yourself about what people really think of you."[25]

Wieand says that emotion, more than intellectual ability, drives executive decision making and relationships—but most executives aren't even dimly aware of who they are, and they often use aggression to cover a vulnerability. Such people extend no invitation for feedback: "You don't know when or why you get defensive, there is no reality testing."[26] So he developed a self-revealing style that has produced powerful results with his clients at AEI. "When you disarm yourself," he says, "you disarm everyone else. I saw that everyone—whether patients in a psych ward or executives in a corporation—wants the same things in life: to be recognized, to be cared for, and be given an opportunity to grow. And if you are authentic and trustful, people will realize that, and they will respond. Authenticity is contagious."[27] And it forces one to reevaluate not only work but also personal life. Wieand found this for himself and he now helps others in their leadership development process.

$$\oplus$$

We can summarize these three levels of learning by characterizing single loop as *incremental learning,* double loop as *adaptive learning,* and triple loop as *transformational learning.* At the single loop level, we question how we are doing in learning a given skill, such as conflict resolution, that we have chosen to learn; at the double loop level, we question whether we are learning the right skill or using the right frame of reference in order to adapt to the given needs of the situation; and at the triple loop level, we question whether the competency we are learning is important to who we are and what we want to be.

Most leadership development work currently takes place at the incremental level by helping people to embody new skills and capabilities. Sometimes the work rises to the adaptive level by challenging people to reshape their patterns of thinking. Seldom, however, do programs go to the transformational level to create a shift in people's point of view about themselves. In a later section, "How to Make a Leader," I contend that leadership development programs achieve little without at least reaching for the transformational level.

MODEL I AND MODEL II BEHAVIOR

Argyris added yet another important dimension to our understanding of action learning. He set up two models of behavior to describe how learning is either inhibited (Model I) or enhanced (Model II). Model I behavior is what Argyris calls defensive behavior, and inhibits learning by acting in ways that are controlling, competitive, and withholding. Model I defensive behavior involves making assumptions about another person's behavior without checking out its validity while advocating one's own without revealing one's reasoning. This behavior is driven by a desire not to embarrass anyone or protect oneself by not exposing thoughts and feelings behind actions. Here people make assertions without inviting inquiry, and attribute things to others without testing them publicly. This leads to hiding things and treating difficult issues as "undiscussible"[28] so the truth is never fully revealed. The result is defensive reasoning and incremental learning.

The fundamental difference between Model I defensive and Model II learning behavior is . . . openness . . . and the courage to be more conscious.

Model II behavior, in contrast, enhances learning by openly sharing information, collaborating, and working together. Model II learning behavior is an open, two-way communication on common goals that looks to surface the "undiscussibles" and reveal the thinking and feeling that drive behaviors. It is a participatory process that includes the views of others in an open forum of mutual influence and decision making. Assumptions are made explicit and tested, assertions are illustrated with data, and difficult issues are brought to the surface and addressed publicly. Ideas are openly debated, and the reasoning behind positions is explored by all. In receiving feedback, for instance, this style of behavior leads us to ask about the assumptions or reasoning behind criticisms as opposed to defending ourselves, rationalizing our position, or blaming others for the situation. The result is productive reasoning and adaptive, even transformational learning.[29]

The parallels to the learning and defensive routines of the Wheel are clear. Holding on to and serving self-interest results in the defensive behavior of Model I, while waking up and opening to others results in the learning behavior of Model II. Model I learning behavior is motivated by a need to control and protect self, whereas Model II is motivated by a desire to learn.

Argyris asserts that most people espouse Model II learning behavior but their actions reflect Model I defensive behavior. In other words, they don't walk the talk or model the way. Some may say they are collaborative and open to the influence of others, but still act unilaterally. Executives often do this when implementing what they espouse as an open and participatory change effort, yet they act unilaterally in making decisions that affect the process. This inhibits learning, undermines trust, and leads to a defensive organizational culture.

The fundamental difference between Model I defensive and Model II learning behavior is the openness discussed earlier, and the courage to be more conscious. In defensive behavior, we hold on and protect ourselves by acting defensively and enclosing ourselves in our cocoon. In learning behavior, we open through awareness and compassion and venture out to learn and grow. Moving from defensive behavior to learning behavior captures in many ways the essence of the heroic journey in the context of a modern organization.

Moving from Model I to Model II leads to the development of personal authenticity. As illustrated by Paul Wieand's story, authenticity is critical to trust and personal influence. Through open inquiry and public testing of assumptions, in a process that Argyris calls dialogue, people can move from defensive behavior to learning behavior. Dialogue, in essence, is awareness and compassion in action. It has been practiced for thousands of years, from Plato and the tribal councils of indigenous cultures to today's Quaker meetings and self-help groups.

Dialogue is a process of mutual influence that balances inquiry with advocacy, in which people open up and genuinely inquire about the positions of others while also advocating their own in ways that invite further exploration (see exercise 3.3). In developing learning behaviors, people also learn to bridge the gap between what they espouse and how they act. Dialogue helps them to surface subconscious motivations that drive their behavior, observe the differences between what they do and what they say, and learn to close the gap between the two. In closing that gap, people learn to align their actions with their words and become more authentic.

THE WHEEL AND THE SPIRAL OF LEARNING

This learning dynamic is also the basic process of the Wheel. As we repeat our learning cycle and learn to access and practice the different learning styles of the Wheel, we move from living in habitual pattern to situational behavior to authentic presence. "Habitual pattern" describes people who are rooted in their habitual ways, and whose learning is at best single loop and incremental. "Situational behavior" describes people who are able to adapt their behavior to the needs of the situation. It is often associated with the notions of personal agility or situational leadership found in today's management literature. Finally, "authentic presence" describes people who are genuine, open, and authentic, and whose learning is triple loop and transformational.

In repeating the cycle, we gradually move up the spiral of learning and progress from incremental to adaptive to transformational learning (from single to triple loop).

In repeating the cycle, we gradually move up the spiral of learning and progress from incremental to adaptive to transformational learning (from single to triple loop). As this applies to you, you become more conscious and translate more of your lessons into action. With each Turning of the Wheel, you move from learning new skills, to reframing experiences, to shifting perspectives about yourself. In the process, you connect to your basic goodness and become more real. You no longer hide as you know your strengths and weaknesses. You have connected with your fundamental truths and that allows you to relax in who you are. The power of this truth dissolves the facade of self-interest, brings you to a place of genuineness and complete sincerity that others trust, and enables you to connect to them. It is the root of your integrity. You have come to your field of power, a place of genuineness so great that it radiates.

This process is summarized in figure 3.2. The path progresses along the three levels, from incremental to adaptive to transformational learning. Openness, in the form of awareness and compassion, drives the process.

The first level starts with mastering technique and developing skills and competencies. As mentioned earlier, it is the primary objective for most leadership development programs. At this level, awareness takes the form of personal feedback and assessment, and compassion takes the form of collaboration with others in the developmental process. The second level proceeds up to situational behavior, as individuals learn to reframe and to adapt their style to fit the context. Here the developmental tools are more amorphous but still distinct, as awareness evolves from personal assessment to reflection, and compassion from collaboration to dialogue. The third level culminates in authentic presence, where individuals surface their belief systems and gifts and learn to shape their actions to make a difference. At this level, awareness evolves into some form of daily reflective practice such as meditation, and compassion evolves into a sense of service to others.

As we travel up the spiral, we also often discover our sense of purpose. In bringing our hopes, values, and beliefs to consciousness, we discover the manner and purpose of how we will use our gifts to make a difference in the world. Wieand and many of the other leaders profiled earlier exemplify this process. Leadership is about making a difference, and that difference can only be achieved through knowing and acting on what we really believe. It is what makes us authentic.

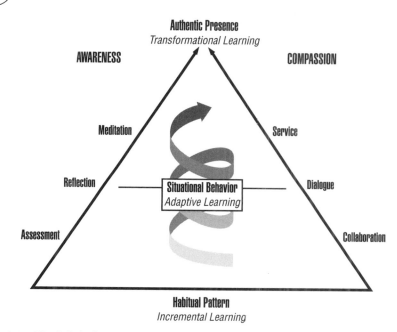

Figure 3.2   The Spiral of Learning

Finding our purpose is the discovery of the innate gifts we use to make that difference in a cause that has meaning. For you that could mean being a teacher helping others develop, or devoting yourself to an organizational mission that you believe in. Charles Handy says, "We find ourselves when we lose ourselves in something beyond ourselves, be it a pursuit of a vocation, a cause or a commitment to a group or an institution."[30] Having discovered that for ourselves gives us the confidence, courage, and personal power to be who we really are in the world. It helps us create meaning out of all experiences, even out of those that may devastate others. Nineteenth-century philosopher Friedrich Nietzsche said that "those who have a why can endure any how, but it is the why that is difficult." Knowing that why is what gives leaders the authenticity, the magic, and the power to achieve great things, while discovering that "why" is the trick, in many ways the whole trick, to developing leadership.

This authenticity is both the same as and different from the authenticity found in the Warrior. It is the same in the sense that it represents the culmination of all the energies of the Wheel working together to bring us to maturity. It is different because it can manifest itself in many forms and in the style of any direction, making it in many ways unique to each individual. Whatever it is, however, it requires work to achieve. It needs to be discovered. As I realized from reading the work of Viktor Frankl. we con't invent our purposes in life, we discover them.[31] In discovering leadership, we discover who we are and what it is to be fully human. This is to discover the hero within—our unique and authentic presence.

THE GROUND OF BASIC GOODNESS

As we progress . . . we discover our true nature, and that nature is to be awake and compassionate.

It is important to remember, however, that authenticity is grounded in basic goodness. As we progress up the spiral of experience, we become less self-absorbed, we learn to see good in ourselves and in others, and we desire to create a better world for everyone. We discover our true nature, and that nature is to be awake and compassionate. Connecting to that nature gives us the confidence to be what we believe in the world.

All spiritual traditions speak to this fundamental truth. The Greeks, for instance, spoke of Daemon, and Jesus taught, "The kingdom of heaven is within you. Seek ye first the kingdom of heaven and all things shall be added unto you." Likewise, Buddhists believe that everyone has Buddha nature, it just needs to be awakened. "Being of good mind and on a good path," is also central to the Native American way.

So it is in Turning the Wheel. As we progress along the path through the different levels of learning and awakening of consciousness, we discover our basic goodness. If we let go of our fears and self-interest and relax in the confidence of who we are, we open ourselves to others. We learn that in letting go we become fulfilled. We gain power by giving it away. St. Francis of Assisi said, "May it be, oh Lord, that I seek not so much to be consoled as to console, to be understood as to understand, to be loved as to love. Because it is in giving that one receives, it is in forgetting that one is found, it is in pardoning that one is pardoned."[32] At work, this may mean being open and honest, having constructive relationships, and being inspired by work.

Although there is little research on basic goodness, the available evidence points to the reality of its existence. Studies of corporate cultures show the power of shared values in corporate performance, and one of the common shared values is a caring attitude toward others. Researchers have shown that the most frequently espoused values in organizational mission statements are integrity, involvement, achievement, quality, innovation, respect, learning, fairness, and service.[33] Similarly, experience shows that when people are asked to develop personal mission statements, one of the most common themes they come up with is to serve others. In writing a eulogy for themselves—a common exercise in leadership programs—people almost always phrase it in terms of the positive difference they made in the lives of others and not in terms of personal achievements.

As psychologist Abraham Maslow pointed out, we have both a higher order and a lesser order of needs. Our lower order needs reflect values such as financial security and professional achievement, but our highest order of values almost always centers on a sense of belonging and service to others. That higher order is what most energizes and inspires. What really excites people is the opportunity to make it on one's own, to do something well, and to do something good for others. This is their basic goodness.

This is also what Wieand and many of the others discussed have discovered. They learned that the first issue of leadership development is discovering one's basic goodness and authentic presence. Having made that discovery for themselves, they now wish the same for others. If more people were to make the same discovery, soon we would have a system that works for us. As Robert Kennedy said, "Each time a man stands up for an ideal, or acts to improve the lot of others, or strikes out against injustice, he sends forth a tiny ripple of hope, and . . . those ripples build a current that can sweep down the mightiest walls of oppression and resistance."[34] In doing so, Wieand and others like him become truly heroic.

HOW TO MAKE A LEADER

PLANTING THE EMOTIONAL HOOK

Leadership development as seen in this way becomes a gradual expansion of consciousness. It goes beyond method and technique, and delves into the questions of who we are, who we want to be, and who we could be. If leadership development programs are to have lasting impact, they must transcend skill development and become transforming. They must hook our energy of becoming and address who we are and what we bring to the world. This reveals our basic goodness and gives birth to our authenticity.

As our examples show our authenticity often emerges from a belief system that is shaped by certain experiences, defining moments, or conscious heroic journeys. What is true of the heroic journeys of Neeleman, Abrashoff, Zander, Chappell, and DePree is also true for the leaders offered as examples of the five primordial ways of knowing and being.

Leadership development as seen in this way . . . goes beyond method and technique, and delves into the questions of who we are, who we want to be, and who we could be.

For Powell and Krzyzewski authentic presence emerged through what they learned from their devoted, working-class, immigrant parents. Feuerstein draws his from a grounding in religious faith. Gadiesh found hers through her experiences in athletics and the Israeli army. Kopp discovered hers through rising to the professional challenge of launching Teach for America. For Wieand, it came by means of the self-exploration that resulted from the demise of a high-flying career. For many others not mentioned, it develops through time spent abroad, the loss of a loved one, or a volunteer service experience.

Warren Bennis and colleague Robert Thomas call these experiences "crucibles," places of challenge and adversity that are meaning-making and that galvanize and shape the sense of self. They evoke the transformational question of "Who am I?" and become turning points in people's lives.

Leadership development is about creating such turning points. Organizational leadership development programs can be made to serve that purpose. The late Sam Johnson, former CEO and current chairman of S. C. Johnson & Son, tells the story of having fired one of his hard-charging professionals four times. He said "I kept hiring him back because he would get things done, but he would put everyone else in the organization into a fit in doing so." The company eventually sent him off to a series of trainings at the Center for Creative Leadership, where he "finally got the message."[5] That person is now the very successful president of one of S. C. Johnson & Son's business units.

GIVING STRUCTURED SUPPORT

Creating such leadership development opportunities is a challenge, for two important reasons. First, it requires a total commitment by the organization. Development programs cannot be treated as add-ons, where people go off for a week or two or more, and then return with no support.

Leadership development must be a continuous effort and integrated into how business is done.

The U.S. Marine Corps provides a great example. The Marines define leadership as their most essential core competence, and they devote enormous energy to developing it. They study leadership, provide leadership training, create leadership experiences, evaluate leadership performance, and develop leadership mentors and pipelines. During the past two decades, GE, Disney, Motorola, and many other business organizations have been learning to do the same.

The most important aspect of developing this organizational support, as Bennis and Thomas say, is to provide opportunities where people practice leadership while they perform in their jobs.[36] (Teams are often effective vehicles for this, as we shall see in the next chapter.) Leadership develops through action learning, and this is where the Wheel serves as an important framework. Leadership development is not an event, or a one-week program—it is a total experience and a lifelong process. Like learning a sport, we study technique, experiment with methods, practice them in live situations, and reflect on and critique the experience. And we do it over and over again.

. . . most people . . . need to be "inspired" from within and feel the "heat" from without, and programs should be designed to achieve this balance.

Second, most people are not prepared to deal with fundamental issues of transformational learning. People tend to be attracted to leadership development programs for practical reasons. They want to learn new techniques and skills for being more successful, but not to look deeply into themselves. For most people, this is scary. They appreciate the need for behavioral change in developing leadership skills, but most simply want silver bullets, concrete methods, conceptual takeaways, and a simple set of steps to make the change happen.

But this is not how it works. As management author Daniel Goleman says, we don't think our way into new behaviors, we behave our way into new thinking.[37] We rewire ourselves through practice, and that practice leads to changes in thinking and being. Behavioral change can lead to transformational change, but it takes tremendous energy, courage, and commitment.

Generating the energy to do this is one of the fundamental challenges in leadership development, and usually requires multiple sources of support. In order to change behavior, people must be both motivated from within and supported from without. In spite of our idealistic intentions, inspiration from within most often simply does not prove to be enough to bring about a desired change. Only a small proportion of people are able to self-start and sustain the necessary energy to change; and when that happens, it often comes in the form of life-changing and life-shaping events.

Thus most people in leadership development programs also need external support if they are to be successful. They need to be "inspired" from within and feel the "heat" from without, and programs should be designed to achieve this balance. Outside pressure can bring people to the program and support their ongoing efforts, but the experience needs to arouse the necessary energy to become self-driven. To have any degree of success, the program needs to awaken people to their real power and their innate desire to individuate. It must hook the energy of becoming and redirect it toward human development.

SUSTAINING ENERGY FOR THE EFFORT

The key to this, of course, lies in lighting the Fire of Self—the Way of the Sage. Awakening the desire to learn and become fully human starts with asking, "Who am I and what is my medicine?" Addressing the meaning of this question taps into the energy necessary for personal development.

Friedrich Nietzsche said, "Life told me this secret: behold, it said, I am that which must overcome itself again and again."[38] This means that human beings are free to create and choose their world, to choose their values, direction, and meaning for life, and impose it upon themselves. He called this "self-overcoming."[39] When we self-overcome, we hook the energy of becoming and create an uplifting, fulfilling, and exhilarating energy This is why Outward Bound and other intense group learning experiences in leadership development are so powerful. People are challenged with their self-imposed limitations and provided an opportunity to overcome them. When people break through, the result is invigorating.

When we self-overcome, we hook the energy of becoming, and create an uplifting, fulfilling, and exhilarating energy.

In the context of the Wheel, self-overcoming is what we do to create balance among the directions. To travel around the Wheel and progress through the three levels of learning, we need to self-overcome—this is the "razor's edge" so often mentioned with respect to living authentically.

To self-overcome, we need to face the fear that arises when confronting self-imposed limitations. Facing this fear requires the openness discussed

In many ways then, fear serves as the beacon guiding us along the path.

earlier, as well as courage and commitment. It requires a willingness to be vulnerable, and to let go of the sense of self through awareness and compassion to realize our fullest potential. As we overcome these fears, we expand consciousness and produce energy. In many ways then, fear serves as the beacon guiding us along the path.

To sustain the progress of self-overcoming requires the development of personal "learning habits," and organizations can help support that process. We need to create regular space and balance in our lives for maintaining perspective and capturing what Bennis and Thomas say are "the lessons learned as well as the lessons about learning."[40] Ken Blanchard calls this the need for "retreat, renewal, and return"[41] and Stephen Covey "sharpening the saw."[42]

All the ancient traditions followed some similar fashion of regular personal renewal to assure balance in life. To this day, Native Americans set aside special places and times for learning. These routines go beyond maintaining physical health, and include mental, emotional, and spiritual renewal.

Today, many people read literature and appreciate the arts for this same purpose; others seek to connect to family, friends, and communities; and still others keep journals, reflect on the scriptures, or do some form of meditation. Community service also provides a source of renewal. Often it is the turning-point experience for people—as in the Peace Corps, AmeriCorps, or Teach for America. Community service can be a source of inspiration and a space for creating context and connecting to others.

Through the past two decades more and more organizations have supported these forms of continued growth by providing on-site fitness programs, family support services, meditation rooms, training programs, and community service opportunities.

WHAT MAKES A LEADER

It is important to conclude by emphasizing the power of the Wheel as a model for both leadership and leadership development. As a model of leadership, the beauty of the Wheel is in its comprehensiveness and elegance. In the introduction I mentioned a number of other models that describe what makes an effective leader. To name a few more, consider the "align, create, and empower," of the U.S. Army, along with the "competence, courage, candor, and compassion" and the " know yourself, know others, and know your stuff"[43] of

. . . the Wheel also tells us that the qualities that promote learning and development are the very same qualities that mark effective leadership

the U.S. military in general. Similarly, there is the "E-Factor"[44] for energy, excellence, enthusiasm, effort, and excitement. All these formulas hold truths, but they are partial truths. The Wheel stands alone in its comprehensiveness because it is based on simple, universal truths.

As a model for leadership development, the Wheel also provides a robust framework to support learning and growth. One of the few things on which the entire canon of leadership research and literature agrees is that leaders are learners. The literature also agrees that leadership is learned through experience. As an age-old model for action learning, the Wheel offers fresh and powerful insights into how learning and development occurs.

Most importantly, however, and intriguingly, the Wheel also tells us that the qualities that promote learning and development are the very same qualities that mark effective leadership. In other words, the factors for learning are the same as those for leading. In the paradigm of the Wheel, the process of learning models the desired result. Likewise, the design of the contemporary leadership development process needs to model the desired outcomes of leadership. Each direction of the Wheel captures a key aspect of learning as well as a key aspect of what makes a leader. Without all these aspects we cannot learn, nor can we lead effectively.

The distilled messages of leading and learning are summarized in table 3.1. These messages go beyond simple competency development. They tell us that leading and learning are in essence five ways of being:

TABLE 3.1 LEADERS AS LEARNERS SUMMARY

The Teacher: Knowing the World. As one of the military aphorisms mentioned above asserts, leaders need to know their stuff as well as their world. Effective leaders consciously participate in a process of acquiring and applying the knowledge and technical expertise needed to master the situation and the context. They are self-directed in their learning, acquiring the skills and competencies required for meeting their goals. They also seek to cocreate and share their knowledge with others.

The Nurturer: Awakening the Heart. Effective leaders also know and learn through what gives them heart. They have an appreciation of their own basic goodness and what they have to offer to other people. This makes them empathic and value-driven, and enables them to engage others in ways that build solid relationships. As a result, they are effective team players, responsible stewards, and good citizens, as they are motivated by learning and a growth for everyone.

The Visionary: Seeing the Way. The learning of great leaders is also driven by a purpose and a constant seeking of the highest view to serve. They are able to step back, take a larger view, and identify what is most important. They have a sense of purpose that integrates life, gives meaning to experience, and drives learning and development. Most importantly, this purpose serves to align them with their calling and draw them to work that carries a meaning that is beyond simply serving themselves. Leadership is a result, not a cause.

The Warrior: Embodying the Way. To paraphrase Gandhi, all great leaders learn to *be* the change they want to see in the world. They have an authenticity that comes from learning to close the gap between knowing and doing, and deploying themselves in ways that match word and deed. They know who they are, what is important to them, and how to act it out in the world. This drives their learning process, gives them integrity, and makes them authentic, real, and powerful for others. They know what they want and will experiment, risk, and persevere to bring it about. This gives them the power to achieve extraordinary results.

The Sage: Learning to Learn. This is the most essential characteristic— the origin from which all the other directions develop. The awareness of the Sage taps into the powers of the other directions and leads to a balanced development of the self. Great leaders know how to learn and this ability engenders a sense of optimism and a feeling of being empowered to take charge of life and circumstance. They are proactive and get the most out of experience. They seize opportunities, turn adversity into meaning-making, and feel like masters of their lives and circumstances rather than victims. This is a seemingly subtle difference in attitude, but one that makes the greatest difference in results.

○ EXERCISES ○

○ EXERCISE 3.1: PREPARING A PERSONAL MISSION STATEMENT

To take the reins of our energy of becoming and realize our authentic presence, we first must know who we are and what gifts we want to bring to the world, our basic goodness. Preparing a personal mission statement can help this process.

A personal mission statement is an expression of our values, principles, or philosophy of life that provides the basis for which all our daily and life-directing decisions are examined. It is rooted in our personal belief system, what we hold most dear and enduring, and serves as a source of personal strength and conviction. It is our personal statement of the intent and principles according to which we would like to live our lives. It forces us to become conscious and think of our priorities, and to align our actions with them. As we do so, the mission statement becomes the touchstone of our authenticity and reminds us that we are driven by something deeper.

Developing a mission statement is not an easy process, because most of us simply do not take the time to ask ourselves about these things. When we do, the answers do not come easily and are often confusing.

It takes time, introspection, and often many revisions before a mission statement takes a form that resonates and is enduring. Like leadership development, it is a journey, a lifelong journey where the process is as important as the product. So even after having developed a mission statement, it is important to revisit it regularly—not only to serve as a reminder for our daily actions, but also to revise and incorporate the additional insights and circumstances that life experience brings. In this way, the mission statement becomes an anchor and a discipline for maintaining focus on our journey. The following activities are designed to help begin this process.

Step 1: Identify your values. Personal mission statements are based on our values. Values are our true motivators. They give us insight into what is right and wrong, and what we consider worth pursuing in life. They reflect our basic goodness, guide our decisions, and lead us to regard what goals or ends are most legitimate.

Most of these will seem important to most people. The challenge, however, is to identify those that are intrinsically most rewarding and inspiring to *you*. We want to identify your most important values—those that are your strongest motivators, your greatest source of joy when satisfied, and your greatest sense of frustration when not.

Identifying personal values is not easy. This exercise helps by presenting an entire list of possible values for guiding our lives. In all my years of doing this work, this is the most effective way I have found for identifying personal values. The exercise presents a list of values and asks you to make choices among them. Many of these will seem important to you, but we want to select those that are most intrinsic, inspiring, and truly motivating. Those that are most rewarding give us the biggest clues as to who we really are.

So in making these choices, ask how your life might be different if a particular value had either a stronger or weaker presence. When there is a tough choice, it may be helpful to consider two values at a time and weigh their relative importance. In going through this process, if a value emerges that is not on this list, or if there is a word that better expresses one, write it in at the bottom of the list.

From the following list of 45 values, check the 15 most important to you.

_____Achievement (reaching goals, getting things done)

_____Adventure (seeking new and challenging experiences)

_____Affection (mutual caring for one another, connecting to others)

_____Altruism (wanting to do good)

_____Authenticity (genuineness)

_____Balance (between work and play)

_____Beauty (appreciating nature, art, and life)

_____Competence (capability, skill, and effectiveness)

_____Commitment (loyalty, dedication, dependability)

_____Competitiveness (winning)

_____Cooperation (working well with others)

_____Courage (risk-taking, toughness)

_____Creativity (imaginative, innovative)

_____Discipline (perseverance, focus)

_____Economic security (financial stability)

_____Equality (equal opportunity for all, low status differences)

_____Fame (being well-known, distinctive)

_____Family happiness (close-knit and harmonious family)

_____Flexibility (agility, ability to adapt)

_____Forgiveness (tolerance, patience)

_____Freedom (independence, autonomy)

____Friendship (companionship)
____Health (overall well-being)
____Inner harmony (peace with self and the world)
____Integrity (honesty, authenticity)
____Involvement (feeling included, participating with others)
____Love (caring, tenderness, intimacy)
____Objectivity (rational, logical)
____Openness (approachable, accessible, vulnerable)
____Order (structure, stability)
____Passion (energy, excitement about life)
____Peace (harmony, conflict-free)
____Personal development (learning, personal growth)
____Pleasure (fun, leisure, enjoyment)
____Power (control, influence over others)
____Recognition (prestige, regarded with respect, social recognition)
____Self-respect (self-esteem, sense of personal identity)
____Service (assisting others, improving society)
____Spirituality (having faith, spiritual, religious)
____Status (level in society)
____Stewardship (responsibility to the whole)
____Vision (clarity, seeing the way)
____Wealth (making money)
____Wisdom (understanding life, insight, enlightenment)
____Other (those not on the list that may be important to you)

Now pick the top 10:

1. _____
2. _____
3. _____
4. _____
5. _____
6. _____
7. _____
8. _____
9. _____
10. _____

Now pick the top 5 and rank them in descending order of importance:

1. _____
2. _____
3. _____
4. _____
5. _____

Finally, for each of the top 5, write a personal definition of what that value means to you. My top value, for example, is freedom, and my definition is "The freedom to explore both my inner and outer world so that I can grow to my fullest potential."

Step 2: Identify your purpose. After bringing your hopes, values, and beliefs to consciousness, we turn to discovering how you will use your gifts to make a difference in the world. Your purpose is how you choose to use your innate gifts to make a difference in a cause that has meaning. A purpose based in deep personal values becomes a source of strength, inspiration, and power. The leaders profiled earlier exemplify how being conscious of a driving purpose gives energy and commitment to achieve the extraordinary.

This exercise is borrowed from the work of Ken Blanchard and Associates.[45] Ken has been an advisor and mentor to me in my professional life, and he introduced this exercise at a workshop he conducted for Cornell University. I find it a very simple and elegant way to help identify purposeful potential.

1. *List some personal characteristics you feel great about. These should be nouns.*
   Examples:

   technical acumen   expertise   energy   courage
   strength   enthusiasm   creativity
   sense of humor   insight   patience

   I have_____

For me these characteristics were coach, facilitator, servant, challenger, and creativity.

2. *List ways you successfully interact with people. These should be verbs.*
   Examples:

   teach   serve   lead

support   inspire   motivate
collaborate   produce   plan

I_____

For me the key words were inspire, motivate, awaken, serve, and challenge.

3. *Visualize what your perfect world looks like. What are the people doing and saying? Write a description of this perfect world.*
My perfect world_____

_____

For me it was: "Everyone has awakened to their inherent basic goodness and they are authentic in being that in the world."

4. *Combine two of your nouns, two of your verbs, and your definition of your perfect world.*
My life purpose is_____

_____

For me it was "I use my coaching and facilitating skills to awaken everyone to their inherent basic goodness and inspire them to be that in the world."

Step 3: Prepare your mission statement. Based on the data generated in the first two steps, prepare a personal mission statement that includes both your values and your purposeful potential. This should be no more than one page. The format is a personal choice: Some are simple narratives, others are poetic, and still others are more visual and artistic. Use whatever style of expression is most inspiring and meaningful for you personally. You may find your mission statement more helpful if you break it down into goals that you have for various roles in your life as a colleague, parent, friend, and change agent. Other perspectives to consider are:

1. What is my ideal for myself as a leader?
2. How do I want to be involved in community?
3. What do I want to create in terms of personal development?
4. What is my unique calling?

My mission statement:

MY MISSION in life is to use my coaching and facilitating skills to awaken everyone to their inherent basic goodness and inspire them to be that in the world.

TO FULFILL THIS MISSION, I will live a life of:

Love: giving and receiving unconditional caring for and from others.

Integrity: acting in ways consistent with my beliefs, even when it is not convenient.

Freedom: making individual choices that enable me to stand on my own and be my own person.

Personal Development: working continually to improve mentally, physically, and spiritually.

Service: supporting others in working toward their heartfelt goals.

THESE ROLES TAKE PRIORITY in achieving my mission:

Father: I help my children to awaken and experience the greatest possible joy in life.

Friend: I am there when my friends need me and serve as an inspiration to their personal growth.

Business: I am a champion of change and constantly work to make work environments more healthy, sustainable, and enjoyable.

Community: I am a generous supporter of promoting healthy communities and involved in making a positive impact.

Share this mission statement with three or four others who know you well, and talk about it with them over and over again until you believe that you believe it. Use it in making significant decisions about your life. And return to it periodically to see if it still carries meaning and whether you should make revisions. Remember, this is a journey and the mission statement itself can serve as a vehicle for clarity as you progress along the path.

○　EXERCISE 3.2: DEVELOPING A PERSONAL LEARNING PLAN

Building on the personal mission statement and your understanding of your various strengths and weaknesses, we now will identify a personal change you would like to make, and we will prepare a personal learning plan for making that change. This change is typically a behavior or skill such as creativity, managing conflict, delegation, or patience that would make you more effective and more able to fulfill your mission.

Learning a new skill or behavior, however, requires tremendous commitment and energy. So it is important to select something that has meaning for you—something that is motivating, takes you out of your comfort zone, and supports your career goals. Otherwise you may lose interest and become caught up in other demands of life. These goals also need to be specific so you can measure them and assess your results. Being better at relationships, for instance, is too broad as a goal because it could mean any number of things. On the other hand, being a better listener is specific and measurable, and also leads to better relationships.

Step 1: Select a personal goal. In selecting a personal learning goal, first look over the results of the previous exercises and ask what potential improvements you might want to make. Among those, select one that is relevant to your personal mission as well as your career aspirations.

For instance, I often have received feedback that I appear to be aloof or disengaged in a group. I must first decide whether it matters enough for me to want to change before considering this as a potential goal. Since coaching and facilitating are important to both my mission and my work, I can't afford to be perceived as aloof and disengaged. If I am going to help people, I have to show that I care. So I selected becoming a more active listener as my goal because I believed this would help me most with this challenge.

Step 2: Prepare a personal learning plan. After selecting a goal, the next step is to develop a learning plan using the Wheel as a guide. As we have seen, the Wheel is an action-learning process. Each direction represents a different set of tactics for single loop learning and developing a new behavior or skill. Traveling around the Wheel using some or all of the learning tactics of each direction ensures a balanced approach to learning as well as a balanced outcome. In using the Wheel as a framework for developing a new skill or behavior, you are also learning to become a more balanced and agile human being. The process models the desired result.

Select a goal and use the following worksheet as a guide for developing your personal learning plan. I have used my goal of becoming a more active listener as an example.

1. *Teacher: Seek feedback and acquire the intellectual understanding and the technical skills necessary for making the desired change.*
   General Learning Tactics:
   •Read books, articles, magazines.
   •Seek role models and mentors.

- Take a course or workshop.
- Ask questions and seek feedback.

*Personal Learning Plan:*_____

_____

_____

Example from my plan:
- Read *The Lost Art of Listening* by Michael Nichols.
- Take a half-day workshop at the university in listening and communication skills.
- Pick a person in this workshop who displays these skills to help me.
- Paula is one of the best listeners I know, so I will also meet with her to ask how she does it.
- I will ask direct observers of my experience for feedback.

2. *Nurturer: Develop the emotional understanding and the relationship skills necessary for that change.*
   General Learning Tactics:
   - Consider your attitudes and emotional reactions to making the change and how you have become stuck in the past.
   - Assess whether these reactions are aids or obstacles and how to address them.
   - Understand how the change may impact others.
   - Involve others in your process and develop a learning partner.

*Personal Learning Plan:*_____

_____

_____

Example from my plan:
- My challenge is that I often feel shy in a group and fear being wrong. Being an introvert, I also need time to ruminate on what I have been hearing before I feel capable of jumping in. After a while, I simply withdraw and stop listening. The combined effect makes me appear aloof and disengaged. I will need to confront these fears in becoming a better listener.

- Alert trusted colleagues in every important group I am in about what I am doing so they can help and provide feedback.
- If I begin to fade, ask one of these colleagues to give me a signal.
- To stay focused, try to listen to the emotions that accompany an expressed statement and identify concerns that are not explicitly stated.
- Note my reactions immediately after the meeting, and approach one of my trusted colleagues later to check the accuracy of my impressions.

3. *Visionary: Conceptualize and develop a plan of action for practicing the new skill or behavior.*

General Learning Tactics:
- Imagine the multiple possibilities for action.
- Identify challenging practice fields.
- Develop a plan and establish goals.
- Prioritize steps.

*Personal Learning Plan:*_____

_____

_____

Example from my plan:
- Identify regular one-on-one relationships or team interactions where listening is important and I can practice.
- In meetings I lead, I will set aside a time where I ask a question and then simply listen.
- Every week for the next four weeks, when I am in a meeting, I will end it by paraphrasing the major points of the conversation.
- At first I will be selective in deciding with whom to practice, working with people who would be open to what I am trying to do, then take on tougher challenges later.
- Roy is one of those tough challenges for me because we have such opposite points of view on things that I often just check out. So after initial practice, I will work with Paula to help coach me on a plan of action for conducting a dialogue with Roy in a way that we both feel heard.
- Before entering my next dialogue with Roy, I will rehearse my plan of action mentally.

4. *Warrior: Take action and follow through.*

   General Learning Tactics:

- Jump in and experiment with new behavior.
- Take risks.
- Act on new opportunities as they arise.
- Be disciplined in practicing, persevering, and following through.

*Personal Learning Plan:*_____

_____

_____

Example from my plan:

- Prepare a regular schedule of meetings with either Paula or my selected partner from the workshop to check in on actions I have taken and results I have achieved.
- Arrange to send myself weekly e-mail reminders to make sure I am following through.
- Capitalize on little active listening opportunities as they arise, whether they are in my plan or not—take every opportunity to practice.
- Confront my fears if I find myself avoiding listening or fading.

5. *Sage: Reflect on experience.*

   General Learning Tactics:

- Take time to reflect on your experience—keep a learning journal.
- Ask what lessons you have learned.
- Discuss with others.
- Consider changes for the next cycle.

*Personal Learning Plan:*_____

_____

_____

Example from my plan:

- Ask trusted colleagues who have seen me in action how well they thought I was listening.
- Keep a learning journal and write and reflect in it after each experience—what lessons I learned, what I would do differently, and what my next challenges are.

• Set aside a number of times each month to review whether my day was appropriately engaged in active listening.

EXERCISES 3.3–3.5: DOUBLE AND TRIPLE LOOP LEARNING— TOOLS FOR THE CONTINUED JOURNEY

The personal learning plan is a specific incremental learning tool (single loop) for improving a particular skill or behavior. Exercises 3.3 through 3.5 introduce more reflective tools for adaptive and transformational learning (double and triple loop) and for helping to deepen self understanding and move the journey forward. They have proven invaluable throughout the ages for expanding awareness and promoting personal growth and transformation.

○ EXERCISE 3.3: JOURNALING

Writing in a journal is one of our oldest methods of self-exploration and discovery, and a powerful exercise for adding texture and meaning to our lives. When we write in a journal, we can reach in and be candid about our inner thoughts and feelings. This helps give us insight into personal growth, and helps access our unconscious to gain a deeper perspective about who we are. Journaling can help us through difficult times, provide a source of creative ideas, and give us foresight by reminding us of past mistakes. It is an effective tool for increasing self-awareness and for discovering our basic goodness and authentic presence.

Journals are not limited to making daily entries of current events like keeping a diary. Rather, journals are intended to help us explore our inner, psycho-emotional world. I have been keeping a journal for many years and used to write almost daily, particularly during times of stress. I found it tremendously helpful in understanding myself and the process I was going through. Now I write only when I know something is percolating just beneath the surface of my consciousness. An event or a thought triggers a glimpse, or flash, of something that I sense is just the tip of something greater that I should write about. So I write to go into it, and often the act of writing my way into it leads to a rush of insight and greater awareness.

I developed this skill after years of following a particular technique that I learned at a workshop based on the work of writer and poet Natalie Goldberg.[46] Her approach is somewhat like the "Zen" of journaling. Basically, her only rule is that there are no rules. This is more difficult than it seems, because for most of us, our rational minds want direction, guidance, and structure. Her

approach, however, is geared toward freeing the mind and tapping the nonra-
tional in order to give insight into deeper fears, desires, and aspirations, and
to surface all those subconscious motivations that guide our daily actions.

Goldberg's technique asks us to journal for ten-minute periods while answering a series of questions. The "non-rules" for answering these questions
are the following:

1. *Keep your hand moving.* Don't pause or hesitate to make sure you are
   making sense. That is your mind trying to take control. If you run
   out of things to say, then simply write "I don't know what to say"
   over and over again until something moves you otherwise.
2. *Don't cross out.* That is your internal judge editing and trying to make
   sense. Even if you didn't mean to write it, leave it. It may provide
   insight later.
3. *Don't worry about spelling, punctuation, or grammar.* This is the same as
   above. No one else is going to read this or try to make sense of it, so
   don't slow yourself down by trying to make it pretty.
4. *Lose control.*
5. *Don't think or get logical.* Remember, you are trying to free your mind.
6. *Go for the jugular.* If something comes up that seems off the wall, go
   right into it. It probably has deeper meaning. Remember, no one else
   is going to read it.

Step 1: Set aside some time to answer some or all of the following questions
with the above set of non-rules in mind.

1. What do I remember most from childhood?
2. What do I find most puzzling about life?
3. Where do I shine in life?
4. What do I fear most?
5. What can I do to nurture myself?
6. Do I live according to my values?
7. What did I learn today?
8. When my friends talk about me they say . . .
9. Ten years from now I can teach others . . .
10. The 27 things I want to do before I die are . . .

Step 2. Go back and circle all the words or phrases that are surprising, meaningful, or insightful for you. Then ask yourself:

1. What do I need to remember in going forward?
2. What changes am I willing to make?

These questions are just a start. If journaling appeals to you, then try to continue on a regular basis. Even if you don't know what to write, start writing about the events of the day and allow anything to surface. You can also develop your own questions. After enough practice, you will make the process your own, and it will become a habit and a partner in your growth.

○ EXERCISE 3.4: DIALOGUE

Peter Senge and others have argued that most of our normal communication in management cultures consists of discussions in which people advocate their position and others push back. They estimate that the majority of our organizations are competitive Model I cultures where the name of the game is winning. In approaching a problem or an issue in such cultures, people often come with a particular view, position, or desired outcome that they promote, and most of what they say is intended to advocate their point. When someone does this, others tend to push back, so the first person pushes harder in return. Positions become entrenched, and everyone ends up hurling alternatives at one another without really listening. These discussions become something like a "ping pong game where we are hitting a ball back and forth."[47] This can be productive when persuasion is required, but it can hinder relationships and developing a more expansive view of the problem or issue.

Dialogue is a style of communication in which the purpose is to go beyond any one person's understanding. It is a learning conversation where people enter feeling safe to explore issues without fear of being wrong. Dialogue has a long history that can be traced back to the early Greeks and indigenous cultures; it is also found today in Quaker meetings and various self-help groups in the style of Alcoholics Anonymous. The word dialogue derives from *dia*, which means *through*, and *logos*, which means *word*, or *thought*. Dialogue is the creation and flow of meaning between two or more people through a conversation that promotes thinking and learning together. It is a reflective practice that is essentially openness, or awareness and compassion, in action. It is a style of conversation in which we communicate through being aware and empathizing with one another to gain a shared understanding of what we are thinking and feeling.

Dialogue, as defined here, is the process of balancing inquiry with advocacy. It involves inquiring into another person's position while genuinely listening to what the other person says and advocating your own position in a way that invites further exploration. In balancing inquiry and advocacy, we try to lay out our thinking so we can create a greater shared understanding in dealing with the issue. This can be scary for many people, because defensive routines and the fear of being wrong often become barriers, particularly in dealing with a sensitive issue. Conducting dialogue, then, like leadership in general, is essentially an act of courage. For many of us, it asks us to step out of the cocoon.

The key aspects of dialogue are:

1. *Take a learning attitude.* In approaching a dialogue, it is important to first check your intent—are you in this to win or to learn, to defend a particular position or to support the collective? If you are convinced you are already right before even opening up to another's point of view, you may miss an opportunity to learn. In wanting to control or manipulate, you can close down and block learning. On the other hand, if you go in willing to accept that you might not know everything that needs to be known, and willing to let go of insisting on a specific predetermined outcome, you open yourself to other people and to potential learning.

   You may be fairly certain of your position, but for the sake of the dialogue it is important to relax that certainty for a moment to at least allow for another possibility. This requires respecting your partners in the dialogue as true colleagues. Martin Buber called this a true turning toward one another, where we appreciate one another not as objects, but as divine beings. It also requires signaling this to your partners in a way that they can believe shows that it is safe for them to enter the conversation.

2. *Use positive language.* In approaching a dialogue, especially one dealing with a difficult or sensitive issue, it is important to pay attention to the language you use. Particularly in advocating your position, there is a fine line between being straightforward and being judgmental. Making attributions and using loaded words like "You're insensitive to others" or "That was a dumb move" puts people on the defensive and provokes them to respond in kind.

   In advocating your view it is important to describe the situation, the relevant behavior, and the impact on you or your perception of its impact on others in objective, nonjudgmental terms. Remember that your views are probably biased until you have heard the other person's point of view. So present information as perceptions and reactions, not facts. Remembering to use "I" instead of "you" in conveying your point of view often helps. For example, "When you did . . . this is what I was thinking," or "I was uncomfortable with that, and I'd like to tell you why" are phrases conducive to advocating our position in dialogue for difficult situations.

3. *Inquire while listening without resistance.* Often it is important to start with a question. As Stephen Covey said, "Seek first to understand, then to be understood."[48] Leading with inquiry helps reveal assumptions and beliefs that may not be in accord with reality. It allows you to "check things out" with others and surface new information to create a greater shared understanding of the issue. It also enables you to surface your assumptions and beliefs that shape your perspective on the situation so you can deal with them publicly.

Your success, however, depends on your ability to listen effectively. Listening without resistance means noticing your own reactions while genuinely hearing the position of others. It requires empathy and slowing down enough to avoid quick judgments, seek additional data, and formulate alternatives. This is difficult because we are always projecting our opinions, ideas, biases, and assumptions. To listen without resistance, you need to let go of these attachments and imagine other people's viewpoints. So as you inquire, probe gently to explore the other person's thinking, suspend judgment to see what you might be missing, and encourage the other person to challenge your view.

5. *Advocate while inviting more inquiry.* Advocacy requires that we state our views in a way that invites further conversation and does not put others on the defensive. As just mentioned, success depends most on your attitude and language. If you come to a conversation with the attitude that you are right, the others will sense it and likely respond in kind. Similarly, if you state your views in a way that does not invite learning from others—for example, "This is what I see, don't you?"— the dialogue shuts down.

Advocating your point of view constructively means simply letting others know what you have observed objectively in a way that invites further discussion. It means revealing your thinking about how you arrived at your point of view and encouraging others to explore it with you. In advocating, you state your view, reveal the thinking that led you to that view (with examples when possible), share your assumptions and interpretations if you know them, and invite others to challenge it.

Perhaps the most important things I have learned in using dialogue are about my attitude and language. When I approach people in an open, positive, and gently probing way, even around the most sensitive of issues, they will often mirror my example and respond in kind. They do not need to be skilled in dialogue to be part of one, as the most important thing is the example I provide. On the other hand, sometimes it doesn't work. There may be baggage in the relationship, or some personal insecurity involved, that makes it impossible. Again, there are no panaceas or silver bullets in leadership. In cases where dialogue is not working, and change is absolutely imperative, it may be necessary to pursue other sources of power and influence—such as a formal performance review.

Step 1: Think of a difficult conversation you should have involving feedback you need to provide or a conflict you need to resolve.

1. Using the principles of dialogue, how would you prepare to have this conversation?
2. How would you convey a positive attitude?
3. How would you talk about the actual behavior or issue and the impact while not making attributions or judgments?
4. How would you ask the other people (or person) about their view and their thinking?
5. How would you present your own view in a way that invites them to explore further?
6. How would you ask about or present alternatives in a way that also invites more exploration?

Share your preparation with a friend or colleague who might be able to help you in your preparation.

Step 2: Conduct the dialogue and then reflect.

1. What did you learn about yourself and the process of dialogue?
2. What might you do differently next time?
3. Where else might you apply this in other relationships or areas of your life?

○ EXERCISE 3.5 MEDITATION

Meditation is both an ancient spiritual practice and a contemporary mind-body technique for relaxing the body and calming the mind. Most meditative techniques have come to the West from Asian religious practices—particularly those of India, China, and Japan—but similar techniques can be found in many cultures around the world. Until recently, the primary purpose of meditation has been religious, although its health benefits have long been recognized in the cultures where these methods originated.

The benefits of meditation are well-documented and include reduced stress, improved relationships, better health, enhanced self-concept, increased perception and memory, reduced alcohol and drug abuse, and greater creativity and productivity. In the present context, however, I will focus on meditation as a daily reflective tool for creating balance, maintaining perspective, and increasing awareness and insight into self, others, and reality.

The two primary aspects of most meditation techniques are concentration and mindfulness. Concentration begins with drawing the meditator's attention to an internal or external object—such as breath, sound, word, and bodily sensations—while minimizing distractions. Then you focus the mind by gently reining in its natural tendency to wander, repeatedly bringing your attention back to the chosen object. This process relaxes, clears, pacifies, and calms the mind through sustained attention. Breath, mantra, and repetitive prayer are the most commonly used forms of concentration.

Mindfulness is awareness of the present moment. To develop mindfulness, meditators attend alertly, but nonjudgmentally, to all processes passing through the mind and body. The idea is to observe experience just as it is. This practice helps us to be awake and alert to all experiences, to meet them with equanimity, and to allow them to pass through the mind and body without holding on to them or rejecting them. These experiences include thoughts, emotions, sounds, and physical sensations. Mindfulness meditation is the practice of seeing these experiences arise just as they are, and letting them go and be without projection or judgment.

The fruits of this practice are clarity, stillness, and insight. By providing a space of ease and interest in which we can become acquainted with the mind's natural reactions to experience, the clarity and stillness achieved from concentration allow insight and reflection to occur spontaneously. We notice aversion, fascination, or restlessness and gain insight into their root cause. We see the mind as constantly moving and changeable, often giving rise to unwholesome desire and associated unpleasantness. As the constant arising and passing of experiences and moods become familiar, it also becomes clear that there is no permanence to them. They are just us—our mind at work. When the mind is still and silent, revealing a bright spaciousness, there are no concrete or permanent characteristics to be found. This is our basic goodness, and through it we relax and see how everything can become workable.

This process is summarized in the following:

Meditation is concentration on an object
- breath
- bodily sensations
- sound
- feelings and feeling

With an awareness of the experience
- as it is
- without accepting or rejecting
- just letting be and letting go

That brings
- stillness
- clarity
- relaxation
- insight

And results in greater
- creativity
- comprehension
- health
- memory
- productivity
- relationships

In essence, meditation is the practice of letting go and letting be. In meditation we do not impose anything on our mind too forcefully, nor do we let it wander. There is no ambition to stir up thoughts or to suppress them. We learn to relate to the world as it is.

Basic Technique: The following is a basic meditation technique as taught by S. N. Goenka, my first meditation teacher. Goenka was born and raised in Burma but he is Indian by descent. He became a successful businessman, then came into contact with his teacher, U Ba Khin, and learned meditation from him. After receiving training for 14 years, Goenka resettled in India and began teaching meditation courses in 1969. These courses now attract thousands of people from across the world and every part of society. While the technique that Goenka teaches has its origins in Buddhism, his approach is nonsectarian. For this reason, his teaching has a profound appeal to people of all back-grounds, of every religion and no religion, of every part of the world.

1. *Sit in a comfortable posture.* Sit in a chair in a comfortable position with your back straight, your feet flat on the floor, and your hands resting in your lap. Keep your head in alignment with your spine, with your chin pointed slightly down. Instead of using a chair some people may wish to sit on a cushion; but do so only if you can remain comfortable in that position without moving for 20 to 30 minutes.

2. *Bring your attention to the breath.* Bring attention to your breath—on your upper lip as the breath passes in and out of your nostrils, or on your abdomen as it rises and falls with your breathing. Either is fine. Just relax and gently bring your attention to your breath as it comes in and out and notice any sensations that arise at your point of focus: hot, cold, tingling—any sensation at all. Just *be* with your breath and these sensations without reacting. As the mind wanders and begins to think or feel about other things, bring it gently back to the breath and observe. The mind's natural tendency is to wander, so don't become perturbed at having to frequently return your attention to the breath. Let go of your wandering thoughts and emotions and return to the breath. You will need to let go hundreds and thousands of times, but in bringing your attention back to your breath remember to do so without judgment or aggression. Just gently bring it back and rest your attention on the breath, let go, and relax.

3. *Sweep attention up and down the body.* After the mind has settled and you have achieved some continuity in your attention, turn your attention to the crown of your head and gently notice any sensations that might arise. Don't force anything, just gently pay bare attention to what is there. As sensations arise—tingling, pleasure, or discomfort—or as thoughts or emotions arise—desire, pain, or indifference—simply let them be as they are and meet them with equanimity without being pulled into reaction. Now spread your attention across the top of your head doing the same—constantly

noticing any sensations, thoughts, or feelings as they arise while allowing them to just be.

Sometimes you will feel things and sometimes not, but do not force. Continue to gently move your attention around the top of your head. Then slowly move it to your face, neck, arms, torso, and so on, sweeping your entire body all the way down to your toes and then slowly back up again to your crown. And repeat sweeping up and down the body, all the while paying gentle attention to any thoughts and sensations and meeting them with equanimity. Continue until you want to finish the session, then bring your attention back to the breath and relax there for a few minutes. Gently open your eyes and end the session.

Meditators often devote anywhere from 20 minutes to an hour to the daily practice of meditation. It is through such a daily practice that we reap the benefits. Meditating just now and then does not allow for the benefits to accumulate and have real impact on our lives. In using the above technique, it is important to spend one-third of whatever time you take on the concentration aspect—the breath—and two-thirds on the mindfulness aspect—the sweeping.

Whatever meditation technique you choose, I strongly recommend that you start with a qualified teacher. My description gives only a basic idea of what meditation is and how it works. There are now hundreds, possibly thousands of meditation instructors and centers available, and they are easily found on the Web. For beginners, I also recommend that you devote at least a weekend to your first experience. I found in my first experience that it took three days before my mind began to still at all; and without experiencing that stillness, you will not have genuinely tasted the power of meditation. Without that taste, you may not have the desire necessary to continue in a daily practice.

4

TURNING THE WHEEL I

TAPPING THE WISDOM OF TEAMS

The honor of one is the honor of all, the hurt of one is the hurt of all.

—Native American saying

One finger cannot lift a pebble.

—Hopi saying

The ancients believed that the three fundamental kinds of work in life for learning and growth are individual, relationship, and community. The Wheel serves all three by reminding us that we are interconnected, and everyone is a part of the vast natural order of the universe. It tells us that the one thing we share in common is loneliness, and we become whole through touching and being in harmony with all things. It also tells us that we learn and grow not by being self-centric, but by awakening ever more fully to how we are woven into the total fabric of the world. To fulfill the vision of the sacred Wheel is to be humble, to relate to other beings and things, and to be responsible for the welfare of the whole community. To the Native American Sioux, living this way is known as *Mitokweyosin:* "With all beings and all things we are as relatives." To survive and flourish in a harsh and constantly changing environment, the Sioux learned to pull together their relationships and strengthen community, bound by the common interests of food, protection, and personal fulfillment.

Individual work comes first, however, as it provides the ground for effective relationship and community work. The early Sioux community honored the sovereignty of the individual, and the freedom to pursue a personal journey. This freedom could have fractured the community if not for the mutual interests that kept people together, and the ability of the individual to find meaning and purpose through making a contribution to the whole. To function properly in a community required a certain selflessness that grew out of individual inner work. Selfishness was dangerous to this society as it could pull the tribe apart. That is one reason why generosity is a sacred virtue to the Sioux. Warriors did not try to stand out from other band members, and strove to act bravely and honorably to help the group in whatever way possible. When glory befell them, they would give away prized possessions to friends, family, and relatives as a measure of their selflessness and awareness of responsibility to the welfare of the community.

The ancients believed that the three fundamental kinds of work in life for learning and growth are individual, relationship, and community.

Ironically, the ground of such inner work is, as twentieth-century philosopher Wei Wu Wei said, the reason you're so unhappy with your life: "Because 99.9 percent of everything you think, and of everything you do, is for yourself—and there isn't one."[1] We learn that we only discover our sense of self—at least of any self worth discovering—through meeting the Other. Only through engaging and participating with others in relationships and community do we grow and develop in ways that have depth and meaning. Just as the heroic myth tells us, the journey that begins with individual work gains fruition only through relationship and community. In learning who they are, people want to know how they belong. All people yearn to belong, and to realize their innate gifts and have them recognized and appreciated by others.

As a living expression of the Wheel, community plays an important role in drawing out and supporting the individual Heroic Journey. Although the universe is a vastly diverse constellation, all things play a part. Every person in the community has a place and a contribution to make. In the Dagara tribe of West Africa, when a woman becomes pregnant, the community seeks answers to why this new person is being sent to them and how that person will contribute. Purpose is not to be *assigned* to anyone, rather it is to be discovered. As an expression of the spirit, this purpose is to be remembered by the individual with the support of the community. Without such a purpose, life

Individual work comes first, however, as it provides the ground for effective relationship and community work.

has little meaning. Dagara elders traditionally play a key role in this process by mentoring the young and challenging them with tasks, trials, and initiations to help them recognize, awaken, and deliver their genius to the community.[2] In the process, the young learn to be individuals without being individualistic, and to belong to a greater whole without losing personal identity. For both the Sioux and the Dagara, this was known as walking in a sacred manner.

The Wheel also provides a framework for integrating the separate journeys with the evolution of the community. It reminds the community to achieve a dynamic balance with all individual elements functioning smoothly in an ordered whole. The community provides a sense of inclusion and potential for everyone to learn, grow, and change. It also provides a working vision that stresses everyone's contribution. For the Sioux, the five directions represent the five clans of the tribe and the different tribes that make up the nation. As Sioux holy man Black Elk said: "The sacred hoop of my people is one of many that make the whole."[3] For him, the Wheel encompassed a set of values and principles for guiding the many aspects of individual, relationship, and community work. It served as a simple yet powerful system for finding meaning, reducing complexity, and dealing with change.

WHY TEAMS ARE IMPORTANT TO ORGANIZATIONS

Modern research on teams bears out much of this ancient wisdom. Aside from leadership and change, there is perhaps no other topic in management literature as popular as teams and team building. Researchers in the 1950s and 1960s focused intensely on teams and groups, but it took the scare from the Japanese and the TQM (Total Quality Management) movement of the 1980s for Americans to pay attention and gain enthusiasm for the findings. Those findings show that collaborating in teams increases motivation, effort, and productivity. They also show that team learning is superior to competitive and individualistic learning, and that it contributes to improved psychological health.

Harvard professor Richard Hackman says that about half of the leading edge companies in this country now deploy most of their employees in self-organizing teams, many of them with remarkable results.[4] Productivity expert

Jack Osburn, for instance, reports that self-directed work teams realized 30 to 40 percent higher productivity at Procter & Gamble, produced in three days as much as entire assembly lines did in fourteen at Tectronix, and reduced service problems by 13 percent at Federal Express.[5] In short, we are relearning that working in community is a social imperative, and another universal and archetypal truth essential to human fulfillment.

Management author Peter Senge and others have pointed out a number of important reasons for this growing interest in teams and their impact on organizations.[6] First, teams bring together complementary skills that exceed those of any individual member. The world is too fast and too complex for any one person to deal with all the issues alone, so many minds working together are better than one. Second, effective teams enable spontaneous, innovative, and coordinated action. Teams form an operational trust and shared vision that allow members to count on one another to act automatically in complementary ways in response to changing events. Each team member knows what the other is doing without needing to coordinate their actions explicitly. Third, teams enable organizational agility and learning. Organizations of all kinds are constantly challenged to keep their products and services vibrant in order to meet the changing and evolving demands of their stakeholders. Success often depends on how quickly they can respond. Teams are more flexible than traditional hierarchical structures, so organizations have turned to them in order to become more nimble, innovative, and continuously self-modifying.

. . .for organizations to succeed, they need involved and committed workers who are self-directed, creative, and inwardly driven to learn . . .

Most importantly, however, for organizations to succeed, they need involved and committed workers who are self-directed, creative, and inwardly driven to learn. Work plays a central role in giving meaning and substance to existence. Teams offer a vehicle for individuals to realize their purposeful potential and find meaning in their work. They give people opportunities to learn and grow in tackling purposeful tasks, and to participate with others in achieving a mutually desired result.

Research shows that this kind of involvement increases not only productivity, but also satisfaction. Work done for the sake of efficiency and to the exclusion of human fulfillment becomes just a job. When people do not find meaning in their work they will make trouble. The workers become alienated and compensate with self-serving maneuvers, social loafing, or other forms of defensive behavior. Teams in striking contrast, offer a vehicle for discovering and practicing leadership.

A study by Richard Hackman of airline in-flight service teams provides a good example of the value of working in teams.[7] After price and schedule, the most important factor in a customer decision for choosing an airline is service. Hackman and his colleagues studied two different approaches—one by an international and one by a domestic airline company—for improving in-flight service.

The international company pursued an engineered approach. Its experts and analysts studied and designed flight cabin services, service delivery routines, and exact workflow procedures for attendants. The attendants then received rigorous training and cabin mocks to reinforce objectives and procedures. The process resulted in predictable and competent in-flight performance. However, the company continued to trail in service innovations compared to its competitors, and often failed to respond to special in-flight needs of customers. More importantly, its flight service personnel left the impression of what some customers described as simply "reading their lines."[8] For flight attendants, it had become "just a job."[9] The system underutilized their intelligence, ingenuity, and initiative and, as a result, the excitement of the work disappeared.

The domestic airline took a self-directed, team-based approach. Attendants received training on company service objectives and methods, but were also provided great freedom in the design and implementation of in-flight services. They were trained in team-building principles—what makes a team and how each individual contributes to the whole—and allowed to develop their own conclusions about how the team was to form and operate. Teams, rather than individuals, became the key unit of operation, and the team decided on its concept, composition leadership structure, schedules, service levels, and procedures. Leadership often rotated among its members, and each person felt fully empowered to provide the shared concept of good service.

As a result, the team clicked, and performed superbly. Customer feedback ratings of the domestic airline were well above those of the international airline. Most important, team members were fully engaged, friendly, and high-spirited. Their work provided them with meaning through autonomy, opportunity, and growth, and contributed positively to their well-being through a sense of belonging. They were committed, self-directed, and inwardly driven to learn.

WHY TEAMS ARE IMPORTANT TO THE INDIVIDUAL

Tapping into the wisdom of a team requires cultivating commitment in each individual member. Hackman and others found a number of essential elements that help teams foster this commitment.[10] Foremost is autonomy, the degree of latitude that the team and its members have in designing and conducting their work. Teams with a clear task and charge work best when the process and performance strategy for achieving the desired outcome is left to the team to determine. When allowed to self-organize, team behavior is normally constructive and mutually supportive in spite of the lack of formal control. A second essential element is that each team member must have a role in the task and know how his or her individual contribution makes a difference to the whole. When members feel their effort is significant and valued, they also feel more responsibility and commitment. A third element is a positive interpersonal dynamic. When members feel mutual respect and support, the sense of fellowship that emerges improves the productivity and functioning of the team. While a positive interpersonal dynamic cannot overcome a poorly designed team, the lack of one can pull a well-designed team down.

Finally, and most important, what most energizes and promotes commitment in a team is a clear and challenging task. The magnetic pull of the task alone is often enough to draw a team together. Effective teams feel they are doing something that really counts, is worthwhile, and provides them with meaning and a sense of fulfillment. This often includes breaking new ground, learning a new skill or behavior, doing something better, making an impact, serving a higher purpose, or benefiting others.

In taking on meaningful roles in a meaningful and challenging task, team members feel they belong, and have an opportunity to realize their talents, capacities, and potential.

As mentioned in chapter 3, there is both a lesser and greater hunger of our becoming spirit. The lesser is driven by a longing for things that sustain life, the greater by things that give it meaning. Satisfying the greater hunger—the sense of belonging, self-actualization, and reintegration with others—is what motivates us and gives meaning to work. It is also what develops commitment and strong teams.

In taking on meaningful roles in a meaningful and challenging task, team members feel they belong, and have an opportunity to realize their talents, capacities, and potential. Serving a challenge or a cause that they believe in, in a way that stretches or fulfills their potential, gets to the heart of what it is to be human. When this meaningfulness is shared with others, it provides the bedrock of an effective team. It frees people from self-interest and makes them more able to appreciate, support, and work with others.

Committed teams, like inspired individuals, have found a way to realize their purposeful potential. Selfishness diminishes, and people become more committed and available. This is what Bertrand Russell meant when he said, "Gradually I learned to be indifferent to myself and my deficiencies; I came to center my attention increasingly upon external objects: the state of the world, . . . individuals for whom I had affections."[11]

The essential challenge for team leaders, then, is to learn how to manage learning and meaning of the group. In chapter 3 I addressed the *why* of the individual, this is the *why* of the team. Success means harnessing the energy of becoming and embarking on a journey that serves the greater hunger of the people involved. It means finding ways to not fall back into self-interest and the defensive behaviors that block learning and development. This kind of success depends not only on the task and the structure of the team, but also the attitude, development, and interpretive frame of the individuals involved.

You may argue that not all team challenges can be expected to provide opportunity for growth and meaning, and that many tasks are boring, routine, and mundane. Yet psychologist Mihaly Csikszentmihalyi argues that even people with the simplest of tasks or the most barren environments can find meaning. He describes an old welder in a worn-down train assembly yard who declined a number of promotions because he found meaning in fixing complex systems.[12] Similarly, campaign volunteers who only stuff envelopes find meaning in their team spirit and the message of the campaign they serve. Counter clerks can do the same through enjoying the quality and efficiency of their service, as well as the satisfaction of helping others.

It becomes clear then, as so many of our wise ancestors believed, that the work of the team is inseparable from the work of the individual.

Even under the most adverse conditions, meaning can be found. Viktor Frankl found that the most important trait of concentration camp survivors like himself was a strongly directed purpose that was not self-seeking.[13] Victims survived not for reasons of self-survival, but rather for the meaning they found in helping others. Their ability to do so depended on their awakening the Fire of Self, and feeling empowered to find meaningful activity, no matter what the circumstance.

It becomes clear then, as so many of our wise ancestors believed, that the work of the team is inseparable from the work of the individual. Teams fail when leaders fail to shape the right team experience, or when members fail to do their individual work. Leaders can help shape the experience, but success depends ultimately on the ability of individual team members to frame that experience in a way that motivates each of them. This kind of shaping and framing is often a reciprocal process as people see how they can use the collective work as a vehicle for doing their individual work. When team leaders and members succeed at this process, productivity and happiness result; when they don't, alienation and drudgery prevail.

Perhaps not all teams can be so inspired, but the point is that the capacity for such motivation lies deep within us and provides the hope, the opportunity, and the ground for designing and building a better personal life and a better society. As Tibetan Buddhist master Chogyam Trungpa Rinpoche said, "If we are to help the world, we have to make a personal journey. It is up to each of us individually to find meaning and work together in realizing an enlightened society."[14] The lesson of both the past and the present is that community work and individual work are not separate. Teams offer a vehicle for both the individual and the collective Heroic Journey, or search for learning and meaning. Framing the team experience as such signals the possible end of work as drudgery and the beginning of work as enrichment and ennoblement.

The question then becomes how to shape, develop, and lead teams in a way that serves the needs of productivity as well as the personal and collective journeys of the people involved.

HOW TO MAKE A TEAM: THE ACTION LEARNING WHEEL AND TEAM DEVELOPMENT

The question then becomes how to shape, develop, and lead teams in a way that serves the needs of productivity as well as the personal and collective journeys of the people involved. Much of the early research on teams focused on generalized stage models of group development, the most popular one being the "forming-storming-norming-performing" model of Bruce Tuckman developed in the 1960s. Recent research by organizational development professors Connie Gersick and Anita Woolley,[15] however, has thrown doubt on the validity of these generalized models. Gersick and Woolley's findings suggest that groups improve performance through an iterative process of doing and reviewing. Teams enhance performance by first engaging the task at hand, then reflecting on their performance, process strategies, and team dynamics.

Finally, they adjust them to improve results. In other words, this research says that teams develop through action learning.

The research that first suggested action learning as a group development process dates back to the work of Eric Trist in the 1940s and 1950s and Douglas McGregor in the 1960s. This early work indicated that the more learning and doing are integrated, the better one can achieve both. It helped us realize that we build a team most successfully by engaging the task and reflecting on the performance of that task. Success in tackling a challenging task with meaningful roles produces trust, caring, and support for one another. To paraphrase management guru Robert Kaplan, we don't build morale to increase productivity of a team, we do it the other way around.[16] Interpersonal dynamics, while important, are simply not the most important point of leverage, especially in the early life of a group. We develop teams primarily through shaping learning and meaning in working on a challenging task.

The Wheel again serves as an important model for understanding, instructing, and guiding this action learning process.

The Wheel again serves as an important model for understanding, instructing, and guiding this action learning process. In moving around the Wheel, team members have a framework to see how they will be challenged, who they are relative to others involved, and what is important to them in terms of the task. They also ask whether they will have a meaningful role, learn, be appreciated, and have autonomy. The responses to these questions help determine the level of commitment and whether they are in or out.

In traveling around the Wheel, the team reflects on these issues while conducting the task. With each repetition of the cycle, the team and its members learn, grow, and develop. Most importantly, they learn how to learn from experience. They move up the spiral of learning from incremental to adaptive to transformational learning. There is no standard order to the process, but it is presented in the following pages in a logical sequence for the sake of clarity.

Just like individuals, however, teams can derail from a lack of balance, overplaying strengths, or clinging to habitual perspectives.

THE TEACHER: KNOWING THE WORLD

Action learning often begins with the Teacher or the Visionary, as in gathering the facts to solve a problem or identifying an idea to move forward. Here we start with the Teacher. In undertaking a challenge as a team, we first want

Just like individuals, however, teams can derail from a lack of balance, overplaying strengths, or clinging to habitual perspectives.

to know the details and reality of the task at hand. We also want to know the composition of knowledge and skills of the group. So we seek data on the current situation, the available resources, and the context of the task to analyze before considering the options. We also want to know what's potentially in it for each of us, whether our personal skills and talents are needed, and how they might contribute and fit together with the others.

A manufacturing team charged with improving delivery at lower cost, for example, needs to know how many orders are typically on the books and plan production accordingly. Otherwise, monthly swings in orders can produce a whipsaw effect that will require constant revision of work strategies and staffing arrangements. They also want to know about the money, time, space, equipment, and staff available to them, whether these are likely to change, and what latitude they have in organizing those resources. They need all this data before they can begin to match the individual skills, competencies, and resources of the group with the task at hand.

Teams can become stuck or derail at this point from members being overly critical of one another, causing mistrust or cynicism. They can also derail from demanding too much information, suffering from analysis paralysis, and striving for the 100 percent solution when the time, information, and resources simply won't allow for it.

THE NURTURER: AWAKENING THE HEART

The Nurturer shapes how members form productive relationships and work as a team. As a team begins to work together, individual members want the others to know what they need from the group, and what the group needs from them. In becoming acquainted with one another, members feel out how they experience and express emotions, how they will deal with conflict, and what kind of interpersonal process will be most productive for the group.

With the Wheel as a model, this step becomes a conscious one by openly reflecting and revealing our thoughts and feelings about our process strategies and our interpersonal dynamic. In doing so, we learn to differentiate ourselves, recognize our mutual support, trust and care for one another, and take ownership for team goals, roles, and procedures. This dynamic evolves into a team ethic that frequently is formalized as a team charter or code of conduct, used to guide and support team functioning. The team ethic represents shared values. It gives shape to a sense of what is important to the team and how we agree to treat one another and conduct business among ourselves and with others. These values are almost always grounded in basic goodness and human virtues such as respect, integrity, and excellence.

Software development teams are good examples of productive team relationships. These teams are effective because they have developed a spoken or unspoken code of conduct that enables members to express themselves openly and be heard directly by others. There is a free and uninhibited exchange of information, ideas, and feelings, yet it is done out of mutual feelings of respect. This kind of interaction defines acceptable patterns of behavior and allows team members to operate freely within those bounds. Outside of the task itself, consciously shared expectations of conduct provide a foundation of trust and an operational bond that holds team members together as they create and respond quickly to changing circumstances.

Teams can derail when a sense of belonging to the group is absent, or when there is a breach in trust or in the code of conduct. If disrespected or not valued for their role or input, members can check out or become disruptive.

THE VISIONARY: SEEING THE WAY

As our team sorts out its situation and interpersonal dynamic, we turn to the Visionary to define purpose and meaning. We want to know what the possibilities are, what matters most, and how the values and interests of the team and our members are served through the achievement of the overall vision. So we work together to determine group goals, roles, process, and vision. We explore how they will organize and create, what process strategies they will follow, and how the big picture aligns with the interests and talents of each individual. We are also given considerable autonomy and freedom to work all this out on our own in order to generate the necessary commitment for follow-through.

To be powerful, the vision must be clear, and it must elicit the emotion and passion of all the members. A truly great team vision speaks to what the team members can become if they truly live their values and aspirations in serving the vision. It provides meaning, taps into their purposeful potential, and enables them to become more of a team. The sense of "we" begins to dominate the sense of "I."

Hackman gives an example of a product development team that was challenged with a deadline to conduct an analysis of a major program launch.[17] The team and its members were given considerable latitude and autonomy in determining how to proceed with their work, sort out and change their individual roles as time went on, and project their own meanings and interpretations into the overall task. The team designed its own process, end product, and performance milestones, and allowed members to move among the different kinds of work to provide variety in experience and the opportunity to expand skills. The result was a successful, high quality product, and a highly committed team.

As Jim Collins and Jerry Porras point out, an observer of people at Netscape once said, "The only people who work this hard are people who want to. The only people who want to are people with enough freedom to do things as they want to."[18] When teams lack such vision and personal alignment, they derail from low engagement and low commitment of the members. They can also derail from having so many options and potential courses of action that they are unable to prioritize and follow through.

THE WARRIOR: EMBODYING THE WAY

As the team and its members establish their vision, interdependent roles, and goals based on the situation and the group dynamic, the Warrior moves the team into action and implementation of the plan. It is through taking action that the gap between knowing and doing is closed, and learning and meaning are internalized.

The most successful teams strive to embody both their task and process goals. Task goals are the ability to achieve objectives and close the gap between the original reality and the desired outcomes. Process goals are the ability to act on the plan in a way that is consistent with the shared values, ethics, and aspirations of the team members. Both are necessary for unqualified success, and as such are key to maintaining momentum, commitment, and an upward learning spiral.

Process goals are often overlooked but are highly important to the team. For our team to internalize the lessons of the work, become authentic, and hold its power, our team actions must be consistent with our shared values. So as we implement their plans, we examine the results in light of our vision, our process, and our values, take stock of the meanings we find, and act to narrow or close gaps between what we know needs doing and what we actually do.

Often, teams need to muddle through the process of doing and reviewing before any of this becomes clear. A newly formed customer service team, for example, may be unable to gain clarity on its direction and process until it has a solid record of experience of trying to implement its existing strategies. The team may take on the task with a well-specified plan and work procedures but it may nonetheless be unable to capture its full potential until it has taken the time to examine the results in light of its intentions, and make appropriate adjustments.

Teams derail when they focus so much on executing the task that they rush to completion before asking whether they are headed in the right direction or how the process serves its individual members. According to Nietzsche, "Many are stubborn in pursuit of the path they have chosen, few in pursuit of the goal." Such collective efforts are so focused on what they want to achieve that they shut everything out and cease to learn and derive meaning from their experiences.

THE SAGE: LEARNING TO LEARN

The Sage governs this doing and learning process by reflecting on and harvesting the lessons of experience. This reflection expands the team's ability to learn how to learn from experience. In traveling around the Wheel, the team openly and publicly reflects on the individual and collective questions raised by each direction, clarifying respective roles, procedures, and goals while building mutual trust, support, and commitment. The clarity and cohesiveness that emerge in turn restrengthen and re-empower members and the team both in doing the task and in learning from the experience.

The team learns, its members learn, and together we learn how to learn. At the same time, we discover meaning for ourselves in the contributions we make and the skills we acquire. We experiment with new behaviors and ways of proceeding in our work, and set up opportunities to receive feedback on those approaches. We reflect on those experiences, make the necessary adjustments, and adapt, learn, and grow in the process. Then we repeat the cycle.

A project management team's members may take time over morning coffee to review what went well and what went poorly during the previous day, and think about what they learned from what happened. They may examine the work planned for the current day, and discuss how the lessons of yester-day's experience might apply for today. They may reorganize the work, and plan to keep in close touch throughout the day to see how things are going so they can fine tune their strategy in response to unanticipated changes. They may even take notes during the day about things to discuss over the next morning's coffee. Purposely taking time to attend to the team's ability to learn goes a long way in building alignment and cohesiveness of the team, and often leads to remarkable individual and collective growth. Teams derail or fall short of desired outcomes when they fail to reflect as a team or actively develop a conscious learning process.

Figure 4.1 summarizes this team action Learning Wheel process. Just as they do for individuals, each step in the Wheel represents a distinct aspect of the team learning and development process: Each aspect is necessary. Each is related to and overlaps with the others. And, although described linearly, the process is holistic and starts at any point.

The Teacher diagnoses the challenge and assesses member contribution; the Nurturer shapes the interpersonal dynamic and how members support and relate to one another; the Visionary finds meaning by identifying and aligning team and member goals; and the Warrior experiments and acts on those goals. This cycle is repeated in an upward spiral of learning and growth, moving the team and its members from incremental to adaptive to transfor-mational learning, and from habitual pattern to authentic presence. The Sage governs this process by driving the doing and reviewing process, integrating the parts, and paying attention to learning how to learn from experience.

DIALOGUE AND THE PRACTICE OF OPENNESS

Just as individuals do, teams travel around the Wheel through openness and the practice of awareness and compassion. As outlined in chapter 3, these qualities are represented by the polar opposites of the Wheel. The Teacher-Visionary axis represents awareness and how we know the world. It com-bines our innate intellectual and intuitive modes of intelligence to discern and make sense of our experience. The Teacher focuses on the concrete and specific, the Visionary on the more subjective and abstract forms of knowing. Operating together, the Teacher and Visionary combine the analytic and the conceptual in ways that allow the team to understand the current reality and see the options available for the future.

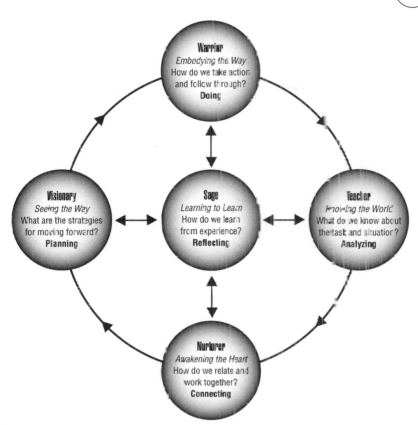

Figure 4.1 The Team Action Learning Wheel

In contrast, the Warrior-Nurturer axis represents compassion and how we engage the world. Here, the powers of feeling and action combine to determine how we relate to others and engage with them in compassionate action. Balancing a concern for self and others with the need to act, the combined Nurturer and Warrior qualities determine how to optimize the talents and commitment of the whole in taking action.

In effective teams, this process is driven by dialogue. As discussed in chapter 3 (see exercise 3.4), dialogue balances inquiry with advocacy; it helps team members open up and genuinely inquire into the positions of others, while advocating their own views in a way that invites further exploration.

In effective teams, this process is driven by dialogue.

Dialogue enables members to learn from one another, access the different directions, and realize the potential of the team. In working on a problem or a task together, members open and share freely while also accepting and supporting others who are doing the same. As they give and receive in this process, they expand themselves, connect more deeply with others, and tap the potential of everyone. Dialogue also helps to build trust by extending the willingness of members to risk learning and growth. They learn to try something new, and to become whole as individuals and as a team.

Dialogue can also be used when our teams can fall into trouble with problems in interpersonal relationships. There are real costs when relationships break down. There are costs to the individual members, with people living with pent-up frustrations and losing out on opportunities to learn. There are costs to the relationship as unresolved issues undermine trust and create frustrations that spill over into other areas. There are costs to the task at hand as the failure to bridge the differences results in wasted effort, misunderstandings, and poor decision making. Finally, there are costs to the team as the inability to pull the different perspectives together undermines the team's ability to tap all its inherent wisdom.

Dialogue helps surface and address interpersonal problems openly and skillfully. This is a real challenge in competitive, individualistic environments, but it is an essential leadership skill. Unless we find ways to work with our differences constructively, we are robbing our selves, our relationships, and our efforts of the lessons.

OTHER APPLICATIONS OF THE WHEEL IN GUIDING TEAM LEARNING AND DEVELOPMENT

RECOGNIZING STYLES

While dialogue is key for traveling around the Wheel, differences in individual style still can interfere with a team's ability to come together. People with different styles may not know the same facts, consider the same possibilities, or foresee consequences in the same way. The team must be able to consciously recognize the differences and pull these differences together to capture its own inherent wisdom.

The Wheel can help bridge the differences by providing a framework for team members to express their points of view in ways that suit one another's natural style. When people of different styles communicate, each person can use the language and perspective valued by the other's. A Nurturer, for example, who wants to convince a Warrior about the importance of including others will explain how inclusion facilitates and enables action. Likewise, Teachers should know that Visionaries will want to know about the possibilities of an issue before looking at the facts. Similarly, if the shadow of that Visionary is strong and creating tension, we may use the language of the Wheel to diffuse it. "I feel we may not need as much of your strong Warrior energy right now. Can you be more of a Nurturer for this?"

The language and the framework of the Wheel depersonalizes the differences, allowing us to work more openly and constructively together. Therefore, every relationship can become a teacher and every conflict a learning opportunity. It is important to remember, however, that the Wheel provides an explanation, not an excuse for being the way we are. To move forward, we must be willing to move out of our cocoon.

CONFLICT RESOLUTION

The Wheel can also serve as a model for dealing with conflict and working with these differences. The energies of the Wheel are an expression of wholeness and balance, and using them can help us appreciate and work with the differences we find with others. In traveling around the Wheel using dialogue, first we turn to the power of the Teacher to *inquire and clarify* the situation. We ask questions and seek a greater shared understanding of the differences. Next we draw on the power of the Nurturer to *respect and support* the relationship by conveying a sense of caring and that everything is workable. We empathize, try to put ourselves in our partner's shoes, and acknowledge the differences in perspectives and feelings. We then go to the Visionary to *identify and discern* the possible options for mutual gain. We brainstorm with our partner to create and inspire commitment around a desirable solution. Finally, we draw on the power of the Warrior to *take action and follow through* on our commitments. The Sage reminds us to be *open and spacious* throughout the process, and captures the lessons learned and how they might apply to other situations. In this way, the Wheel provides a neutral framework for people to feel freer to differentiate themselves from one another and learn from those differences. Controversy can even be promoted, deliberately structured, and managed for the sake of learning.

RECOVERING FROM THE SHADOW

What do we do when we blow it, lash out in anger, or say something we regret? This is usually the shadow speaking. Recovering from such situations skillfully offers important opportunities not only to learn but also to build a ground of trust in the relationship. When a shadow flares up we need to address the situation openly. We need to see it, point to it, and ask what evokes it. Perhaps we erupt in anger and say something like "You were a jerk to file the report the way you did!" Then we stop, apologize for the language, explain that the anger was about not being included, and invite exploration of what invoked it. We can also do this for our partners when their shadow flares up by serving as these people's mirror. The principles are the same, we simply point to it: "This is what I just saw, what was that about? Is there something we need to do differently?"

This is not to say that all difficulties in interpersonal relationship can be addressed through dialogue and using the Wheel as a framework for communication. Sometimes the baggage and the neurosis of one participant or another is just too great to break through. In such cases, we may need to use other means. It is to say, however, that we should try these approaches first, and only later use stronger tactics. Doing so creates safety, trust, and synergy, the very bedrock for building effective teams.

TEAM DESIGN

The Wheel can also be used to design the composition of a team. Like individuals, teams can have a particular style. Team style is determined by the mix of the directional styles of its members. Studies show that diversity in style and perspective within a team promotes productivity, learning, health, and positive relationships. Teams create not when pulling in the same direction but when pulling in different directions. As Thomas Jefferson once remarked, "Difference of opinion leads to enquiry, and enquiry to truth."[19] Thus, in assembling a team, leaders can design the composition of its members to represent all styles. The challenge in having such a mix, however, is that differences often degenerate into conflict. The more embedded people are in their own perspectives and unable to consider the perspectives of others, the lower the quality of decision making. To leverage differences, members must use dialogue and the Wheel to be aware of and appreciate individual differences, and how to disagree with one another while confirming one another's strength.

DECISION MAKING AND CREATIVE PROBLEM SOLVING

Finally, as in conflict resolution, the Wheel may serve as a process model for decision making and problem solving (see exercise 4.4 below). Although a balanced team design is desirable, it is not necessary. If membership of the team is skewed in three or fewer directions, the team can use the Wheel as a process model for approaching its task instead of reconstituting membership. As the team travels around the Wheel using dialogue, individual members can learn by stepping out of their natural tendency, taking on another perspective.

They first call on the energy of the Teacher to collect data and diagnose the issues. Then they evoke the intelligence of the Nurturer to exchange feelings and interpretations, then the Visionary to brainstorm and select options for moving forward, and then the Warrior to act and implement. The Sage again governs the process and reviews the outcomes to capture the lessons learned. These process steps parallel the decision-making and creative problem-solving models found in management literature. Groups can be creative, in spite of their inherent reservations, if they follow the steps.

. . . in practicing the processes of the Wheel, a team becomes more balanced and complete, more aware and compassionate, and more authentic and powerful.

I cannot overemphasize, however, the importance of having the team's process model the desired result. This is as important for teams as it is for individuals, whether applied to action learning, conflict resolution, or decision making and creative problem solving. In using the Wheel as a process model for their work while practicing dialogue, the team and its members develop wholeness and balance through emulating the different directions. That practice not only brings balance to the team members, but also moves them into authentic presence and basic goodness. Thus in practicing the processes of the Wheel, a team becomes more balanced and complete, more aware and compassionate, and more authentic and powerful.

The executive team of *Midwest Living* magazine, a company of the Meredith Corporation, provides a good example of using the Wheel as a framework for action learning and building a team. The existing group and its new president were brought together to conduct a scenario-planning process to address the recent lackluster performance of the magazine and reposition it for the future. (Scenario planning is an organizational planning and learning methodology developed and made famous by Shell Oil and now widely used throughout all kinds of organizations.) The *Midwest Living* group conducted its process through a four-month period, during which it alternated team retreats with individual and subgroup work assignments.[20]

The process started with collecting and distilling contextual information and bringing it to the first retreat for the group to digest. Before sorting through the data, however, the team was introduced to the Wheel as a means for understanding the dynamics of teams and the change process, and for establishing ground rules and norms for how the team would work together. This step also introduced dialogue as a means for opening the team to the perspectives of each member and tapping their combined wisdom.

After agreeing on these norms and digesting the data, the team outlined four possible futures and the implications for vision and strategy. The team members condensed these into a half-dozen objectives around which they self-organized for taking action. The team continued to meet to review progress, reflect at regular intervals on its strategies and performance, and adjust goals and behaviors accordingly. The scenario planning process became integrated into the team members' way of working together and conducting business.

In sum, the team traveled around the Wheel—from Teacher to Nurturer to Visionary to Warrior to Sage—to build and execute the plan. In the process, the team members also built their team. Traditional boundaries dissolved, new and refreshing ideas emerged, and the group coalesced around exciting prospects for the future. After six months, the executive team had moved the magazine to record distribution levels and advertising placements.

TURNING THE WHEEL: TEAM LEADER AS DESIGNER

As mentioned earlier, when the ancients in the Buddhist tradition wanted to receive a teaching, they would ask their wisdom keepers to "Turn the Wheel." In a similar vein, current management authors talk about leaders as designers—meaning leaders whose primary focus is to design and guide the learning processes of their teams and organizations. Guiding this process re-

In contrast to the high profile, directive style of leadership, the leader as designer is humble—often operating behind the scenes . . .

quires a different kind of leader. In contrast to the high profile, directive style of leadership the leader as designer is humble, often operating behind the scenes to shape systems, structures, and procedures in ways that tap into the inherent talents and commitment of others.

Like the elders in the Dagara tribe, such leaders work to draw out the gifts of others. Lao Tzu knew about this kind of leadership more than two thousand years ago, when he wrote: "A leader is best when people barely know that he exists, not so good when people obey and acclaim him, worst when they despise him. 'fail to honor people, they fail to honor you;' but of a good leader, who talks little, when his work is done, his aim fulfilled, they will all say, 'we did this ourselves.'"[21] When leaders operate at the center of action, it is often out of self-interest and often becomes a cause for derailment. Enduring leaders are driven by learning and commitment to wholeness, not to self-acclaim.

Leaders also create conditions through which others become effective. They design the learning and meaning-making processes of the team, and channel the energy of becoming toward individual and collective fulfillment. As Walt Disney once said about building his famed animation teams, "Of all things I have done, the most vital is coordinating the talens of those who work for us and pointing them towards a certain goal."[22]

Thus the overarching team-building strategy for you as a leader is to focus on developing an experience through which team members have an opportunity not only to meet some prior expectation, but also to go beyond it in a way that creates a sense of forward movement in novelty and accomplishment. Team leaders strive to provide a sense of achievement, identity, and opportunity for growth. When they succeed. alienation gives way to involvement, and helplessness gives way to empowerment. This is why providing a strong challenge and a clear task is so important for the team leader. Teams respond to challenges that offer them the opportunity to achieve something they have not done before. What matters most is that the task be significant and require growth to achieve.

In addition to providing a challenging task, team leaders can promote and design the right conditions for effective team development by learning to "Turn the Wheel." Drawing on the primary lessons of the chapter, table 4.1 summarizes the points of leverage for using the Wheel to design and make an effective team.

TABLE 4.1: TURNING THE TEAM ACTION LEARNING WHEEL

Teacher: Knowing the World

1. *Form a real team.* It is essential that each team member offer an important perspective or skill for contributing toward the task. Otherwise the team is not really a team. Often mistakes are made when existing teams are asked to take on new challenges without considering complementary skills or whether everyone has a contribution to make in the new effort. When a person's talents are not required, it often leads to low commitment and a dysfunctional dynamic.

2. *Provide information and resource support.* It is important that the team have access to the information, resources, and training necessary for accomplishing its mission. Team members need the information, skills and organizational resources necessary for tackling the task. Otherwise, they become frustrated and discouraged, and negatively affect the dynamic of the team.

Nurturer: Awakening the Heart

3. *Develop team values and norms.* The leader can help support the development of a positive interpersonal dynamic by ensuring the team has defined a clear sense of values and acceptable patterns of behavior. Asking the team to develop a values statement serves to develop group culture and provide the framework for discussing interpersonal dynamics (see exercise 4.3).

4. *Process the interpersonal dynamic.* The team needs to take time periodically to reflect on its interpersonal dynamic. When this is not the habit of the team, problems often emerge and prevent members from interacting honestly and openly with one another. Team leaders can ensure this reflection takes place by intervening as necessary and regularly scheduling times to debrief the dynamic.

Visionary: Seeing the Way

5. *Shape shared vision and process goals.* Effective teams have a clear, shared vision of the goal and planned steps for achieving it. That clarity

helps the team members work interdependently without becoming burdened with the need for frequent meetings or bureaucratic controls.

6. *Co-create to motivate.* Teams are motivated through having the authority and latitude for deciding how to proceed in their work. That freedom and autonomy allows members to cocreate their goals, methods, and processes, aligns their talents with what gives them most meaning, and helps them own and commit to their role.

Warrior: Embodying the Way

7. *Support follow-through.* Team leaders can promote follow-through by regularly scheduling time to discuss progress toward goals. This sets a benchmark for teams to gauge their effectiveness, plan and revise their activity, and keep leaders apprised of any obstacles they may need to address for the team. This also establishes a culture of discipline for closing the gap between idea and reality.

8. *Encourage walking the talk.* As part of the follow-through discussions, team leaders need to address the process of the team. This means discussing not only progress made toward goals but also how those goals are being achieved in terms of the values the team espouses and deems important. This strengthens the team culture and gives the team authenticity.

Sage: Learning to Learn

9. *Foster action learning.* Effective teams integrate learning and doing and adopt an action learning process that enables them to learn from experience. This means adopting a process of "do and review," where the team engages the task and periodically reviews its process in traveling around the Wheel to capture the lessons learned and make necessary adjustments (see exercise 4.4). Leaders can play an important role by ensuring a discipline of reflection.

10. *Practice dialogue.* The team needs to practice dialogue to "Turn the Wheel." The practice of dialogue is essential to the team learning process. It helps create an atmosphere of openness, build effective interpersonal relationships, and tap the individual talents and resources of the team. When dialogue skills are not practiced, differences can undermine openness, trust, and learning and derail the team. Team leaders help by serving as a model.

⊕

RICHARD FARR AND LEE YOUNGBLOOD of the Research Triangle in North Carolina are good examples of leaders as designers. As local business executives and campaign chairs for the United Way programs of Durham County and Wake County, respectively, they saw advantages to merging their campaigns and agencies with the Orange County United Way. They designed an effort that eventually overcame entrenched positions and parochial views of their respective boards and agencies and resulted in a merger that became a national model for United Way regionalism.

Even though there were vast differences in the size and budgets of the respective counties, Farr and Youngblood convinced their boards to appoint a team to explore the opportunity of merging, with equal representation from each county. The initial requirement of such equality was key in establishing the openness and the ground of trust that would eventually lead to success.

In convening the team, they designed a group process that included making decisions by consensus, focusing on win-win solutions, recognizing the uniqueness of each county, and targeting actions that were feasible to implement. They also set up a shared goal structure through which each county could see the benefits of cooperation. That mix of procedures resulted in an assessment of each county, taking steps to communicate and involve agency staffs, and developing shared implementation goals down to the operational level. To paraphrase one team member, the equal representation, operating principles, and shared goals were key to overcoming fears and cooperating fully. So thorough was their communication and involvement that they received unanimous approval from their boards to merge within two years.

The results were an immediately reenergized agency staff and an instant double-digit increase in funds raised. In reflecting on the leadership of Farr and Youngblood, team members said that their success as leaders was not to be found in their personalities, but in the procedure and process they implemented and developed. "They are leaders because they are consensus builders, team-oriented, respectful of differences, and not defensive," said one team member.[23] "Additionally, they know how to facilitate, capture, and communicate a vision, set and achieve goals, and have a low ego need. They don't personalize issues, and they don't need credit."[24] Farr and Youngblood were characterized as quiet, contemplative men whose expertise is in thinking through processes and developing models to learn and to achieve consensus. They were so focused on results that few who benefited from their leadership even knew who they were. They were leaders as designers.

⊕

SUMMARY

Like the ancients found in their cultures, we have found in our own that cooperation and working together in a community are essential for human productivity, growth, and satisfaction. We are created not for isolation but for relationship, and the team, or community, serves as a vehicle that enhances the individual and collective journeys of learning and meaning. These journeys are not separate; each builds on the other.

We also see how the Wheel provides a simple yet compelling model for guiding these journeys. Realizing the power of the team requires the commitment of each team member. The Wheel helps nurture that commitment through helping to discover and articulate the learning and meaning needs of each member of the team.

In invoking and emulating the power and unique intelligence of each direction, the team and its members awaken and realize their fullest potential. They travel up the spiral of experience, move from self-interest to other-interest, integrate with others and the community, and access a system of archetypal and universal values. In so doing, they realize their authentic presence and enter the realm of basic goodness. As we shall see in the next chapter, the result serves as the hope and ground for creating an enlightened society.

○ EXERCISES ○

With the following series of team exercises, the primary focus shifts from developing self to developing others, and from the inner to the outer dimensions of leadership. Facilitating these exercises is a powerful means to build on the work of the previous exercises and further develop leadership skills. Facilitators are good listeners, observers, communicators, diagnosticians, and designers of group activity. They also model learning behavior, empathize and develop their trust with the team, provide encouragement and support, and monitor and change personal behavior as necessary. Finally, good facilitators practice dialogue, and help the team learn to balance inquiry and advocacy. These are all important leadership skills, and what they require makes clear why personal work is necessary before doing relationship and community work.

To find opportunities to practice these exercises, it is best to work with a team where you are not in charge, or where you are simply a member. In general, team leaders do not make good facilitators because their position of power and influence can dominate the discussion and make it difficult for everyone to be objective. On the other hand, if you are the group leader and still want to use the exercises, there are a few options. First, you can have a neutral party—someone who is not part of the team—facilitate. As the team leader you still learn in the process, and the whole group benefits. Second, if another team member has the appropriate level of understanding and interpersonal skill, you might have this person facilitate. This would be an important developmental opportunity for that person, and it would demonstrate to others your desire to develop the team as a whole. Third, if you have open and trusting relationships with the members, you may choose to facilitate yourself. You should not facilitate, however, if there are issues or strained interpersonal dynamics already operating between you and any team members, or between other members of the team. Deciding whether to facilitate yourself is tricky.

○ EXERCISE 4.1: THE LEADERSHIP WHEEL TEAM ASSESSMENT

This is one of those rare team activities that works every time and I am indebted to my friend Rodney Napier for the basic idea. The activity can be used with a new team coming together for the first time, or with an existing team looking either to change its current dynamic or just to take a fresh look at it. The purpose is to introduce the team to the Wheel so its members can explore its meaning and application together. It is fun and engaging and requires very little facilitation. As people assess where they are on the Wheel, and identify both their strengths and weaknesses together, it creates an atmosphere where it is safe to "own" their profile. People become open to changes they may need to make, and the openness and humor set a positive tone.

Step 1: *Presentation of the Wheel.* The success of the activity depends on the team's ability to appreciate the historical, cultural, and even spiritual context of the Wheel. So the first step is to present that information in a way that engages people's interest.

I often introduce the Wheel by talking about Carl Jung's discovery of the four psychological types and about the Wheel's appearance in other traditions, especially the Native American and Tibetan Buddhist traditions, as outlined in chapter 2. Then I walk the team through the Wheel, taking no more than about 15 minutes, briefly describing the wisdom and shadow aspects of each direction. I do not describe the Sage at this point, leaving it instead to the end of the activity, as the Sage is a qualitatively different archetype.

After traveling once around the Wheel, I explain how each of these traditions also believe that when we are born, we come into the world through one of these 'doors' or 'gateways' and that place is our 'home' or preferred style. I add that the purpose of life in all of these traditions is to become whole or complete by learning to access the qualities of each of the other directions, so that as we grow older and mature, we tend naturally to internalize more of the other directions.

As a facilitator I then ask team members to identify their original home, or preference, the place where they are comfortable most of the time. For some people this is difficult because they have already learned multiple styles. In this case, I ask what happens to them under stress, because that is when the preferred style often emerges. "Teachers tend to put their nose to the grindstone to figure this out. Nurturers huddle with their friends and colleagues to get through this together. Visionaries brainstorm the possibilities and ways out. And finally, Warriors tend to 'kick-ass and take names.'" If a person's preferred style is still not obvious to someone in your group, then ask that person to pick just one style for the sake of this activity, admitting that the person may have multiple preferences.

Step 2: *Team Discussion*. Ask the group to self-sort into groups of homogeneous preferences—East, South, West, and North. If one of the directions is underrepresented, then ask a member from another direction, who also has affinity for the underrepresented style, to switch. Then give the groups about 15 minutes to discuss the following questions among themselves:

1. What do you like about this style?
2. What do you find that is problematic or gets you into trouble?
3. What do the other styles need to know to work effectively with you?

After the time is up, go to each group and ask its members to present their answers to these questions while also asking for reactions from the other groups. The discussion is always quite open and humorous as people quickly begin making fun of themselves and the problems they have with people of other preferred styles.

Step 3: *Applications.* Finally, with the team as a whole, discuss the potential applications of the Wheel. It is usually important to begin by asking where leadership is found on the Wheel. The answer, of course, is that leadership can emerge from any direction, but people are quick to point out that leadership is in the middle because it is important to be agile and adjust style to the needs of the situation. This is also when to introduce the Sage, explaining how it is the governing archetype and the one responsible for learning and developing agility. Then ask for other applications in the following areas:

1. Teams—in terms of making sure there is balanced representation of each direction.
2. Communication—using the language of other directions to improve communication.
3. Conflict—turning differences that are natural sources of tension into opportunities for creating synergy.
4. Learning and change—how the different directions work together as an action learning model for individual, team, or organizational development.
5. Decision making—how following the action learning sequence in a decision-making process ensures robust decisions, even in unbalanced teams.

○ EXERCISE 4.2: TEAM DEVELOPMENT

This activity is very powerful for opening up the possibilities for both personal and group learning. It levels the playing field, creates an open atmosphere, and identifies areas of strength and needed development. It is an excellent follow-on activity to the previous exercise.

Step 1: *Individual Assessment.* Give team members about 15 minutes to work alone on the following questions:

1. Where do I see myself on the Leadership Wheel—what are my most preferred areas?

2. What are my areas of strength and weakness relative to each direction?

3. What things must I start or stop doing to be a more effective team member relative to that assessment?

4. What one or two changes am I willing to make to become a more effective team member?

Step 2: *Team Sharing.* Ask each of the team members to take about ten minutes to share with the whole group their answers to the preceding questions. In sharing this information, it is important for individuals to first ask if the team agrees with where they see themselves on the Wheel. This gives everyone an opportunity to receive feedback and continue to build self-awareness. The process also helps identify and clarify individual roles and contributions to the team.

Having identified one or two personal changes that an individual wants to make, and after making sure that everyone on the team understands them, the team as a whole then explores how the team might support the individual member in making the change(s). One of my areas of needed development, for instance, has been to be more Warrior-like in presenting and standing by my beliefs. So I have asked teams to check in with me periodically and ask what I "believe," given the issues on the table. This little signal then gives me permission to practice that skill.

Step 3: *Team Assessment.* Next the whole team should assess the balance of the group given the styles represented. The team composition may be skewed toward one or two directions. When that is the case, it is important to ask what adjustments the team as a whole might need to make to ensure a balanced approach to the work agenda. A team with underrepresented Visionaries, for example, might commit to taking some time at each meeting to discuss the issues from the perspective of a Visionary. Placing oneself in the shoes of another direction is easier than it might seem, and it is great practice for learning to access another direction.

Step 4: *Follow-up.* Finally, make sure the team periodically revisits these individual and team change commitments to assess and reflect on everyone's progress. For personal learning, this usually requires setting aside a whole meeting at regular intervals to discuss everyone's progress. At meetings dedicated to this purpose, team members share the progress and efforts they have made, and ask for feedback and suggestions. For the team as a whole, however, this reassessment can be done by taking a few minutes at each meeting, or every other meeting, to discuss and reflect on the team's process and progress toward its commitments. This does not take much time, and is a powerful tool for increasing team awareness and development.

○ EXERCISE 4.3: TEAM VALUES, MISSION, AND VISION DEVELOPMENT

Developing a values, mission, and vision statement is a powerful tool for clarifying team objectives, purposes, and modes of operation, identifying individual roles and responsibilities, and invigorating and inspiring a group into action. Team values are those set of beliefs people share about how to operate in conducting the team's business. They lead us to believe that some means and ends are more important than others. These values often are subliminal and operate just below our radar screen. Surfacing them and achieving agreement on them is important to developing and sustaining a team culture.

A mission statement defines the core purpose of a team, its reason for being. The mission is typically given to the team in the form of the task or challenge it is charged to address. It is extremely important, however, for the team to develop a shared understanding of that mission, because often members are on different pages.

Finally, vision is the overarching dream or goal, and a clear description of what will be different or accomplished when the mission is fulfilled. A team mission, for example, may be to develop a new product in the field of hand-held communications. Its vision may be to produce the first hand-held product to incorporate audio, visual, and digital communications at a cost affordable to the mass market.

Step 1: *Values Development.* In developing a team values, mission, and vision statement, we typically start with values. They lay the foundation for mission and mission for vision. Developing team values is often the trickiest step. As discussed in exercise 3.1 (the personal mission statement exercise in chapter 3), people are often quick to identify a number of values important to them without giving sufficient thought and consideration to what is most deeply important. The result is a statement that is hollow and empty because it hasn't really touched the minds and hearts of the members. Thus, a team often needs to struggle with identifying its members' values in order to give them more life and meaning.

The Team Values Ranking Form that follows is the best one I have come across in this regard. It is adapted from the work of the late Brendan Reddy, a highly regarded team consultant who often worked for National Training Laboratories.[25] Have each team member take about ten minutes to complete it.

Team Values Ranking Form

From the list of twelve values below, number your personal top three values from 1 to 3 in order of importance for what you value in teams, with 1 being highest. Also number, from 10 to 12, the values you consider the lowest in importance for what you value in teams.

    ____ *Achieving:* making a worthwhile contribution in meeting the needs of the team and the organization.

    ____ *Nurturing:* making team members feel they belong and are safe enough to relate to one another well and openly.

    ____ *Learning:* offering stimulating, active opportunities for members to grow, develop, and express themselves

    ____ *Automomy:* providing a place where members can make choices, express their independence, and participate in team decisions.

    ____ *Harmonious:* fostering group harmony and solving problems rather than blaming and finding fault.

    ____ *Creative:* developing an atmosphere in which team members can be innovative and take risks in finding new solutions.

    ____ *Purposeful:* having a clear sense of team purpose to which everyone is committed and in relation to which results can be evaluated.

    ____ *Flexible:* being responsive to needs, open to change, and not bound by traditions when they are not functional.

    ____ *Structured:* operating by a clear set of team practices and procedures that makes clear what is expected of team members.

    ____ *Resourceful:* having the necessary resources, tools, training, and rewards to get the job done.

    ____ *Successful:* having a visible and credible team that has good growth, productivity, and service record.

    ____ *Camaraderie:* encouraging friendly and informal relations with an emphasis on enjoying fellowship.

    _____ (Write in values not provided in the above that you find important and rank this item.)

After the members have individually ranked their items, have them share their results and engage in a group dialogue to create consensus on the top five. Consensus is defined as:

1. I can live with this value.
2. I can defend it publicly.
3. I can model it.

The tendency when the group disagrees is to aggregate its members' responses—for example, combining Creative and Resourceful. It is important not to do this, because the process of forcing people to make choices increases the clarity of the values held most dear. Once consensus is achieved, then the group is free to customize the language and interpretations into a polished statement.

Step 2: *Mission Development.* The next step is to ask each person to take ten minutes to develop on their own a one-sentence definition of the team mission. The mission is typically given to the team, but it is important to create a shared understanding of its meaning and interpretation. One of the challenges, however, is frequent confusion concerning the difference between mission and vision. So I often provide some examples from organizations as well as from teams. I use organizational examples because they are better known and resonate quickly with people.

> *NASA in the 1960s*
> Mission—to explore outer space.
> Vision—to put a man on the moon by the end of the decade.
> *Ford in the 1920s*
> Mission—to make automobiles.
> Vision—to build a car for the multitude (one affordable to everyone).

I also use team examples from my own experience. The team mission for the Institutional Planning and Research department at Cornell was: "To support the institutional planning and decision-making process." Our vision in the 1990s was: "To create a new institutional planning process model that provides both data research and organizational development support." The organizational development component was a new departure for us, as up to that point in time the team's focus was primarily on data support and analysis.

After people have prepared their statements, put them into groups of two or three to share and discuss their one-sentence definitions, with the goal of preparing a common mission statement that everyone in the small group can agree with. Then, as a whole group, discuss the small group statements and select the best aspects of each.

Step 3. *Vision Development.* Follow the same process described in Step 2, but this time to do it for vision rather than mission development.

Step 4. *Statement Preparation.* At this point, the team has basically generated the raw data for a values, mission, and vision statement. It is now ready to be polished. Rather than do this as a team, it is better to have one or two people prepare a statement that will be critiqued later by the team as a whole. Here is an example from an internal organizational development team:

> *Mission:* To provide internal consulting services to teams and the
> department in organizational development.
> *Vision:* To change the culture so that our organization is acknowledged
> as one of *Fortune* magazine's best places to work.
> *Values:* To be the best for our clients, we will provide services in a way
> that models fun, achievement, creativity, and team play.

Step 5: *Follow-up.* To sustain and bring this statement to life, make sure the team periodically reviews how it is doing in modeling it. To do this, have every member anonymously rate on a scale of 1 to 5 how well the team is fulfilling each of the components of the statement. Compile the responses and share them with the group as a whole for discussing how the team might do better.

○ EXERCISE 4.4: TEAM PROBLEM SOLVING AND DECISION MAKING

In taking on its task, a team can adapt the Leadership Wheel as a decision-making, problem-solving, or action-planning tool. The team travels around the Wheel answering a series of questions related to each direction while practicing dialogue by probing the issues and the possibilities. In this exercise, the team leader or facilitator simply walks the group through the following or other related questions. Depending on the magnitude of the issue or problem, the team may move through the questions in one meeting or several meetings.

1. *Teacher: Develop a shared understanding of the current reality.*
- What is the issue or situation?
- What are the current and available facts?
- What more do we need to know including feedback on our progress?
- What is our skill set and do each of our own skills complement each other's?

2. *Nurturer: Identify sources of resistance and support for change.*
- What are the sources of resistance (people) that keep us from moving forward?
- What are the emotional benefits or incentives to not changing?
- What are the sources of support (people and emotional) for moving forward?
- What do our values say, and are there other behaviors or cultural norms that help or hinder progress?

3. *Visionary: Forge a shared vision and strategy for the future.*
- What are the alternatives and possibilities for resolving the issue?
- What is the best possible solution and vision for the future?
- What strategies and process steps will close the gap between the vision and current reality?
- How do we address the sources of resistance and support?

4. *Warrior: Develop and execute action plans.*
- What are the immediate tasks at hand?
- Who will be responsible for them?
- What is their deadline?
- How will we follow through to make sure it happens?

5. *Sage: Reflect on lessons learned.*
- What happened?
- What are the lessons learned?
- What revisions do we need to make?
- Do we have the right people and resources involved?

I often provide the team with another shorthand version of the Learning Wheel (see figure 4.2) to help people remember and consciously follow this process. I call it the five Ds:

1. Diagnose the current reality.
2. Digest emotional and relationship impact.
3. Design a shared vision and strategy for the future.
4. Do the plan.
5. Debrief the lessons learned.

Consciously following this action learning process is often the only team building a group ever needs. In debriefing each step taken in tackling the task, the team learns to adjust its strategies and its internal dynamics over time. At the same time, the members and the team as a whole learn, grow, and develop.

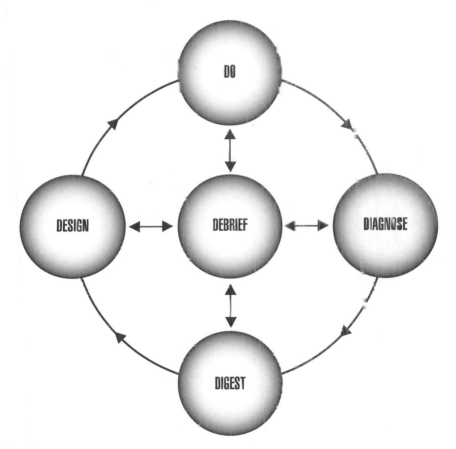

Figure 4.2   The Team Problem–Solving Wheel

○ EXERCISE 4.5: PEER COACHING

Partnering with another member on your team to serve as your coach is a powerful tool for helping develop a new skill or become a better team member. Team members see you in action and are able to provide feedback, insight, and support in your process. The process builds personal skills, as well as trust and a stronger sense of team.

Coaching is an important leadership skill. Leaders work through others and are able to empower, mentor, and develop people. Good coaches listen well, build trust, and connect with people. They show that they care and are committed to the other person's growth and development. They are also tough and able to challenge people when necessary. They know how to stretch others and ask the right questions. Finally, good coaches are also committed to their own learning and this helps them equip others to learn for themselves. They know how to learn from experience and use that insight in helping others.

There are several important challenges to becoming a good coach.

Building a Partnership. Good coaches need to build a partnership so that others will want to work with them. This means building an atmosphere of openness, safety, and trust through demonstrating that they have their partner's best interests in mind.

Understanding the Other Person. Good coaches are able to understand the other person. They learn how the other person views the world and what that person cares about. This requires good listening and dialogue skills for probing and gaining a deeper understanding.

Managing Motivation. Good coaches are able to identify and help manage their partner's motivation. They understand that a coach does not motivate a partner per se; rather, good coaches detect what excites and moves their partners, and then play on that. Different people are motivated in different ways. Some are motivated out of affiliation with others, others out of a sense of achievement, and still others out a sense of autonomy. A good coach is able to discover and leverage these dispositions to help people grow and develop.

Challenging People to Grow. Finally, good coaches are able to challenge partners in new ways and provide them with constructive feedback. Here again they use their dialogue skills to test, challenge, and critique their partners in ways that do not put them on the defensive. The result is a powerful learning experience for both the partner and the coach.

The coaching process itself follows the action learning cycle of the Leadership Wheel. Using dialogue skills, the coach starts by working with the energy of the Teacher to help create an awareness of the need for change, then the Nurturer to identify potential emotional blocks and barriers, the Visionary to explore the possibilities and develop a plan of action, the Warrior to act and follow through on plans, and the Sage to reflect on the experience and the lessons learned. The most important point in the initial stages of the relationship is for the coach to find an area of change that the partner is motivated to address, and then to use the Wheel as a guide to develop a robust action learning plan.

The following is a sample set of questions a coach might use in helping a partner.

1. *Teacher: Create awareness of the possibility for change.*
   - What feedback have you received? If none, how do we set it up?
   - What are areas that you think you might want to work on?
   - Why? What makes you think these areas need change?
   - What reasons might there be to change?

2. *Nurturer: Identify emotional aids and barriers to change.*
   - How do you feel about looking for ways to do this differently?
   - What concerns do you have about making change?
   - What have been your emotional blocks and barriers to change in the past?
   - What support from others do you need in order to change?

3. *Visionary: Choose a key area of attention and make a plan.*
   - Which areas of potential change are most important to both the job and you personally?
   - What goal(s), then, do you select for yourself?
   - What specific steps, following the action learning process of the Wheel (see exercise 3.1), do you plan to ensure a robust learning plan?
   - What is a reasonable outcome or goal?

4. *Warrior: Follow through and act on plans.*
   - What are the first things you are going to do?
   - When are you going to do them?

•What else do you need to consider?

•When should we meet to discuss progress?

5. *Sage: Reflect on lessons learned.*

   •How do you feel about your progress?

   •What have you learned from your experience so far?

   •In hindsight, what would you do differently?

   •What are the next steps?

To develop coaching partners, simply divide the team into groups of two or three. Three is preferred because a third person adds insight to the discussion and serves as an additional source of support and feedback. Then set up a time to discuss and coach one another. At the first meeting, make sure you share your learning intentions, or your plans from exercise 3.1 or 4.1. Then, using dialogue and the Wheel as a guide, critique and support one another on your plans. Make sure you meet at least every other week to follow up and maintain momentum.

I often integrate peer coaching partners into teams and cohorts in leadership development programs. The experience is very rich for people. It often creates not only progress on learning plans and development of coaching skills, but also a lasting network of relationships for exploring future issues together. It builds tremendous social capital in the organization, and is an important tool for creating synergies and making things happen.

5

TURNING THE WHEEL II

CREATING ENLIGHTENED ORGANIZATIONS

This we know: the earth does not belong to man, man belongs to the earth. All things are connected like the blood that unites us all. Man did not weave the web of life, he is merely a strand in it. Whatever he does to the web, he does to himself.

—Chief Seattle[1]

We must learn how to see the company as a living system and to see it as a system within the context of the larger system of which it is a part. Only then will our vision reliably include return for our shareholders, a productive environment for our employees, and a social vision for the company as a whole.

—Phil Carroll, former CEO of Shell Oil[2]

What we've seen in earlier chapters about interconnectedness and clarity of purpose becomes even more relevant at the organizational level. If we are to make capitalism better serve our needs, we need to redefine the fundamental purposes of business. So, as previous chapters explored the *why* of the individual and the *why* of the team, here we explore the *why* of business.

The purpose of most modern businesses is growth and profitability. Yet to address the problems discussed in this book's introduction, the business must become more than an instrument of profit. While profitability is a necessary condition for business, it is not a sufficient purpose. Businesses that truly excel in the future will be those that discover how to tap people's commitment and desire to learn, and pursue purposes that are more consistent with the needs of the planet and humanity's higher aspirations. Such businesses will learn to direct

Businesses that truly excel in the future will be those that discover how to tap people's commitment and desire to learn, and pursue purposes that are more consistent with the needs of the planet and humanity's higher aspirations.

their energies in ways that go beyond simply making profit, and expand their goals to protect the planet, serve the greater good, and release the human spirit.

What this means in reality and how it is actually manifested, however, is something that every company needs to work out for itself. Business surely is still about profit, but it is to be profit for a purpose, or for a greater cause. Peter Drucker has said that if a business fails, "It is because they missed the part about business in the community, business as life rather than livelihood, and business as a neighbor."[3] Profit is simply the test of the validity of that purpose, not the purpose itself.

We again return to the Wheel to help us find that purpose and make this shift. As we have already seen, the Wheel serves as a guide for individual, relationship, and community work. It keeps us aware of our interconnectedness. It teaches that the great laws and principles governing the patterns and cycles of the universe also govern the evolution of both the individual and the community.

We see that we are part of a complex web of life, and that what we do to others and the earth, we also do to ourselves. Chogyam Trungpa Rinpoche said, "When human beings lose their connection to nature, to heaven and earth, then they do not know how to nurture their environment or how to rule their world . . . healing our society goes hand in hand with healing our personal and elemental connection with the world."[4] Thus we cannot harm one without harming the other, or heal one without healing the other.

To serve human fulfillment, then, we need to create balance and harmony among all levels and all things. Individual work provides the foundation for teamwork, and teamwork for system work. As we progress along this path, we internalize the message of the Wheel. This unhooks us from the destructive cycles of self-interest, and opens us to learning, growth, and the greater possibilities of the universe. One of those possibilities is the creation of more enlightened organizations and, in turn, a more enlightened society.

ORGANIZATIONS AS PURPOSE-SEEKING SYSTEMS AND AGENTS FOR SOCIAL CHANGE

In the last few decades, management literature has provided a number of important perspectives for shaping organizational purposes that are consistent with the messages of the Wheel. Systems theorists Russell Ackoff and others show, for example, that the behavior of each element of an organization has

As we progress . . . we internalize the message of the Wheel. This unhooks us from the destructive cycles of self-interest . . . and opens us to . . . greater possibilities. . . . One of those . . . is the creation of . . . a more enlightened society.

an impact on the whole and is interdependent with other elements in the system.[5] Whatever that system does, its elements and its surrounding environment are also connected to and interdependent with that process. Thus for an organization to endure, there must be a shift in mind from seeing it as separate from the world, to connected to the world and its actions interdependent with it. When systems ignore these interdependencies, they eventually fail.

These systems are teleological in nature, meaning they seek and pursue purposes. Ackoff points out that organizations are inherently ideal seeking systems where the individual elements operate together in a natural process to pursue an overall ideal, or purpose, and where progress toward that purpose leads to further purposes.[5] Organizations, then, are purposeful systems that are also part of one or more purposeful systems. There are the purposes of the organization, the individuals interacting with that organization, and the system that contains that organization. This means that for an organizational system to achieve a dynamic equilibrium and survive in the long run, it must serve the ability of all stakeholders to pursue their purposes. Said in another way, the purpose of business, or any organization, is to be the instrument that allows others to find and fulfill meaning. As professor Peter Koestenbaum says, "business is a vehicle for personal and organizational greatness."[7] Enduring organizations are purpose-seeking systems where the values, beliefs, and purposes of the individual, community, and environment function together in serving mutual ends.

Ackoff concludes that the purpose of business is not only to improve the quality of life of others, but to do it in a way that enables everyone to satisfy their needs while also being responsible to others, the organization, and the containing systems.[8] He said that business is a vehicle that serves human development and within which human development takes place, where people work together to increase their ability to satisfy their hungers as well as those of others. In learning to appreciate the interconnectedness of things, people also learn to aim for the greater good. From this view, then, the process as well as the output, the means as well as the ends of business is human development.

There are already many examples of successful businesses working with this broader sense of purpose. Jim Collins, first with Jerry Porras, and then later in a separate study,[9] found that the most enduring and highly successful companies have a clear and balanced purpose that enables them to continually adjust over time. Instead of purpose seeking, they called such companies visionary because their purpose went beyond making money. These companies know what they stand for—they have a soul and conscience that arouses people's commitment and empowers them to learn and develop to meet their desired ends. They have a core ideology, based on a sense of shared values and purpose that inspires and motivates in moving toward their goals. Their examples include:

From this view, then, the process as well as the output, the means as well as the ends, of business is human development.

Merck	To preserve and improve human life
Fannie Mae	To strengthen the social fabric by continually democratizing home ownership
3M	To solve unsolved problems innovatively
Hewlett-Packard	To make technical contributions for the advancement and welfare of humanity
Cargill	To improve the standard of living around the world
Disney	To make people happy
Lost Arrow Corporation	To be a role model and tool for social change
Sony	To experience the joy of advancing and applying technology for the benefit of the public
Mary Kay	To give unlimited opportunity to women

These are all very successful companies—businesses with a clear purpose that transcends simply making money—and they are dedicated to human fulfillment. Companies such as these are also often modeled after the ideals of their leaders and founders. Henry Ford said that any business that is simply about making money is not much of a business. He wanted to make a car for the multitude. Similarly, David Packard said that money is the result and not the cause of business[10]—companies exist to make a contribution to society. He wanted to advance human welfare through technology. In addition to those already mentioned, others have founded companies solely for the purpose of pursuing a social cause. Ben Cohen and Jerry Greenfeld, for example, founded Ben & Jerry's Homemade Ice Cream based on a three-part mission statement emphasizing product quality, profitable growth, and a commitment to the community.[11] John Mackey founded Whole Foods to provide an alternative model for business and work for the greater good,[12] and Anita Roddick founded The Body Shop to promote environmentally and socially conscious body care products. These business leaders show us that social change can originate within business enterprise.

These companies have been both purposeful and purpose-seeking—purposeful by making a positive contribution to society in a way that inspires, uplifts, and motivates, and purpose-seeking by operating on a set of principles that nurtures the pursuit of purposes of all stakeholders—customers and employees alike.

This purpose-seeking is the energy of becoming and the Heroic Journey manifesting itself at a system level.

This purpose-seeking is the energy of becoming and the Heroic Journey manifesting itself at a system level. Just as individuals need to harness *their energy of becoming*, organizations too need to work with this energy *at the collective level*. The companies listed are focused on building an organization that serves the learning, development, and meaning-making of all rather than making a specific product or hitting the market just right. Bill Hewlett and Dave Packard wanted to first start a company and then decide what to make,[13] just as Sam Walton said that "companies are not vehicles for products, but products are vehicles for companies."[14]

Unfortunately, the successors to these founders have not always followed the founders' principles. In the case of Wal-Mart, for instance, the original ideals have been displaced by growth and market dominance strategies. The point, however, is that when businesses do pursue learning, meaning, and purpose seeking at every level, they succeed and endure. Their overarching purpose enables purpose seeking in their people. It constitutes an ideological core that gives the organization its ability to adapt and learn by providing autonomy to individuals to find their own way while giving themselves over to the cause.

It also serves the organization to foster this purpose seeking in the surrounding community. MIT professor Michael Porter and consultant Mark Kramer insist that by investing in the social and economic goals of the environments in which they operate, companies improve their long-term business prospects. DreamWorks SKG, for example, a film production company, created a program to teach low-income students in Los Angeles the skills needed to work in the film industry. The social benefit is better education and increased employment opportunities for low-income citizens, and the economic benefit is greater availability of a skilled workforce and a more robust local business cluster on which the company depends.

Porter and Kramer point out that "Social and economic goals are not inherently conflicting but integrally connected. Preserving the environment benefits not only society but the company too, because reducing pollution can lead to more productive use of resources and help produce goods that consumers value." They conclude that the "most effective tool for addressing the world's pressing problems is often to mobilize the private sector in ways that benefit both society and companies."[15]

. . . by being sensitive to the interdependencies of the systems in which they operate, companies learn to serve the needs beyond profit and growth and become agents for social change.

There are now many other examples of businesses creating such positive social change by investing in the environments and communities they touch. Cummins Inc. built schools in Brazil to prevent stealing of metal by school-less children. Green Mountain Coffee Roasters eliminated the middlemen to deliver Fair Trade prices to local farmers in Peru and Mexico while saving costs for the company. General Mills invested in small businesses owned by minorities in the inner city of Minneapolis and created 150 jobs that gave employees an ownership stake. Finally, Herman Miller's Environmental Quality Action Team, a volunteer group of 300 employees, was instrumental in recycling 23 million pounds of waste and reusing another 21 million pounds for fuel to heat the main plant.[16] There are many more.

The point is that by being sensitive to the interdependencies of the systems in which they operate, companies learn to serve the needs beyond profit and growth and become agents for social change. They are not purely altruistic, and they are not perfect. They are learning, however, that serving the long-term interests of the community does indeed serve the long-term interests of the business. It's the only way to sustain a dynamic equilibrium.

MANAGING CHANGE IN PURPOSE-SEEKING SYSTEMS

To sustain that dynamic equilibrium, managing change in purpose-seeking systems must be both evolutionary and directed. It is evolutionary in the

Henry Minzberg said that . . . while the evolutionary approach "suggests no control, the directed approach suggests no learning." Companies must find ways to do both . . .

sense that there is no direct control over learning and change, only the self-regulated control achieved through modeling the governing values and purposes. The ideological core enables a level of freedom and autonomy at the local level that leads to new ideas and innovations that the organization adopts if it fits the global picture. Instead of pursuing something known and fixed, direction is found through a process of discovery that comes through experience, and not foresight. As Collins and Porras said, these companies tend to "try a lot of stuff and keep what works."[17] Their examples include American Express's unintended evolution into travel services, Motorola's into advanced electronics, Hewlett-Packard's into computing and 3M's into abrasives.

In contrast, change is also directed in the sense that the ideological core provides an indirect control that helps govern the action around emerging ideas. A directed change process can also help organize and shape thinking in turning emerging ideas into clear directions and driving strategic initiatives through the system. New market entries, product launches, acquisitions, turnarounds, reengineering, and major systems implementations are all examples of change efforts that are more directed in nature. But even here, to be successful, the evolutionary principles of meaning making must still be at work.

The key, of course, is to create a balanced approach between the two. In his critique of strategic change, professor Henry Mintzberg said that evolutionary change efforts are often "slow and lacking in focus," and directed efforts are "rarely a source of new ideas." So while the evolutionary approach "suggests no control, the directed approach suggests no learning."[18] Companies must find ways to do both—top-down as well as bottom-up. This means that in managing change, to be both purposeful and purpose seeking, businesses must place a degree of control into the hands of those who will be affected by the change itself. Otherwise the change effort does not generate the motivation and commitment necessary for successful implementation. Nor does it hook the collective energy of becoming in a way that manifests a concern for the greater good.

This purpose-seeking process describes an enlightened learning culture. People have choices on defining their purposes relative to the whole, how to achieve them, and how they relate to personal needs. This maximizes commitment and learning because individuals will make the choices they find most intrinsically rewarding. In this context, people are more likely to choose goals that will stretch them and help them grow, and are more likely to monitor them and learn from the results. This also makes them resilient in the face of change, because the overall purpose and the choices they have made give them meaning, and they are both more patient and more tenacious in bringing it about. Finally, this frees them to help others, because finding meaning takes them out of their defensive mode and enables them to be supportive of others, just as they need others to be supportive of them in pursuit of their own journey. The result is an open, collaborative, learning culture that is able to adapt to changing conditions in serving the overall cause while also attending to responsibilities extending beyond the organization.

As elements of an action learning model, the five directions of the Wheel become the five disciplines for managing organizational learning and change, and for creating an enlightened organization.

THE ACTION LEARNING WHEEL, CHANGE, AND ENLIGHTENED ORGANIZATIONS

The Wheel offers a simple yet compelling paradigm for capturing the lessons of research and experience, and guiding the purpose-seeking process of organizations. Just as it does for individuals and teams, the Leadership Wheel also serves as an action Learning Wheel for organizational learning and change. It can be used to shape new purposes, strategies, culture, or any other process of systemic change, and in the process creates an enlightened learning culture. This is a dynamic and organically unfolding process that respects the interconnectedness of its elements and its containing systems. It is also a continuous and iterative process where the steps are not necessarily sequential or discrete. It can start at a number of different places, and each aspect can be revised and revisited at different times. It changes constantly as we refine and adjust strategies while we gain experience. As such it is a dynamic model for conducting business.

As elements of an action learning model, the five directions of the Wheel become the five disciplines for managing organizational learning and change, and for creating an enlightened organization. The process often starts with either the Teacher or the Visionary exploring the current reality or the possibilities for the future. Here again, we will start with the Teacher for the sake of a logical sequence.

The Teacher represents the ability to acquire knowledge of the current reality and build the case for change. We then move to the Nurturer to build broad-based support and develop a shared understanding of the need for change. Next, the Visionary helps us determine what is most important and chooses an overall direction and strategy. And finally the Warrior takes us into action and executes that plan. The Sage helps us govern this process by focusing on the organization's ability to learn from the experience. With each iteration of the cycle, the system refines and adjusts its understanding processes, visions, strategies, and actions. It learns to learn from experience, and moves up the spiral of experience to become a learning organization and a more enlightened culture.

THE TEACHER: KNOWING THE WORLD—MANAGING KNOWLEDGE

At a systems level, the Teacher is about managing the knowledge of the organization. It serves as the organizational radar in generating and managing the knowledge necessary for supporting organizational learning and change.

The Teacher represents the ability to generate, capture, and share data and combine it with human judgment to shape shared meaning, purposes, and mental models.

It is focused on anchoring thinking in the here and now and continually developing the organizational ability to see reality clearly and objectively in managing and building the case for change.

The Teacher represents the ability to generate, capture, and share data and combine it with human judgment to shape shared meaning, purposes, and mental models. It seeks the unvarnished truth of things, free from bias, so we can base actions on a foundation of intellectual honesty and realism. Therefore it seeks data that will help the organization identify and achieve its goals, manage its performance, and enhance its ability to learn from experience. Often this data is used to create a sense of urgency that propels the organization into action. It is a valuable approach for overcoming complacency, denial, and even arrogance.

The knowledge management effort of the Teacher is important to both the direction-setting capacity and the learning capacity of the organization. Change efforts fall short if they simply focus on information related to the strategic direction of desired change. For change to succeed, the knowledge management effort also must focus on information related to its people, its management processes, and its ability to learn from its experience. These areas of focus are important to managing the capacity for change and the ability to harness the commitment and energy necessary to continually learn, adjust, and adapt purposes.

As in the case of individuals and teams, systems also can derail through overuse of the qualities of a direction. Peter Senge called the inhibitors to change *learning disabilities.*[19] I call them derailment factors. For the Teacher, organizations can suffer from accumulating so much data that it is difficult to internalize, so overly aggregated that it loses meaning, and so structured and compartmentalized that it limits systems thinking. Organizations can also fall victim to the belief that data has more predictive powers than is warranted, causing them to make very costly and time-consuming investments in data collection to minimize uncertainty. Unfortunately, that attitude often simply overloads change efforts with data and paralyzes decision making.

As in the case of individuals and teams, systems also can derail through overuse of the qualities of a direction.

Data can help us prepare for the future and the unknown, but it is not the panacea for dealing with uncertainty. It must also be combined with human judgment and insight that emerges from experience and robust dialogue. The following are some principles for managing knowledge of a system.

Develop a Norm of Inquiry. The first challenge of managing organizational knowledge is to develop a norm of inquiry and information sharing. As discussed in chapter 3, Orit Gadiesh believes that getting results begins with establishing a set of facts as the point of strategic departure. For her, information is the foundation for the right solution and it must be collectively obtained and understood.[20] Data enables the change process by providing the context and feedback necessary for shaping purposes, taking action, and learning from experience. However, as Mintzberg found, many organizations separate the data collection process from the execution process, and in so doing disempower and undermine the commitment of those implementing the change.[21] Separating the analysts from the doers can create a gap in understanding and motivation. For the doers to buy in to change, they must also own the data and its truth.

Data collection and interpretation, then, need to become the responsibility of everyone, not just the analysts. To empower change, organizations must develop cultures that support data inquiry at every level. This is not to say that data collection should not be a specialized function or be managed by professional planners, but it is important that the doers participate in generating and interpreting that data, and in shaping new mental models.

Likewise, studies have shown that personal discussion of the data, in the form of a face-to-face dialogue, is far more influential than impersonal reports in affecting action. Simply sharing the data carries little meaning, as doers have not digested or absorbed it, or had the opportunity to add their perspectives. Generating, sharing, and interpreting data through broad-based dialogue, in contrast, provides the organization with an opportunity to build trust and commitment along with its diagnostic capabilities.

Measure What Counts. The data we collect influences what we pay attention and give meaning to because, in many ways, we manage what we measure. When data content is skewed by what is quantifiable and easy to measure, it can bias our understanding and decision making. Again, Henry Mintzberg said that hard data biases decisions toward the economic and away from the social and cultural aspects of change.[22] The traditional content of data collection often ignores these influences, and mirrors our existing compartmentalized view of the world. An extreme example of this is ignoring air pollution in the costs of production because there is no easy measurement. Similarly, looking at easily quantifiable purchasing patterns of consumers provides clues on trends, but says nothing of the underlying reasons.

Ideally, effective change processes draw on a variety of sources of data that support the informed judgment calls and intuition necessary for a dynamic, interactive, and synergistic process of change. Information must take into account not only the hard data related to performance and context, but also the soft data that comes from the experience of the doers immersed in the work, and from the customers and clients receiving the product or service.

For the change process to be effective, the content of the data collection effort must model the essential components of the change effort itself. If the goal is to develop a purpose-seeking, learning, enlightened organization, then it is important to measure and monitor the factors essential to that process. The basic idea is that we focus only what we measure so we need to measure the right things.

Here the Wheel offers a balanced set of criteria for measuring the organization's performance relative to its goals as well as its ability to learn from experience. The framework of the Wheel ensures both execution and learning. So, just as we have seen with respect to other processes, it is important that the nuts and bolts of the data collection effort itself model the results we are trying to achieve. This approach is similar to the Balanced Scorecard concept made popular by Robert Kaplan and David Norton that has been so successfully implemented in many Fortune 500 companies including CIGNA, Mobil, and UPS.[23] With the Wheel as a framework, the measurements reflect the following perspectives:

Teacher: The picture of the current reality including the internal strengths and weaknesses of operational processes as well as the external threats and opportunities to the organization.

Nurturer: The attitudes, values, and satisfaction of all stakeholder groups including customers, employees, shareholders, and community members.

Visionary: The specific and measurable objectives, critical success factors, and process measures to ensure forward movement toward desired ends.

Warrior: The performance results of those objectives and critical success factors at the individual, team, and organizational level.

Sage: The learning processes including the competencies and the lessons learned from experience at the individual, team, and organizational level.

Foster a Shared Understanding of Reality. As mentioned earlier, one of the key challenges in managing strategic change is creating sufficient shared understanding of the situation to both motivate change and coordinate action. John Kotter speaks to the importance of using data to create a sense of urgency for change,[24] while Peter Senge points to the need to create shared mental models to coordinate action and movement.[25] Because people are often compartmentalized in their activities and not educated to a larger view, creating such shared understanding is one of the bigger challenges of the change process. Compartmentalization inhibits their ability to be fully informed and committed participants in the change effort. It also inhibits organizational learning, because without a shared understanding of the current reality it is difficult for people to think together in creating a shared future. The data collection effort offers an opportunity to address this challenge by doing what Marvin Weisbord and others call "bringing the system into the room."[26] This means that to ensure development of shared knowledge, we

bring the data into a room along with representatives of all affected stakeholders—internal and external—to engage in a dialogue on its interpretation
and meaning. This dialogue serves to break down barriers, educate those
present about these issues, and ensure a broader shared knowledge of the
system and its dynamics. More important, developing shared understandings
and mental models through face-to-face dialogue also serves to develop a
commitment for coordinated action.

This dialogue can be conducted through large meetings or a series of
small meetings. Search conferences and other large scale intervention
methodologies are held over periods of one to three days and can include
hundreds and even thousands of people. A search conference of the Seneca
Nation helped participants surface a shared understanding of the problems
caused by proposed organized gambling on the reservation and led to a decision at that time to not pursue the opportunity.[7] Alternatively, a series of
smaller meetings that brings the system into the room can also foster the
shared understanding necessary to motivate people and bring about coordinated efforts. Creating forums for such dialogue is discussed more in the context of the Nurturer (also see exercise 5.2).

THE NURTURER:
AWAKENING THE HEART—BUILDING SOCIAL CAPITAL

The Nurturer builds the social capital necessary for collective action. Social
capital is the glue that makes collective movement pos-

*The Nurturer helps
form social capital
by identifying the
norms of behavior,
or values, that
people model . . .
[and] providing
networks of
participation
through which
people engage in a
meaningful
dialogue . . .*

sible. It includes the values, norms, trust, and networks
of any group gathered for a common purpose. The Nurturer helps form social capital by identifying the norms
of behavior, or values, that people model in working
with one another in order to build trust and effective relationships. These values typically include service,
equality, collaboration, and mutual support. They are
rooted in our basic goodness, and they arise out of a
feeling of connection to the whole. As such they form
the foundation for encouraging teamwork and the sharing of power, information, and resources.

The Nurturer also helps build social capital by providing networks of participation through which people

engage in a meaningful dialogue to help interpret, design, and implement the purposes and methods of the organization. Dialogue becomes increasingly meaningful as people see how they share the risks and rewards of actions to be taken. This dialogue pervades each activity of the Wheel in the system change process: managing knowledge, developing vision, taking action, and learning from experience. It also empowers the change process, by providing people with a voice and opportunity to exercise their free will in making choices about it. This is not to say that people have complete freedom in exercising those choices, but they are provided with meaningful opportunities to help influence their direction.

Building social capital enables change efforts to be both directive (top-down) and evolutionary (bottom-up). Executives can decide to enter a new market and then test the idea and work it through the system through a dialogue of implications cascading down the organization. Similarly, a new product idea can emerge from the lower ranks where a company-wide dialogue serves to gain attention and build support throughout the organization. The bottom line is that the process must develop a sense of social capital, or cohesion and community, so that the eventual decisions are robust and accepted by the critical mass necessary for successful implementation.

Change efforts often derail when there is an imbalance in this process. Overly directive efforts that simply drive change through the system can run roughshod over the social capital by being overly controlling, and undermine the imagination, learning, and commitment within an organization. In contrast, wide open, evolutionary efforts can provide so much leeway that they waste time and resources, and fail to gather the social momentum necessary for taking any direction. The Nurturer tends to err on the evolutionary side of the equation by leaning toward equality in voice and participation. Creating an optimal balance between control and freedom must be done in a way that builds trust, otherwise the defensive routines will prevent the open dialogue needed to genuinely test ideas and build the necessary commitment for change. The following principles from the wisdom of the Nurturer can help in this process.

Identify Core Values. The culture and social capital of an organization rest on its values. Values, again, means the shared set of beliefs and principles about how to operate together and with other stakeholders in conducting business. These provide the moral foundation of the organization. They guide how we commit to and work with others in keeping with ends and means that we consider more legitimate and correct than others. Tuning in to values plays a critical role in guiding, aligning, and galvanizing the organization. Organizational values are built on personal values; so encouraging people to engage in an organization-wide dialogue serves to motivate and inspire, and helps to create an environment that supports positive relationships and the development of trust. Discovering and articulating these shared values provides the ground for identifying purpose and guiding future actions.

As we saw in earlier chapters, when we take time to explore our values, the result reflects our inherent goodness. When people explore what is most important to them, they tend to discover a higher order of needs that includes self-realization and contribution to others.

The practice of openness in traveling around the Wheel helps in this process. It reveals our true nature and inspires us to reach toward our inherent higher order of aspirations, including caring for all and the development of self and others. Values that typically emerge from this process include terminal values such as quality, excellence, and service, or instrumental values such as integrity, teamwork, trust, and openness.

Identifying such values sets the stage for developing an open culture where it is safe to explore issues openly in an environment dedicated to human fulfillment. Values provide the ground for extending out and serving others, and the bedrock for creating an enlightened organization and, in turn, an enlightened society.

Values, however, are only as good as the fervor with which they are lived. If values are espoused and not lived, then they become a source of destructive cynicism. If, on the other hand, people "walk the talk," they become a force for building trust and inspiring authentic and purposeful action. Facing the scare of the Tylenol poisonings in the early 1980s, Johnson & Johnson pulled $100 million of product off the shelves even though it was clear that the poisonings were not attributable to anyone in the organization. They repackaged the product, moving from capsules to caplets. Public trust increased so much that within a few months of introducing the new package they had increased their market share beyond what it was before the disaster. Their action was based on the values stated in their credo: "We believe our first responsibility is to the doctors, nurses, and patients who use our products."[28] Closing the gap between espoused values and lived values becomes a developmental challenge—and opportunity—for the organization, and provides an important strategy for building lasting trust and commitment.

Establish Social Networks. To ensure a robust dialogue on the issues of change at each stage in the process, especially as these issues relate to each direction of the Wheel, it is important to establish the forums of exchange. Former CEO of Allied Signal Larry Bossidy describes these as the social operating mechanisms that he nurtured at Allied Signal and also while at GE.[29] These can be formal and informal meetings, team discussions, workshops, or even e-mail exchanges where people can network around the issues. The dialogue in these social networks serves to educate, generate new information, test and validate ideas, nurture relationships, develop shared understanding and commitment, and reflect on the lessons of experience.

Special events or regularly scheduled meetings serve equally well in this regard. GE, for instance, uses the regular meetings of the Corporate Executive Council of the top 35 executives for this purpose. The council meets two and a half days quarterly to review all aspects of the business and to learn from one another. This type of vehicle needs to be in place at all levels of the organization.[30]

Lou Gerstner, former CEO of IBM, was known for creating company-wide dialogue through his regular e-mails to the entire company.[31] Likewise, Herb Kelleher, former CEO of Southwest Airlines, conducted company-wide "town meetings."[32] The U.S. military uses "After Action Reviews." Mechanisms such as these foster a consistent framework for creating shared mental models and generating the critical mass of support necessary for implementing change. Bossidy called them vehicles for shaping common ways of "thinking, behaving, and doing" in the organization.[33] To work effectively, however, the agendas and results of these events need to be linked so that the messages are consistent throughout the organization and drive development, culture, strategy, and operating processes at all levels.

Build Trusting Relationships. It is difficult to overemphasize the importance of building trust and relationships in a learning organization. The lack of trust and good relationships between people is one of the most important reasons that most change initiatives fail. Without mutual trust there can be no relationship, and without relationship there is no basis for developing the collective commitment necessary for concerted effort. Achieving this kind of trust requires becoming clear on the system of driving values and making sure that interactions emulate those values. It also requires paying attention to the impact of interpersonal dynamics on thinking and learning and making sure that our behaviors and norms are supportive and consistent with learning and change. This combination makes for a culture of openness where everything can be discussed, even the most difficult and sensitive issues.

For the social network to work most effectively, it is important that the dialogue be open, frank, and supportive, so participants can think aloud without fear of criticism and judgment, and conduct critiques without rancor. We saw in earlier chapters (see in particular exercise 3.3) that people must be skilled in balancing inquiry with advocacy to deal with conflict and difficult issues openly and constructively. Otherwise, defensive patterns break down trust and relationships, and become a barrier to effective change.

Leaders play a particularly important role in this process through modeling the desired behaviors. Openly addressing issues of job security and career change in a reengineering effort, for instance, helps to build trust and commitment, even though it may run against the short-term interests of those involved.

THE VISIONARY: SEEING THE WAY—FORGING SHARED PURPOSES

The Visionary harnesses the knowledge and social capital of the organization to shape a compelling direction. A Visionary identifies the purpose as well as the path toward that purpose, and communicates it in a way that connects people to meaning and energizes and uplifts them. Visioning is a discipline of constantly interpreting and reflecting on our purposes and objectives for the future. It is an ongoing dialogue to clarify what is important based on the lessons of experience, and to surface, test, and improve our mental models for future action.

A visionary identifies the purpose . . . and communicates it to people in a way that connects people to meaning . . .

Not everyone is a systems or strategic thinker, but as Larry Bossidy points out, all benefit from the process of working in a group guided by someone who has a comprehensive understanding of the business and its environment.[34] In focusing on the excitement of formulating possibilities, setting the future direction becomes a powerful means for communicating and motivating the hearts and minds of the people involved. The result reflects what we care most about and is built on our sense of values.

Emerging from our basic goodness and as a natural outcome of following the unfolding process and wisdom of the Wheel, these values provide the foundation of an enlightened culture. Purposes and objectives built on these values provide a core ideology that attracts commitment and energy by drawing on our deepest yearnings. As noted in the study by Collins and Porras, companies guided by a core purpose and ideology outperformed other companies by a factor of twelve over a 75-year period.[35]

Experience also shows, however, that establishing meaningful purposes and objectives is one of the most challenging aspects of managing change, and often a cause of derailment. Developing a compelling direction for the future often requires new ways of thinking and establishing broad-based support. Yet the diversity of agendas and fragmented interests of defensive organizational cultures often makes the challenge of forming a shared purpose an insurmountable one. Attempts often turn into generalized and watered-down statements that inspire no one, and provide such leeway that almost any course of action can be justified. As a result, change efforts often bog down from a lack of inspiration or a fragmentation of effort. Meaningful directions and shared purposes are difficult to develop, and evolve gradually through an iterative process mirroring the wisdom of the Wheel. The following key processes are those of the Visionary.

Develop a Shared Vision of the Future. The vision includes both the overall purpose and the overarching goal of the organization. The purpose is the contribution an organization makes to society. For Disney, it is "to bring happiness to millions."[36] Such purpose is built upon values, is lasting, and serves to guide and inspire. Along with the values, the purpose constitutes the core ideology of the organization. The overarching goal is what is to be achieved in serving that purpose. Again, for Disney it has been "to build Disney World in *our* image."[37] This kind of goal sets the direction for the future and is commonly known as vision.

Thus values fan into purpose and purpose fans into vision. As Collins and Porras show, often the core ideology of values and purpose is enough in itself to inspire and move the organization. Companies such as Hewlett-Packard and Tom's of Maine founded their enterprises by first defining their core ideology—who they are, what they stand for, and who they serve—and then building their business out from there. A core ideology empowers people by connecting them to their aspirations, inspiring them with a common and noble cause, and allowing them freedom to make choices for implementing their share.

A vision can take that one step further by providing an overarching goal. In his discourse on servant leadership, Robert Greenleaf defines vision as the "overarching goal, the big dream, the overarching concept . . . something presently out of reach . . . so stated that it excites the imagination and challenges people to work for something they do not yet know how to do."[38] Collins and Porras call these BHAGs—Big Hairy Audacious Goals[39]—for stimulating progress and making forward movement. Compared to the core ideology, they are more temporary in nature and serve to provide a tangible, energizing, and highly focused goal for fulfilling the purpose. The purpose of NASA in the 1960s was to explore outer space. Its vision was to put a man on the moon by the end of the decade. Similarly, the founding purpose of Sony was to elevate Japanese culture and national status, and its vision was to change the worldwide image of Japanese products by creating the first pocket-sized transistor radio.

It bears repeating, however, that arriving at such a singularly clear and compelling vision is difficult to achieve. Visions tend to take time, evolve, and emerge only after several iterations of the learning cycle. Often when they do appear, they can be too lofty, overreaching, or abstract to hold meaning. In this case it is important to bring the message down to earth and develop a few shorter term, bite-sized strategies for fulfilling the core ideology that are easier to connect with. Leaders play an important role in this process by actively working with people to break down a vision or to make future directions relevant to the different players so they can connect and feel aligned with the direction.

Take a Systems Approach. As mentioned in the discussion of the Teacher, managing change needs to address the organization's direction of change as well as its capacity for change. This means that once the values, purpose, and vision are clear, the next step is to ensure that the systems for bringing them about are in place. The ends as well as the means, the goals as well as the path, need to be clear. Moreover, the organization not only needs to know how it will achieve its purpose but also how it will adapt its approach to changing needs and conditions in its fulfillment. It needs to provide a developmental environment by building its purpose-seeking ability. Collins and Porras call this a process of "clock building,"[40] meaning a focus on building the company itself rather than its specific products. This includes how the organization will allocate resources, develop human capital, structure incentive systems, interact with customers and the environment, shape the organizational culture, and design the organizational structure, systems, and processes to align with the overall direction.

At GE, for example, Jack Welch said that he wanted to foster an environment "where people would dare try new things, where they would feel assured in knowing that only the limits of the creativity and drive would be the ceiling on how far and how fast they would go."[41] Although Welch's leadership style is not always admired, his insights here are cogent. Hewlett-Packard and 3M are other good examples of companies that have engendered this kind of developmental climate. Creating this climate requires a discipline of engaging in an ongoing dialogue with all stakeholders—internal and external—to continually align efforts with evolving conditions and directions.

Taking a systems approach often means extending developmental opportunities into the surrounding community. Investing in the developmental or purpose-seeking potential of the containing system provides social benefit, creates goodwill, and serves the long-term business interests of the company. Porter and Kramer mention Cisco's Networking Academy as another good example of doing this well.[42]

Cisco is the world's largest producer of networking equipment. As the information technology industry continued to grow, companies worldwide began to face a chronic shortage of qualified network administrators. To offset the problem, Cisco developed a program to donate equipment and train people to build and operate computer networks. The project began as an effort working in secondary schools but soon evolved into the Cisco Networking Academy—a Web-based distance learning program serving secondary and post-secondary students worldwide. The academy soon attracted other partners including Sun Micro-Systems, Hewlett-Packard, and Adobe Systems. Cisco now operates 9,900 academies in all 50 states and 147 countries. As a result, Cisco enlarged its market, increased the sophistication of its customers, and added billions in incremental earnings for those who joined the workforce as a result of the academy.[43]

Educate to Communicate. For the vision or core ideology to have power, it must be broadly shared and owned, otherwise the people most needed for carrying out the core ideology and vision will not follow. Participation in the vision development process and the ongoing dialogue around implementation serves to help develop common ground and communicate future directions. However, simple communication and participation in a dialogue are often not enough. For people to be motivated for change, they must find personal meaning in it.

Chris Argyris found that meaning and motivation stem from the ability of the individual to learn, to have choices on personal goals and the path to those goals, and to align those goals with those of the organization.[44] To generate the broad-based appeal necessary for bringing it to life, a vision or core ideology must tap into the hopes, dreams, and aspirations of those involved. So the process must be developmental for the organization as well as for the individual. It engages people in a way that helps them expand their frame of reference, develop new ways of thinking, and find meaning.

Such a process requires that people have done their personal work. Shared visions are built on personal visions, and personal work is the bedrock for creating the future. People need to know what is important to them, so they can determine how future directions of the organization connect with their own aspirations. As Tom Chappell says: "To know who you are, your values, your gifts, and what you care most about in life, these are the clues to finding meaning in work."[45] Self-knowledge is the path to meaning and commitment, and organizations can help in this process. Thus the most successful change efforts go beyond simple communication programs and include training opportunities to help people find meaning and their place in the organization.

Motorola U, Disney U, the HP (Hewlett-Packard) Way, Tom's Learning Institute, Crotonville at GE, and others are examples of attempts that organizations make to help people along the way and to encourage them to truly connect with the purposes of the organization. It is part of a total effort to build what Collins and Porras call "cult-like cultures,"[46] where people feel such ownership of the core ideology and purposes served that they are willing to give themselves over to it.

THE WARRIOR: EMBODYING THE WAY—TAKING ACTION

Once the purposes are formed, the Warrior takes action to get it done. Warriors integrate the wisdom of all the other directions of the Wheel to turn plans, beliefs, and visions into reality. As we have seen,

Warriors integrate the wisdom of all the other directions of the Wheel to turn plans, beliefs, and visions into reality.

organizational change is both a directive and evolutionary process where plans emerge from a broad-based dialogue and are then tested through experience. It is through taking action that feedback is obtained, and it is from reflecting on that feedback that plans are revised and gain clarity. This is the action-learning process inherent in the wisdom of the Wheel. The Warrior is essential to this process by playing a role not only in implementation of plans but also in their formulation. Here the planning and the doing are merged into one. Plans are operationalized through taking experimental action, focusing on short-term wins, pushing the action down the organization as far as possible, and adjusting plans based on the lessons of experience. This demands a culture of authenticity where people show up, engage fully, and take realistic action.

Many failed organizational change efforts are the result of poor execution of well-laid plans. Effective execution depends on the wisdom of all the directions, not just the Warrior. However, it can break down with the Warrior from too much emphasis on control and serving the needs of bureaucracy and people at the top. Many change efforts are designed for control and simply driving through prescribed plans. When there is too much control, the change process becomes an extension of vested interests and the entrenched power structure of the organization, which undermines creativity, learning, and commitment. Here are some helpful principles from the perspective of the Warrior about how to create a balance between control and freedom so that good ideas can emerge into strategies from anywhere in the organization.

Instill a Culture of Authenticity. Successful organizations are grounded in a core ideology that is widely shared by all their members, and that allows the organization to thrive in the most uncertain of environments. But this only works when the ideology is brought to life and modeled at every level of the organization. Instilling a culture of authenticity is about the organizational embodiment of the core ideology, and about closing the gap between idea and reality in our purposes and our conduct. It is about challenging the process, being effective in bringing goals to reality, and having integrity in bringing espoused values to life.

Closing these gaps is the developmental challenge for every level in the system, and as such is the motor of growth and learning. That developmental challenge holds the promise of basic goodness and creating enlightened society, but the promise must be fulfilled in actions. No matter how clear we are on our goals and values, the process of internalizing them must be a disciplined exercise in trial and error. The Warrior engages in ongoing dialogue that examines actions in the context of the goals and values, and affirms and adjusts them based on the lessons of experience. This dialogue is integrated into the very fabric of the organization's experience, so that planning and doing work hand in hand, and the organization walks the talk.

Orit Gadiesh says such organizations have a true north: Like the difference between a compass set to magnetic north and one that finds true north, these organizations' ideological core does not change with the shifts in the business environment. She says that you can tell just by walking in the door whether a company has a true north.[47] True north is the culmination of the corporate search for truth and the emergence of spirit in the workplace. Companies that have a true north embody their core ideology in every respect. They embody their purpose and beliefs in action. They translate their core ideology into everything they do—including their goals, processes, and behaviors. They create strong cultures where the signals are so consistent throughout all levels of the organization that it is impossible to resist the pull of the overarching purpose.

Again, this is part of what Collins and Porras meant by cultlike cultures. The leadership and direction are authentic, and that authenticity engenders trust, commitment, and confidence among employees as well as customers. Organizations that are authentic are likely to attract the most creative employees, because the environment of personal mastery allows people to find meaning in their work. Likewise, they are more likely to attract loyal customers. People want a good product, but, given the choice, they will choose to be served by those who model the higher human aspirations that are the same as theirs. This kind of modeling requires vigilance, constant discipline, and the intention to adopt, abide by, and internalize the purpose of the organization.

Aaron Feuerstein of Malden Mills and the Johnson & Johnson Credo mentioned earlier are good examples of the power of organizational authenticity. Tom's of Maine is another: Rather than continue selling a problematic deodorant, Tom's pulled the brand off the shelves to reformulate the product. When they reintroduced it, they achieved public trust and a greater market share because they modeled their mission of "serving our customer's health needs with a mission of responsibility and goodness."[48]

Experiment and Create Short-Term Wins. In their examination of visionary companies, Collins and Porras found that many made their most important moves through experimentation, not as the result of a grand plan.[49] Successful companies build on their core purposes by trying a lot of new things and keeping those that work. HP's move into the computer business, for instance, was made simply to power its line of instrument products. Likewise, Motorola ventured into advanced electronics simply to add features to the company's televisions and radios. These were unplanned strategies guided by a core purpose, and they came to life through an evolutionary process of trial and error. These companies did not rely exclusively on centralized planning departments studying every move. Rather they focused more on developing environments conducive to action learning, where people could fulfill their own developmental purposes in serving the overall purpose.

Wal-Mart is another example of a company that achieved great success through a series of incremental steps that had no overall plan based on foresight, but simply remained true to the founding vision. An executive of Wal-Mart said: "We live by the motto, 'Do it. Fix it. Try it.'"[50] The only guiding theme is the core ideology and the intention of learning and developing through experimental change. Once experiments achieve some success, they are developed through company-wide dialogue and promoted with pilot programs to create short-term wins. Those short-term wins are consolidated through an organizational dialogue that shares the lessons learned and addresses the question of where and how to apply them in other areas of the organization. Experiments thus evolve into strategy, and build credibility and momentum to sustain efforts.

Rudy Giuliani's approach to crime provides a good example. When Giuliani took office as mayor of New York in 1994, the city was suffering from a serious crime problem. He was elected on a platform of public safety and knew that he would have to achieve some short-term wins to build momentum for some of the longer-term, more significant changes he planned. He therefore decided to focus on eradicating the highly visible problem of the "squeegee men" who approached cars stopped at intersections, washed windshields, and then demanded money with varying degrees of menace. He instructed police to give these men tickets for jaywalking the moment they stepped off the curb to clean cars—a recognized offense, so no new laws were required. Ticketing allowed police to look into the offender's prior arrests and, in many cases, they found that the men were wanted for more severe crimes. The police were then able to remove them from the streets. Within one month, Giuliani had completely eliminated the squeegee-man problem and made a highly visible first step toward cleaning up New York City.[51]

Localize the Action. To empower experimentation and short-term wins, it is important to move decision making down the organization to where it is closest to the action. Exercising choice in the decision-making process gives people control, inspires their learning, creativity, and motivation, and fosters the conditions necessary for finding meaning in work. The people closest to the action also have the best insights for making informed judgments and are in a better position to respond quickly. The core ideology and vision provide the umbrella of control for empowering small, self-organizing units with latitude for developing and implementing strategies to meet specific needs. Conversely, that umbrella also provides the freedom to achieve short-term wins, and to experiment with new ideas and approaches that allow new and promising strategies to emerge quickly from anywhere in the organization.

This is what is commonly known as thinking globally and acting locally, what Collins and Porras call "ideological control, operational autonomy."[52] Localized decision making combines all the elements of the Wheel in taking action. It combines data and judgment, planning and experimentation, feedback and dialogue, and thinking and action in an unfolding search for solutions and alternatives.

3M is a classic example of the benefits of local decision making. After the nearly fatal early days of 3M, CEO William McKnight wanted to build an organization that did not depend on him for setting future directions but that would continually evolve and move forward based on the initiative of employees. The company went from mining to sandpaper to Scotch Tape to Post-it Notes and a host of other products, all without the benefit of an overarching strategy. People worked in small self-organizing teams that were fully empowered to realize their core ideology to "solve unsolved problems innovatively."[53]

THE SAGE: LEARNING TO LEARN—
PROMOTING CONTINUOUS LEARNING

The Sage governs the overall change process by focusing on the organization's ability to learn and develop from experience. The challenge for today's organization is not simply implementing the latest innovation, it is to learn how to grow and develop in the face of both planned and unplanned change.

The Sage is about paying attention to this learning process, seeing how we tap into our creative intelligence, developing insights into our experience, and translating its lessons into action.

As management author and consultant Arie Degues said, "An organization's only long-term competitive advantage may indeed be its ability to adapt and learn faster than the competition."[54] Organizations need to be able to drive change initiatives through the system as well as capitalize promptly on opportunities as they arise from experience. The literature of the 1990s refers to this capability as the agile, resilient or learning organization—meaning that the organization has the ability to constantly improve, innovate, and change in concert with changing market conditions in pursuit of its purposes. The Sage is about paying attention to this learning process, seeing how we tap into our creative intelligence, developing insights into our experience, and translating its lessons into action.

Failing to pay attention to how the organization learns is one of the root causes of many derailed attempts at organizational change. During the 1990s Cornell University went through an alphabet soup of organizational change methodologies to increase efficiency and productivity and become "the best-managed university."[55] These included TQM, strategic planning, process reengineering, and a major systems implementation. Many argue that each of these successive attempts failed to take hold and have the planned impact on the organization, yet never did the institution take time to reflect on the lessons learned from the previous experience. Instead, mistakes from earlier efforts were repeated. Each time, the effort failed to build an effective leadership coalition, develop trust among the various stakeholders, or provide adequate networks for communication and participation.

As with individuals and teams, the ability to learn from experience is perhaps the most essential competency for organizational change. It must become part of the organizational dialogue and consciousness. The following are some important principles from the perspective of the Sage for building this ability.

Manage the Learning Process. The organization must actively "Turn the Wheel" and manage the change process as well as the process of learning from experience. The Sage attends to the learning process to capture and expand on the lessons learned. Often this function is achieved through a "design team," or through a leadership team, a steering committee, or an office of organizational learning whose sole purpose is to design and attend to the overall change process and capture the lessons learned from experience. In performing this function the design team considers a host of issues, including the desired outcomes to achieve, the developmental steps to take, the stakeholders to involve, the hidden agendas to dissolve, the lessons of experience to capture, and the adjustments to make as the effort unfolds.

Again the Wheel serves as a useful guide for developing the learning and change process. Turning it ensures that each essential component of the Wheel is incorporated into the change process itself. As in other areas, the design of the change process should model the desired result. If the desired result is to develop a learning, agile, and resilient organization, then the path should mirror that desired result. Since the Wheel itself represents an action-learning and developmental process, we design the learning change process by incorporating the perspectives of all five directions.

Teacher: Track the knowledge necessary for managing change.

Nurturer: Build the social networks necessary to create shared understandings of reality and possibilities for the future.

Visionary: Develop shared futures and design structures, systems, and processes to work in concert with the overall direction.

Warrior: Develop tangible mechanisms to make plans and emerging directions actionable.

Sage: Pay conscious attention to how the organization learns from experience.

In managing this process, the design team leverages the organization's social network mechanisms to develop shared understandings from each perspective of the Wheel, and to capture the lessons learned from experience, both good and bad.

Build the Leadership Team. The leadership team plays a critically important role in inspiring generative learning and change in the organization. As mentioned before, Kotter's research shows that visible leadership at the top is the single most important factor distinguishing adaptive, learning organizations. Success requires that the leadership team members not only support and champion learning and change, but also embody it as role models for others to emulate. Leaders must have the courage and discipline to challenge change, model appropriate learning behaviors, and learn the skills essential for actively managing and engaging in the change process. As such they must be willing to take risks, model openness, collaborate with others, and inspire a sense of stewardship for all stakeholders and resources of the organization. Modeling the way is a Warrior trait, but it is discussed here with the Sage because of the important role the leadership team plays in enhancing learning and governing the process of change.

To play that role effectively, the leadership of the effort must also be shared and extend beyond the inner circle at the top. Leaders from across the organization must act in concert in championing, modeling, and engaging in the change process. This is what Kotter refers to as building a leadership coalition.[56] The team at the top must work together in not only developing the skills necessary for managing change but also modeling them as the whole organization watches. Otherwise one weak link in the team creates what management author Daryl Conner calls a black hole,[57] where the change message goes in but nothing comes out. Thus as the leadership team learns and develops, so, too, will the rest of the organization.

Pass It On. The last responsibility or outcome of the process is to pass on to others what has been learned, as Sages do with their students. As the organization learns about learning and change, and what it takes to create and sustain a more enlightened organization, it is important that it share this wisdom with others. Going back to our discussion of the Heroic Journey, this is where the boons of the journey are shared with the community. In sharing the lessons learned, we set in motion an awareness that compounds and multiplies the impact in every direction and helps everyone improve, grow, and develop.

This also helps those who are doing the sharing. As we all know, teaching others helps further clarify and internalize the lessons. This is why Noel Tichy said it is important for executives to coach and teach in the development programs of their institution. Roger Enrico of PepsiCo was among the first to gain visibility for doing so, and later on Jack Welch of GE did the same thing.[58] Now many management gurus and prominent business leaders alike claim that coaching, teaching, and developing others is perhaps the most important role of today's leaders. Welch invested millions to overhaul Crotonville, GE's fabled leadership development center. He wanted a place "to reach the hearts and minds of people," a place to form "the glue that held everything else together."[59] And executives played the lead—mastering the lesson, modeling it, and passing it on to others.

Passing it on includes the external stakeholders of the organization. In addition to the DreamWorks film school, Cisco's networking academy, and other examples already mentioned, Tom's of Maine provides yet a different type of example. The company promulgates its message of social responsibility and environmentally conscious personal care products to its customers and surrounding community through its packaging, commercials, web site, and annual reports. In passing it on, they have learned that one of the reasons people buy their products is the company's commitment to people and the environment: "To inspire all those we serve with a mission of responsibility and goodness."[60] In purchasing their products, customers are purchasing

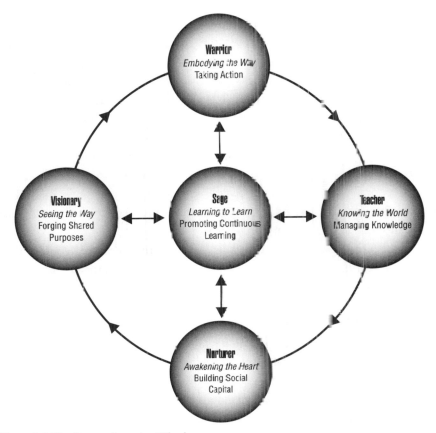

Figure 5.1 The Systems Learning Wheel

Tom's core ideology, even if at a premium. Enlightened organizations are value-added in the minds of many, and modeling that in business conduct serves the greater advancement toward enlightened society.

The most effective change efforts balance the natural tensions between control and autonomy, the individual and the community, and the task and the process.

Figure 5.1 summarizes this process. The Wheel shows us that systems change is a dynamic, purpose-seeking process that relies on the free exchange of information and ideas, and a coalescing social fabric to create an order for action. It also shows us that change is a continuous action-learning process in which collective thinking and acting identify directions that only become fully known as the directions themselves are undertaken. Finally, it shows that change is a developmental process that individuals, teams, and the organization come to identify with, align their purposes with, and develop their capacities to fulfill them along the way.

Each direction of the Wheel is essential to these processes and interdependent with the others. The knowledge of the Teacher anchors actions in reality; the participation of the Nurturer develops community support for new directions; the insight of the Visionary arouses and aligns aspirations around purposes; the discipline of the Warrior turns those plans and beliefs into reality; and the consciousness of the Sage continues to adjust and learn from experience. This overall dynamic is repeated in an upward spiral of learning and growth, moving the organization to a learning culture that is open, supportive, and committed to its purposes.

The action learning process of the Wheel is both deliberate and emergent. It can serve as the model for directed change such as driving through a systems implementation, as well as for evolutionary change such as creating the conditions for continuous improvement and innovation. The most effective change efforts balance the natural tensions between control and autonomy, the individual and the community, and the task and the process.

As in earlier venues, capturing the wisdom of the Wheel at a systems level requires openness and the foundational practices of awareness and compassion. These are again represented by the dynamic tensions between the polar opposites of the Wheel. The Visionary-Teacher dynamic is awareness and helps the organization form shared understandings for current reality and future directions. The Warrior-Nurturer dynamic is compassion and shows how to engage the social order for taking meaningful action.

At each step in the process we engage in the practice of dialogue to understand the data, generate the social fabric, develop a shared vision, act in coordination in its fulfillment, and learn from experience.

As mentioned in past chapters, awareness and compassion are also important to accessing the individual qualities of each direction. In a systems change effort, this takes the form of dialogue. At each step in the process we engage in the practice of dialogue to understand the data, generate the social fabric, develop a shared vision, act in coordination in its fulfillment, and learn from experience. Dialogue is the experience of openness. When there is openness there is less self-interest and a greater sense of other and responsibility toward the whole. As we travel around the Wheel in a systems effort, then, we begin to connect to purposes beyond ourselves, and to our responsibilities to one another and the planet.

Thus the compounding, cumulative impact on the organization in traveling around the Wheel is not only learning and development, but also a growing commitment to service, human fulfillment, and socially conscious endeavor. As we open, we open to the needs of all in the world, and to the highest aspirations of human fulfillment. By following the inherent messages of the Wheel, we create opportunities to make a better world and an enlightened society. In so doing, we transform modern capitalism to serve as a vehicle for personal as well as organizational greatness.

TURNING THE WHEEL: THE LEADER AS DESIGNER II

As we saw in chapter 4, the leader's role in managing change is as challenger, designer, and architect. Enduring leaders do not unilaterally direct and mandate change; rather, they initiate and create the conditions necessary for change. They know the process of change and how it works in organizations. They take a stand for the development of their organization and their people, and they work to provide enabling conditions at every level in the system. They challenge others to build purpose and search for opportunities, and they strive to develop the purpose-seeking and learning ability of the organization and its people. And they can use the Wheel as their guide by using the learning and change principles I have discussed to create the necessary conditions. As summarized in table 5.1, leaders "Turn the Wheel" by promoting the 15 principles of systems change of the Wheel.

Most important, however, enduring leaders understand that the success of the collective work is predicated on individual work, just as the ancients found that the creation of enlightened society is dependent on the Heroic Journey. This is true for those at the top, as well as for those at every other level in the system. To succeed in creating a better world, leaders must first set the stage by committing to the awakening of the individual. So they mentor, coach, and promote learning wherever they can. This is what Vaclav Havel meant when he said, "The salvation of this world lies nowhere else than in the human heart."[61] It's also what Trungpa Rinpoche meant when he said, "To create a better world we must first discover what we have to offer."[62]

So in designing the conditions necessary for change, the leader must begin by first knowing the self, and then challenge, help, and empower others

TABLE 5.1 TURNING THE SYSTEMS ACTION LEARNING WHEEL

The Teacher: Knowing the World—Managing Knowledge

1. *Develop a Norm of Inquiry:* To empower and create the impetus for change, organizations must develop cultures where collecting and interpreting data and knowledge is the responsibility of everyone.

2. *Measure What Counts:* To ensure both execution and learning, organizations must use a balanced set of performance measures using the perspectives of the Wheel as a guide. What is measured along the path should model the desired result.

3. *Foster a Shared Understanding of Reality:* To enable collaborative thinking and action, organizations must foster a systemwide understanding of the data and knowledge.

The Nurturer: Encouraging the Heart—Building Social Capital

4. *Identify Core Values:* To establish the foundation of the desired culture, organizations must identify and nurture values to guide daily actions.

5. *Establish Social Networks:* To ensure a robust dialogue and shared understanding at each stage of the process, organizations must establish regular forums of exchange.

6. *Build Trusting Relationships:* To promote an open and honest dialogue around the issues, organizations must pay attention to building trusting and collaborative relationships.

The Visionary: Seeing the Way—Forging Shared Purposes

7. *Develop a Shared Vision of the Future:* To energize and align commitment, organizations must develop a shared vision or core ideology that connects people to their aspirations.

8. *Take a Systems Approach:* To ensure a developmental climate, organizations must design organizational systems that are aligned with learning and the overall direction and in concert with the containing system.

9. *Educate to Communicate:* To develop broad buy-in, organizations must communicate future directions through actively engaging people in a developmental process.

The Warrior: Modeling the Way—Taking Action

10. *Instill a Culture of Authenticity:* To bring the vision to life, organizations must build an authentic "cultlike culture" and learn to model it at every level of the system.

11. *Experiment and Create Short-Term Wins:* To create movement and momentum, organizations must create opportunities for short-term wins.

12. *Localize the Action:* To empower new experimentation, organizations must localize decision making and allow the core ideology to govern action.

The Sage: Learning to Learn—Promoting Continuous Learning

13. *Manage the Learning Process:* To increase the capacity for learning and change, organizations must actively manage the learning and change process.

14. *Build the Leadership Team:* To provide the visibility and credibility necessary at the top, organizations must develop a coalition of leaders who model the way and actively engage in the process.

15. *Pass It On:* To challenge others to pursue a similar course, organizations must pass on the lessons of proactive social change.

to do the same. For many people, the Heroic Journey is not natural. They need to be encouraged to discover themselves and live in a way that provides meaning, especially in work settings. Only when their personal work is done are people able to work with others in a way that serves the greater good. This is the leader's work: Leaders commit to support the full development of their people and gain commitment in return. There is no loyalty up, if there is no loyalty down the organization.

Finally, a point that cannot be overemphasized—to create the necessary conditions, *leaders must model the new way.* People in organizations pay attention to what leaders say and do, and visible leadership is the most important leverage for change in an organization. To create the conditions for change and develop more enlightened organizations, leaders must comport themselves in ways that are consistent with the core ideology and espoused values of the organization. They have to set the example, be a role model for others, and not ask others to do anything they wouldn't do themselves. They model learning by engaging in dialogue, leading with questions, dealing skillfully with conflict and difficult issues, and criticizing without rancor. This requires that they have done their personal work, embarked on their own Heroic Journey, and are able to engage their world from their position of truth.

⊕

JIM GOODNIGHT, CEO and cofounder of SAS Institute, is a good example of such a leader. SAS Institute, the world's largest privately held software company, had an unbroken record of double-digit growth from its founding in 1976 through the late 1990s. Even with the technology industry bust of the new century, SAS continues to grow. Ranked over and over again in *Fortune* magazine's 100 Best Companies to Work for in America, and called "Sanity Inc." by *Fast Company*,[63] the institute's culture is a model that others are beginning to follow.

Mirroring the lessons of the Wheel, Goodnight attributes his success to designing SAS's culture around serving the needs and purposes of people. He developed elaborate systems to listen to the needs of his 3.5 million customers, and practiced what he preached by investing an unprecedented 30 percent of his revenues in research and development to meet their needs. He also invests in his people and in the culture of SAS that supports them. SAS is designed to nurture and encourage creativity, innovation, and quality. Company policy supports a flexible 35-hour work week, for instance, because Goodnight believes that tired programmers make mistakes. SAS also supported on-site child care, health care, residential living, and fitness centers long before such benefits were commonplace because Goodnight believes that supporting the life purposes of the individual creates an environment of trust, respect, and commitment.

The results are legendary. SAS employees are renowned for their talent, motivation, and loyalty to SAS. A 16-year veteran says, "When I came on board I figured I'd stay five years, but after that I realized I was having too much fun."[64] Goodnight extends this sense of responsibility to the containing system through philanthropic efforts in the surrounding community. He helped bail out a small airline for $22 million whose loss would have been a major blow to the local economy, and created a private school alternative, the Carey Academy, designed to be a model school integrating technology into all facets of education. In sum, he has built a world-class organization that dominates in a highly competitive industry by developing a work environment based on trust and respect for stakeholders in and outside the organization, and his model is now being emulated by others.

⊕

SUMMARY

Building on the themes of the last three chapters, we have seen the Wheel serve learning, change, and development for individuals, teams, and organizations. Each level of work is necessary for effective change, and levels are mutually interdependent. Teams and organizations provide the vehicle for personal work, and personal work is the premise for effective teams and organizations. Beginning the Heroic Journey lays the ground, but to engage it fully is to engage at all three levels. Each level is a purpose-seeking process that is a manifestation of our search for meaning, and our natural urge to become and reach wholeness.

The challenge for the modern organization, then, is to harness this purpose-seeking energy and direct it toward life-sustaining ends. This can, in fact, be a natural process. In doing the individual and collective work discussed, people learn to appreciate the intricate web of life and the inherent limits of self-interest, and aim for the greater good. Self-interest is no longer paramount; instead, learning and improvement in pursuit of something greater is the goal. In practicing the principles of the Wheel, we harness this energy of becoming and channel it toward human fulfillment. The natural outcome of this work, then, is a growing commitment to human development and the creation of enlightened society.

○ EXERCISES ○

The following two exercises incorporate many of the action-learning messages of the Wheel. Exercise 5.1, Getting Started, focuses on the Sage and provides a basic approach for building the leadership coalition, vision, and strategy necessary for the change effort. Exercise 5.2, The Large Group Conference, provides a tool for building the networks and social capital necessary for implementing the effort. It is presented here as a way of creating a shared understanding of the future (Visionary), but can also be adapted to develop a shared knowledge base (Teacher), to plan and coordinate the action steps (Warrior), or to debrief the lessons learned (Sage).

○ EXERCISE 5.1: GETTING STARTED

There are three main challenges to beginning the process of developing a learning, more enlightened organization. The first one is to identify a rationale for making the desired change that is acceptable to others. Change efforts, especially ones based on the premise of human fulfillment, are usually met with skepticism and a reluctance to go along with the latest management fad. To overcome the early resistance, it is important to sell the program on the basis of the bottom-line benefits the effort is intended to produce—such as improved performance, better customer service, increased competitive advantage, enhanced innovation, and greater organizational agility. To promote the rationale for the effort on any other basis tends to simply produce opposition.

The next challenge is to determine a point of entry, tool, or vehicle through which changes will be made. Developing a learning and more enlightened organization requires fundamental shifts in attitudes, beliefs, assumptions, and skills. These changes are not taught—they are learned through experience. Buckminster Fuller said that if you want to teach people a new way of thinking, don't bother trying to teach them; instead, give them a tool, the use of which will lead to new ways of thinking. In an organizational setting, this point of entry or vehicle often takes the form of strategic planning, process reengineering, total quality improvement, or organizational mergers. Whatever vehicle is chosen, it needs to provide the structure and practice field through which learning takes place.

The final challenge is to develop an example of the new way for others. This new way is one of openly thinking and learning together about a shared set of ideas about the future, and aligning people around what they care about. It is often so different from past experience that most people need an example before they can make the attempt. Pockets of people ready for this change often exist throughout the organization, but they frequently do not survive unless they are leveraged upward. Thus to provide the visibility and the credibility necessary for moving forward, the example often needs to come from the top.

There are certainly risks involved with the leadership team serving as a model. If the leadership team is viewed as the only driver of the process, it could feel like an entirely top-down initiative and cause resistance. Here as in all other applications of the Wheel's wisdom, the process of change should model the desired result of change—in this case, openly thinking and learning together. Therefore, forming a separate design team to work in conjunction with the leadership team is often an effective way to open the process and help model the new way. The design team typically represents a vertical slice of the organization and is charged with working with the leadership team to design, guide, and evaluate the change effort. In addition to modeling the new way, this approach also empowers and helps develop future leaders of the organization.

Step 1: *Form a Design Team*. The design team should consist of a diverse set of stakeholders in the organization—including key people from the top, middle managers, and lower-level employees. Such diversity is necessary for establishing credibility, and for avoiding the risk of falling back into entrenched ways of thinking and acting and thus becoming a top-down process that results in the same old stuff. Members should include people who have a natural commitment for making change, as well as credible critics who could add value to the dialogue and credibility to the effort if persuaded. Depending on the complexity of the organization, the team can range from 8 to 24 people. Of course the larger the team, the more need there is for a skilled facilitator.

Step 2: *Train and Develop the Leadership and Design Teams*. The purpose of the training is to orient people to the scope and charge of the change effort, educate them on how change works, and develop shared expectations of the process. This training can be done with both teams together or separately. Doing it together helps create a common framework and establish relationships, but executive schedules often will not permit that. If done separately, the leadership team is trained first so they understand the reason for and purpose of the design team and fully support it. Training often is conducted in a two- to three-day retreat.

1. *Establish the business question*. It is important to provide an overview of why the effort is being undertaken while also having people buy in and reflect deeply on the challenges it poses. One way to start is to ask people to think about the best team experience they have ever had as a professional or in their extracurricular activities, and then to consider the following: What was the structure of the team like or what aspects of behavior among the members made the team successful?

- How did they interact with one another and with people outside of the team?
- What are the differences between this team and the one most typical of your experience?

The responses and the ensuing dialogue will describe a learning organization. People are most fulfilled and energized when they are serving their higher order of needs, and most will have had such an experience on a team at some point in their lives. As the discussion unfolds, list the key points on a paper while asking them to enhance the definition as they go along to fit the ideals and aspirations of the group. Then ask the following:

- •If we brought this issue to an organizational level, what would happen as a result?
- •What would it bring us?
- •What stands in our way?
- •How will we know if we are making progress?

Reflection on these questions broadens the depth of understanding necessary for considering the effort, and plants the seed that grows into the commitment necessary for making it happen. Just as importantly, the results of the discussion help to clearly establish the central business question the effort is addressing—how to create a more enlightened organization—and are used to shape choices made in the process.

After the business question is established, provide an overview of how change works using the Wheel as a guide. It is important to make the point that, for change efforts to succeed, the process must be applied at the individual, team, and systemwide levels—the individual work provides the foundation for teamwork, and teamwork for system work. Thus the primary training agenda for retreat is to design a change plan for individuals on the team, for the team itself, and for the system it is serving. This drives the change effort down to the level of the individual and makes it real for the team and its members. The remaining agenda for the retreat looks like the following.

2. *Conduct individual work.* Walk people through some of the personal exercises in this book including the Life Line activity, the Heroic Journey, the Leadership Wheel Self-Assessment, the Personal Mission Statement, and the Personal Learning Plan (exercises 1.1, 1.2, 2.2, 3.1, 3.2, in chapters 1 through 3). This serves to:

- •Deepen the sense of undertaking a journey and introduce an understanding of the Wheel,
- •Provide a foundation, at a personal level, for the organization people want to create, and also ground the effort in basic goodness,
- •Develop personal expectations around managing change and learning plans to follow through and model those expectations, and
- •Use the design team itself as a vehicle for the personal change effort.

3. *Conduct team work.* Then walk the team through the chapter 4 exercises, including Team Assessment, Team Development, and Team Mission and Values Development—shaping the latter in the context of the culture the team wants to create. This means developing a mission and values statement for the desired organization that is later floated in front of others as a straw man, or test case. Also include Peer Coaching to provide support for one another in personal learning efforts, and the dialogue exercise from chapter 3 to enhance team communication. This serves to:

- Develop the team and the relationships among team members,
- Deepen the understanding of the Wheel and its application in a team setting,
- Clarify the mission, vision, and values of the desired organization, based on things the individual members care about, and
- Provide additional support for the individual learning plans.

4. *Conduct system work.* Finally, ask the team to design a process for systemwide change using the team mission, vision, and values statement and the 15 points on the Wheel discussed in this chapter as a guide. No single approach works for all systems; therefore it is important to apply the principles of the Wheel in a way that works best in the context of your organization. The key outcome here is to design a process that transforms the system experience into knowledge about a learning, enlightened organization that is accessible to everyone. If training for the leadership and design teams is done separately, this component is first developed by the design team and then discussed with the leadership team. This step serves to:

- Develop buy-in from team members on the design of the process so they can be informed and committed thinkers and participants in the process,
- Further develop and deepen people's understanding of change and how it works at the system level, and
- Sensitize team members to their responsibilities to the containing system.

Step 3: *Develop Next Steps.* After the initial retreat, the team identifies next steps. The important thing to keep in mind is that the design team does not do all the work. In fact, it is important for the team to draw others in the organization into to the process by asking for input and involving them in planning the future and implementing the different initiatives of the effort. This spreads participation and increases the buy-in.

○ EXERCISE 5.2: THE LARGE GROUP CONFERENCE

A large group conference is an important method for communicating, testing, modifying, and achieving buy-in for the change effort. This basic approach can also be used to develop a shared knowledge base for thinking together, to review progress of the effort to date, and to capture the lessons learned. The large group conference engages hundreds, even thousands, of individuals in building collaboration and commitment toward shared goals. These conferences are large-scale dialogues that often result in faster, richer change than the traditional cascading approach of slowly rolling out plans to those who implement them.

The fact is that the vast majority of change efforts fall short because the key people who are interested in and affected by the changes are not included in planning and implementing them. Traditional organizational planning efforts tend to rely on small groups at the top that develop and advocate new directions. This approach often prolongs the change effort through iterative cycles of seeking additional information, feedback, and confirmation from different sources. It exhausts energy for the effort, and also minimizes the potential solutions because all the best thinking is not brought to bear simultaneously on the issues. As a result, these change efforts fail to develop the thinking or broad-based commitment necessary for creative, long-lasting change, and people become disillusioned and frustrated at every level of the organization.

In contrast, the large-scale conference brings the whole system into the room to analyze and cocreate the future. It is not a cascading down or a rolling out of a program; rather, it is a genuinely broad-based participation and involvement in learning and creating a shared destiny.

Tackling problems of change requires leveraging the talents of the entire organization. The complexity of today's world is such that no small set of individuals has the ability to fully grasp and synthesize all possible variables or options. Bringing large groups of people together increases the pace of the process and makes the interconnections necessary to leverage organizational knowledge a hundred times. The discussion of the future and how to create it also energizes people. This is not to say that small groups are inappropriate, only that the limitations of small groups need to be complemented by the diversity and richness of large group interactions.

The foundation of the large group approach has its roots in the research of Kurt Lewin and his successors, including Fred Emery, Eric Trist, Ron Lippitt, and Marvin Weisbord. It is also characteristic of indigenous cultures where entire villages gather to come to decisions on issues that affect everyone. The various methodologies that have evolved over the past several decades include the Search Conference, Future Search, Work-Out, and Real Time Strategic, and they involve anywhere from 80 to 2,400 people. The basic principle of the large group approach is to bring the whole system into the room to think about the context of the larger environment and plan for change.

This means going beyond simply inviting people to an organization-wide forum and informing them about how the future will be different. For real change to occur, there needs to be a systemwide shift in understanding that results in a collective will for action. This does not occur without involving people in deep and meaningful ways. The involvement needs to be structured and genuine, and include input on the formulation and implementation of the effort. It is through the process of involving people that the social capital, broad commitment, and sense of community necessary for change develop.

The approach presented here is a blend of some of the conference methods previously mentioned. Unlike some of the methods that literally start from scratch, this approach uses the conference to test a straw man for the future. This straw man could be a plan developed by the leadership and design teams. The reason for using a straw man is that it is often too difficult to bring everyone up to the level of strategic and systems thinking necessary for creating a compelling future. People are simply not informed enough and their jobs do not demand it of them, so the result is often incremental and watered down. Discussing the straw man elevates understanding and puts everyone on common ground for thinking together about the future.

This approach calls for a one-day conference for groups of up to 100 people. Groups larger than this are difficult to manage, and working with them often results in a less engaging and meaningful experience. Therefore, it is important for larger organizations to use a series of conferences that eventually include everyone in the system. In the latter case, the design team serves as the link for weaving the overall results together.

The approach also calls for including a representative group of external stakeholders—customers and community members—in the conversation. This serves to ensure that the dialogue is sensitive to external concerns.

The design team manages, presents, and facilitates the conference. Executives play a lesser role in order to level the playing field and invite broad participation. The following is a sample design for the one-day conference.

1. *Provide an overview.* The purpose is to engage everyone in thinking and planning for the future. So present an overview to the whole group of how this process works and why we are doing it.
2. *Ask for a reality check.* Break the large group into small groups and ask what is currently working or not working well. This allows the large group to lead the process, and it avoids potential biases that could be brought about by sharing the straw man first. Record the responses and use them as a check against the straw man later.
3. *Present the straw man.* The straw man is the plan, mission, values, or strategies of the effort. The intent of the presentation is to educate and share information and not to preach, lecture, or sell a particular approach. It is to bring everyone onto the same page about the business environment affecting them and the possibilities for the future.
4. *Ask for feedback.* Break the large group into small groups and ask them about concerns, omissions, and other ideas for the straw man. Drawing on their reactions and results of the reality check, ask each group for three to five changes they would make. Asking for changes invites them to participate fully in the process. If the design team has done its homework well, the straw man is generally supported with some minor changes.
5. *Respond to feedback.* If possible, it is important for the executives to take time to respond to the whole group about the feedback—what changes they will consider making or not making, and why or why not. Failure to close the loop by responding to the feedback leaves people with an empty feeling and often deflates momentum. Leaders need to take the opportunity to share the reasons for their position. This serves to educate and inspire further participation.
6. *Ask what needs to happen to make changes achievable.* Again break into small groups and ask people about barriers to making changes and about helpful norms, behaviors, and practices for moving forward.

The design team compiles the results of the conferences and then, working with the leadership team, adopts a plan for moving forward. This plan becomes the basis for unit action planning efforts.

6

THE HEROIC JOURNEY IN ORGANIZATIONS

DESIGNING THE TOTAL EXPERIENCE

We have not to risk the adventure alone, for the heroes of all time have gone before us. The labyrinth is thoroughly known. We have only to follow the thread of the heroic path, and . . . Where we had thought to travel outward, we will come to the center of our own existence. And where we had thought to be alone, we will be with all the world

—Joseph Campbell[1]

The health of our economy, our society, our planet, and our spirits calls for a new and more pervasive kind of leadership. It calls for inspired men and women who balance self-interest with caring for the welfare of the whole. The Heroic Journey provides a wonderful metaphor for engaging the essence of this new style of leadership. It is an archetypal truth that kindles the imagination, touches the heart, and makes even greatly diverse people aware of what unites them.

This journey is the story of a mythic struggle to bring order, meaning, and purpose to complex and uncertain times. Revolutionaries, political leaders, and business people of all times have cultivated courage, compassion, awareness, discipline, and authenticity to make the world a better place. These are traits of the heroic spirit, an archetypal pattern acting in all who face challenges head-on with an open heart.

The real challenge of this journey, however, is not a larger-than-life heroic quest; rather, it is to change the world from right where you are, one step at a time. The heroic spirit is alive among all who are committed to action in the face of adversity. The Heroic Journey is about becoming fully mature and authentic by discovering and integrating the different parts of our selves. It is about learning how to bring your natural gifts to the world. It is about aligning your words and actions with your values and beliefs. It is about learning how to share the boons of this activity and empowering others to do the same.

Our teams, organizations, and communities offer opportunities for this journey. We are called forth to it every time we're asked to do something of significance that requires us to change. Sometimes we're thrown in, sometimes we're lured in, and sometimes we stumble into the upward spiral of learning and growth that it requires.

In an organizational setting, this journey can take many forms. It could be starting a new team, experiencing rapid growth, or merging with another organization. It could be a reengineering effort or new strategic initiative. But whatever it is, the challenge is to engage the change process in a way that makes you more capable, more resilient, and more whole as individuals. The boon of the effort is more enlightened leaders, organizations, and communities.

The call to go forth and do something, however, often feels overwhelming. The journey is demanding, and sometimes it seems to call us to something "larger than life." There are times when you may choose not to take the risk, and instead remain in your comfort zone. There are other times when you may start out full of energy but turn back because of fear, despair, mistakes, or fatigue. There are times when you may feel so burdened that you may even begin to feel victimized. The truth is that the complexity and difficulty of facing change is often undersold. We often underestimate what is required and shrink back from the call. When we do this, we underestimate both ourselves and the power within the opportunities we face.

The real challenge of this journey . . . is not a larger-than-life heroic quest; rather, it is to change the world from right where you are, one step at a time.

Challenges such as these help us see why personal change needs to be inspired from within as well as supported from without. As a developmental process, it works from the inside out *and* from the outside in. It needs to be a total experience, one that operates across the full spectrum of individual and collective endeavor. Not seeing this two-way nature of the dynamic is one reason why the wisdom of the ancients is so often unavailable to us in our current struggles. Without appropriate support and grooming for future leaders or their successors, many of the enlightened principles of leaders such as Hewlett, Packard, Walton, and Disney are often lost. There is no systemic vehicle to gain and build momentum.

In contrast, the disciplines of the ancient warrior and spiritual traditions offer total efforts to shape and mold the individual through systematic training, practice, mentoring, and evaluation. Only through recapturing this systemic discipline can we again learn to leverage the lessons of the past and accumulate momentum and hope for the future. Without it, we may wither in unsuccessful efforts. This process must start with the individual and be actively supported by the system. It is an interdependent process, in which the individual discovers self through serving the aims of the collective, and the aims of the collective are met through serving the individual.

The Wheel is a comprehensive paradigm for shaping the journey and creating this total experience. Comparative studies by Linkage Inc.[2] and the Center for Creative Leadership,[3] both top providers of leadership development programs, show that action learning is the most effective component of such programs. People learn and develop most by tackling real problems and challenges that impact the bottom line. The Wheel is a complete, robust paradigm of action learning that applies through the full spectrum of individual, team, and system levels of experience and promotes a leadership style and organizational culture dedicated to human fulfillment.

The truth is that the complexity and difficulty of facing change is often undersold.

Most leadership programs, however, do not start with the premise of human fulfillment; and few, if any, apply this premise to all three levels of experience. Linkage Inc.'s research shows that programs most often target the team and system levels of learning, frequently to the exclusion of the individual. The result is that most programs take the heart out of leadership development. They focus on technique and quick fixes, developing a narrow set of competencies that serves a defined set of team and organizational objectives. But as the Wheel shows, leadership development rests on the premise of human fulfillment, and that begins with the individual. Starting there means going beyond skill development and focusing on personal transformation. It also means working at all three levels, beginning with the individual and using teams and organizational change as vehicles.

A BASIC DESIGN FOR A TOTAL EXPERIENCE

As a developmental process, it works from the inside out and from the outside in. It needs to be a total experience . . .

I have worked with a number of organizations in developing programs that provide such a total experience. These programs are designed primarily around a series of three experiential workshops over a six-month to one-year period with action learning assignments in between. The first workshop begins with a focus on the individual and then moves to the team and system level of experience. Drawing on the exercises of this book, many of the participants claim their lives have been changed as a result of the program.

INDIVIDUAL WORKSHOP

The key objective for the first workshop is to hook the energy of becoming, the desire to learn and develop, through insight into the self and increasing self-awareness. Much of the material that I use in this workshop appears in the individual exercises given in this book. Processing the feedback from these exercises, along with other personal assessment instruments used in the program, serves as a gateway for taking a deeper look at self and inner motivations. The workshop helps participants frame the feedback and uses individual and group activities to confirm, extend, and deepen self-understanding. This is an emotional experience that strikes at a gut level, opens participants to larger questions, and launches them on their journey.

The lessons are reinforced through ongoing activities and support after the workshop. First, participants follow through on their personal learning plans and develop learning strategies that mirror the action learning process of the Wheel. Second, participants meet regularly in their coaching teams to assess progress on the learning plans, share feedback, and revise plans. This serves the triple purpose of supporting the learning process, developing coaching skills, and practicing dialogue in delivering constructive comments. Third, learning plans are shared and discussed regularly with a mentor to further interpret and support the learning process. Often the mentor is a professional coach, such as one of the program instructors, or a senior person in the organization who can help guide choices on both professional and personal developmental plans. Finally, participants are asked to practice dialogue further by addressing one difficult interpersonal problem they have with another person and sharing the results with their coaching team and mentor. Dialogue is emphasized because of the role it plays in both the individual and collective learning processes.

The key objective of these interim assignments is to strengthen the sense of the Sage that was aroused in the first workshop. The Sage awakens all the other directions—it is the latent governing urge to individuate and develop. It is feeling empowered to learn how to learn from experience, and to double- and even triple-loop learn. Feeling personally empowered and learning how to learn are the two root ingredients for the lifelong journey of leadership development. If we have these two, then everything else unfolds naturally from them. Through experiencing success on personal learning plans, people are encouraged, supported, and emboldened to do more.

TEAM WORKSHOP

The second program is a workshop on building relationships and teams. This program builds on the experience of the previous workshop and is often considered an even more powerful interpersonal experience. Again drawing on many of the exercises of this book, the overall objective of this workshop is to develop trust and relationships through continuing the practice of dialogue in building teams.

Here, participants divide into teams, take on a series of tasks, and follow the action learning framework of the Wheel to achieve their task and build their teams. After processing the results, these teams then change roles and become team-building consultants for other teams in the workshop. The teams again use the action-learning framework of the Wheel to diagnose, design, carry out, and debrief a team process intervention activity for one of the other teams. The process continues to build self-knowledge and insight into effective relationships and group dynamics. In essence, participants learn to know themselves through others and at the same time begin to experience a true Model II learning culture. For many, this is the first taste of this experience and plants the seed for them to want to recreate such an experience in the workplace.

After the team session, the participants continue to work in their coaching teams and with their mentors to make progress on their personal learning plans. These plans may change with experience, and they often do; but the point is to ensure a discipline for following through and developing a habit of learning from experience. In addition, participants also identify and take on a team-building opportunity in their workplace. This can be an existing work team or an ad hoc team working on a special project. The purpose is to identify an experience through which the participant can apply in a real-life situation the lessons learned as the team leader or as a facilitator of a team intervention in the team workshop. Coaching teams and mentors help the participant identify, design, and debrief the experience to capture its lessons.

SYSTEM WORKSHOP

The third program in the series is a workshop on managing and leading change at a system level. The key objective here is to learn to use change efforts as a vehicle for developing leadership skills and building a learning culture. Participants use the Wheel as a model to learn about the theory of change and how it works, and then engage first in a simulation and then in a live case study to design and implement a strategic system-level change process. Issues they deal with include the full range of the 15 principles for managing change, including forming the leadership team, gathering data and diagnosing the system, engaging social networks and capital, designing the process, taking action on plans, and managing organizational learning. They gain insight into how to manage change, overcome inherent resistance to change, and motivate and align people to the effort.

Most change efforts fail due to poor execution, and poor execution is most often the result of insufficient shared understanding and commitment of the people affected by the change. The simulation focuses on how to achieve that commitment. As in the first two workshops, one of the important takeaways is to understand that the process of change must model the desired result. In other words, the process of creating a learning culture must itself mirror learning behavior—the process and the result must model what is to be learned. After the simulation, participants present and critique one another's design and implementation processes in order to learn from one another's experience.

After the systems session, participants work either in teams or in their individual units on the system change effort they identified. They continue to work in their coaching teams and with their mentors for guidance, feedback, and revision. This support often includes one-on-one coaching with program facilitators and executives, and regular meetings of the group as a whole to discuss progress and the lessons learned. The key here is to continue to reinforce the habit of learning how to learn from experience.

FOLLOW-UP

This overall process has proved to be a powerful experience for participants, but the impact can be short-lived if the leadership team has not engaged in a similar experience. As already emphasized, leaders are the most important organizational influence on shaping strategic direction and culture. Unless leaders emulate learning behavior, it is difficult for pockets of learning culture to take hold and grow. Therefore, in inaugurating a leadership development program it is important to start at the top, with the leadership team participating in the process as a cohort.

Going through the process as an intact team, especially at the executive level, is the most powerful use of this methodology for creating a learning culture. Participants deal with real issues and relationships, and as a consequence have the opportunity to break through entrenched patterns and renew and reinvigorate their relationships. They also create a common language, framework, and vision for dealing with a range of issues including leadership, strategy, and culture that they want to model for others in the organization. In experiencing this as a cohort, the group develops a sense of team and mutual support for sustaining and continuing their learning.

The power of the cohort is often an overlooked vehicle for deepening and building on the experience. The bonds and relationships established through shared experience provide the energy, commitment, and support necessary for continued growth. Sharing insights and perspectives with participants in subsequent workshops helps executives reinforce their lessons learned and model the way.

To promote continued learning after the workshop series, many organizations also employ a structured review process that focuses on the ongoing developmental efforts of the individual and succession planning. Here, people receive feedback on their progress and revise their latest developmental goals on a regular basis. They are also considered for readiness in the next step of their career, as in potential job or rotational assignments in their professional development cycle. Often at the heart of this process is a 360-degree assessment based on the leadership competency models of the organization. As mentioned in chapter 2, however, these competency models are based on the existing culture of the organization, which may or may not be conducive to learning. Incorporating the Wheel as the competency model in the assessment of leadership promotes not only the development of a learning culture, but also the principles of human fulfillment in all its aspects. It provides the ground for creating enlightened teams, enlightened organizations, and enlightened communities.

Finally, a few organizations incorporate community service as part of the leadership development process. This reinforces the message of extending beyond the self, and the boundaries of the organization, to serve the greater whole. As we saw earlier, doing this serves the mutual development of the individual, the organization, and the community. It is another way to awaken the heart and realign our energy of becoming, which makes it another practice field for working on leadership skills. Abbott Laboratories incorporates community projects into their leadership development program in order to challenge participants to think differently on how to lead, meet the needs of others, and have an impact. Community service also helps nurture a commitment to doing well while doing good for the world. This means doing more than simply volunteering for an activity or dispensing charity from a distance; it means active involvement and creating genuine relationships in promoting a meaningful endeavor.

When community service clicks, people begin to think about reaching out and creating developmental opportunities for all in real and meaningful ways. Such is the bedrock for creating an enlightened society.

○ EXERCISE ○

○ EXERCISE 6.1: SERVICE LEARNING

As emphasized throughout this book, it is in an organization's interest to be responsible to the communities in which it operates. Businesses can promote social responsibility by integrating community service initiatives into their leadership development programs. Known as service learning, these initiatives are most often found in undergraduate experiences in institutions of higher education. However, they can also provide an important developmental opportunity for business organizations.

The intent of service learning is to prepare people and organizations for living responsible lives in an interdependent world. Service learning goes beyond simple volunteerism, in which people become aware of social issues, to actually engaging people in altering the systems that are at the root of many of the problems. More importantly, this engagement fosters an understanding of the community not as something separate but as an extension of the organization. People learn to consider the well-being of the whole and to conduct business as part of an integrated network in which all may flourish.

Service learning serves multiple purposes for the organization. First, it is a vehicle for empowering people as learners to develop and practice their leadership skills. Working in teams to take on projects in the community provides an important practice field for honing new behaviors and intellectual skills. Second, it informs people and creates a deeper understanding of the world we live in, and instills a greater awareness of the interdependencies within the whole. Third, it imparts a value of responsible citizenship. Engaging in projects in the community helps people further appreciate that the integrity and effectiveness of our system as a whole depends on our sense of ethics and social responsibility toward all.

In taking on a service learning project, it is important to work in small teams. Team members are able to learn from one another and to provide mutual support in sustaining the effort. Teams also provide the context for peer coaching, and for assessing and supporting one another on personal learning plans. The following provides a basic approach for undertaking service learning projects.

Step 1: *Identify Projects.* My experience shows that the selection of the projects should be driven by the participants, who otherwise may not have the energy or commitment to follow through in meaningful ways. Thus I ask them to think about something that they care about such as youth, health, the elderly, and people with disabilities, and focus on potential services in those areas that they can launch or improve.

Step 2: *Identify and Contract with the Client* In considering potential projects, it is important that people also identify a client in the community—a potential service provider or community partner—who is also committed to making a change. I have seen many projects falter because the client was interested in seeing what the participants might come up with, without ever truly committing to making changes. Therefore, once mutual interest has been gauged, ask participants to negotiate with the chosen community partner to shape the purpose, expectations, and mutual roles in the project. Often this takes the form of a letter of mutual expectations.

Step 3: *Evaluate Progress.* At regular intervals, the team, the sponsoring business, and the community partner should evaluate progress. This serves to keep the project on track and give participants opportunities to reflect on the lessons learned. As part of this review, team members assess one another on their contributions to the team as well as their progress on personal learning plans.

Over time, the service learning projects can have a very significant impact on the community. Since our inception, the Roy H. Park Leadership Fellows in the Johnson School at Cornell University have undertaken many projects in the local community—ranging from working with youth, to environmental nonprofits, to health services, to supporting local start-up businesses. Everyone benefits from this process—the students from their learning experience, the community from the better programs, and the university from stronger local relationships.

FOR MORE INFORMATION

For more information about leadership, team, and organizational development programs and services involving the Leadership Wheel, contact:

THE LEADERSHIP WHEEL

215 Forest Home Drive
Ithaca, NY, 14850
E-mail: ccs7@cornell.edu

NOTES

INTRODUCTION

1. John Naisbitt, *Megatrends 2000* (New York: Avon Books, 1990), xxii.
2. Paul Hawken, Amory Lovins, and Hunter Lovins, *Natural Capitalism* (New York: Little, Brown & Company, 1999), 1–6, 241; Paul Hawken, *The Ecology of Commerce* (New York: Harper Business, 1993), 1–35.
3. Charles Handy, *The Hungry Spirit: Beyond Capitalism* (New York: Broadway Books, 1998), 31.
4. Ibid., xiv.
5. Vaclav Havel, "A Joint Session of the U.S. Congress," in *Toward a Civil Society: Selected Speeches and Writings, 1990 - 1994*, 31–45. available from (accessed October, 2004).
6. Handy, *Hungry Spirit*, xv.
7. Adam Smith, *The Wealth of Nations* (1776; New York: Knopf, Random House, 1991).
8. Adam Smith, *The Theory of Moral Sentiments* (1759; Cambridge, UK and New York: Cambridge University Press, 2002).
9. John Maynard Keynes, "Economic Possibilities for our Grandchildren," in *Essays in Persuasion* (New York: Harcourt Brace, 1932).
10. John Kotter and James Heskett, *Corporate Culture and Performance* (New York: Free Press, 1992), 83–93.
11. James McGregor Burns, *Leadership* (New York: Harper & Row, 1978), 2.
12. Alfred North Whitehead, *Process and Reality* (New York: Free Press, 1969), 53.
13. Carl G. Jung, ed., *Man and His Symbols* (New York: Doubleday, 1964).
14. Mihaly Csikszentmihalyi, *Flow* (New York: Harper Perennial, 1991), 235.

CHAPTER I

1. William Wordsworth, *Palgrave's Golden Treasury* (1807), available online at http://www.bartleby.com/106/278.html (accessed October 2004).
2. William Shakespeare, *The Tempest* 4.1.156–57, Harvard Classics edition available at http://www.bartleby.com/46/5/41.html (accessed October 2004).
3. John C. Maxwell, *The 21 Indispensable Qualities of a Leader* (Nashville: Thomas Nelson, Inc., 1999), 139, 140.
4. Peter Gold, *Navaho and Tibetan Sacred Wisdom* (Rochester, VT: Inner Traditions, 1994), 127.
5. Lee Bolman, "Reframing Leadership," talk given at the third annual Friends of the Center Leadership Conference, Kansas City, MO, May 30, 2001.
6. James Wynbrandt, *Flying High: How David Neeleman Beats the Competition Even in the World's Most Turbulent Industry* (Hoboken, NJ: John Wiley & Sons 2004), 135.

7. Ibid., 223.
8. Dan Rather, "Jet Blue Flying Higher" (June 3, 2003), 2.
9. Ken Howe, David Tong, Steve Zuckerman, David Armstrong, George Raine, Carolyn Said, Jeanne Cooper, Steve Corder and Colleen Benson, "On the Record: David Neeleman Jet Blue Airways" (, San Francisco Chronicle, September 12, 2004), 8.
10. Ibid., 8.
11. Ibid., 8.
12. James Wynbrandt, *Flying High: How David Neeleman Beats the Competition Even in the World's Most Turbulent Industry* (Hoboken, NJ: John Wiley & Sons, 2004), 224.
13. Ibid., 223.
14. Captain Michael D. Abrashoff, *It's Your Ship* (New York, Warner Books 2002), 4.
15. Ibid., 4.
16. Polly LaBarre, "The Agenda—Grassroots Leadership," *Fast Company* 13 (April 1999), 1.
17. Ibid., 3.
18. Ibid., 2.
19. Warren Bennis, *On Becoming a Leader* (Reading, MA: Addison Wesley, 1989), 69.
20. Chogyam Trungpa Rinpoche, *Shambhala: The Sacred Path of the Warrior,* (Boston: Shambhala Publications, 1988), 60–64.
21. William James, *The Principles of Psychology,* vol. 2 (1890), 110, available at http://psych-classics.yorku.ca/James/Principles/prin19.htm (accessed October 2004).
22. Harriet Rubin, "The Power of Words," *Fast Company* 21, 141–145 (January 1999).
23. Ben Zander, "Music as a Metaphor for Leadership," talk given at the Johnson School of Management, Cornell University, Ithaca, NY, November 28, 2001.
24. Polly LaBarre, "Leadership—Ben Zander," *Fast Company* 20, 110–115 (December 1998)
25. Ibid.
26. Ibid., 115.
27. Ibid., 110.
28. Ibid., 114.
29. Chogyam Trungpa Rinpoche, *Shambhala,* 35–41
30. Chappell, *Managing Upside Down,* (New York, William Morrow and Company, 1999), 40–43.
31. Ibid., 43–46.
32. Eric Patterson, "Values' Vital to Tom's of Maine Business," interview with Tom Chappell, Boulder County Business Report, 1995, 2
33. Chogyam Trungpa Rinpoche, *Shambhala,* 158–172.
34. Ibid., 25–34.
35. See Alvin Toffler, *The Third Wave* (New York: Bantam Books, 1990); Herman Maynard and Susan Mehrtens, *The Fourth Wave: Business in the 21st Century* (San Francisco: Berrett-Koehler, 1993).
36. Maynard and Mehrtens, *Fourth Wave.*
37. Max DePree and Frances Hesselbein, "A Conversation with Max DePree," *Leader to Leader* 6, 19 (Fall 1997).
38. Ibid., 20.
39. Ibid.
40. Carl G. Jung, *The Essential Jung,* ed. A. Storr (Princeton, NJ: Princeton University Press, 1983), 390.
41. Rod Napier, Clint Sidle, and Patrick Sanaghan, *High Impact Tools and Activities for Strategic Planning* (New York: McGraw-Hill, 1998), 279.
42. Chogyam Trungpa Rinpoche, *The Great Eastern Sun* (Boston: Shambhala, 1999), 11.

CHAPTER 2

1. William James, "Energies of Men," *Science N.S.* 25, no. 635 (1907): 321–332; available online at http://psychclassics.yorku.ca.James_energies.htm (accessed October 2004).

2. See the discussion of the Five-Factor Model by Gordon Allport and H S. Odbert, in Howard J. Pierce and Jane Mitchell, *Big Five Quick Start* (Charlotte, NC: Center for Applied Cognitive Studies, 1995), 2.

3. Michael Lombardo and Robert Eichinger, *Preventing Derailment* (Greensboro, NC: Center for Creative Leadership, 1999), 7–11.

4. Max DePree, *Leadership Is an Art* (New York: Dell Trade, 1989), 11.

5. Mary Guthrie, "True North: Keeping Your Bearings in the Business World," *Cornell Enterprise Magazine,* Fall 2000, 21–22, developed from a talk given by Orit Gadiesh on September 7, 2000.

6. "Orit Gadiesh," *Harvard Business School Working Knowledge Special Reports,* September 5, 2000, 2.

7. Guthrie, "True North," 21–22.

8. Chogyam Trungpa Rinpoche, *Cutting through Spiritual Materialism* (Boston: Shambhala, 1987), 225.

9. Daniel Goleman, "What Makes a Leader" *Harvard Business Review* (Boston, Nov–Dec 1998).

10. Warren Bennis, *On Becoming a Leader* (Reading, MA: Addison Wesley, 1989), 169.

11. Peter Senge and Fred Koffman, "Communities of Commitment," *Organizational Dynamics* 22, no. 2, 5–19 (autumn 1993).

12. Mike Krzyzewski with Donald Phillips, *Leading from the Heart* (New York: Warner Business, 2000), 11.

13. T. E. Lawrence, *Seven Pillars of Wisdom,* introductory chapter (1926); available online at http://etext.library.adelaide.edu.au/l/l42s/introduction1.html (accessed October 2004).

14. Ben Heskett, "Chambers' Tale of Icarus," CNET Networks Inc, 1995–2002, 2; available at http://www.CNETnews.com (accessed October 2004).

15. John Waters, *John Chambers and the Cisco Way* (New York: John Wiley & Sons, 2002), 73.

16. Ibid., 91.

17. Ibid., 160.

18. Ibid., 90.

19. Johann Wolfgang von Goethe, *Maxims and Reflections* (New York: Penguin Group, 1999), no. 689.

20. James Post, "Aaron Feuerstein—A Socially Responsive Owner" *Business and Society,* 9th ed., 1999, 10; Michael Ryan, "They Call Their Boss a Hero." *Parade,* September 8, 1996, 5.

21. Post, "Aaron Feuerstein," 10–15.

22. Ryan, "They Call Their Boss a Hero," 4–5

23. Carlos Castaneda, *Tales of Power* (New York: Pocket Books, Simon and Schuster, 1974), 106.

24. Gibran, Kahlil, *The Prophet* (New York: Alfred A. Knopf, 1979), 56.

25. Peter Block, "Quest for Accountability," talk given at the third annual Friends of the Center Leadership Conference, Kansas City, MO, May 30, 2001.

26. Oren Harari. *The Leadership Secrets of Colin Powell* (New York: McGraw Hill, 2002), 215.

27. Ibid., 219.

28. Ibid., 215.

29. James Collins. *Good to Great* (New York: Harper Business, 2001), 21.

30. Wendy Kopp, *One Day, All Children . . .* (New York: Public Affairs, 2001), 23.

31. Carl G. Jung, *Man and His Symbols* (New York: Doubleday, 1964), 168–176.
32. Charles R. Swindoll, *Strengthening Your Grip* (Dallas, TX: Word, Inc., 1982), 204.

CHAPTER 3

1. Erwin Schroedinger, *What is Life? Matter and Mind* (Cambridge: Cambridge University Press, 1967), 136.
2. Hannah Riley, "Rudy Giuliani: The Man and His Moment," *Kennedy School of Government Case Program* (Cambridge: President and Fellows of Harvard University, 2002), 1–2.
3. Morgan McCall, Michael Lombardo, and Ann Morrison, *The Lessons of Experience* (New York: Free Press, 1988), 122.
4. Hyemeyohsts Storm, *Seven Arrows* (New York: Ballantine Books, 1972), 5.
5. Ibid.. 26.
6. W. Brian Arthur, Jonathan Day, Joseph Jaworski, Michael Jung, Ikujiro Nonaka, C. Otto Sharmer, and Peter M. Senge, "Leadership in the Context of Emerging Worlds: Illuminating the Blind Spot," *McKinsey-Society for Organizational Learning Leadership Project* (summary paper on Ongoing Research Project, 1999–2000), 5.
7. Daniel Goleman, *Destructive Emotions* (New York: Bantam, 2003), 3–27; Daniel Goleman, *Emotional Intelligence* (New York: Bantam, 1997).
8. Albert Schweitzer, *The Philosophy of Civilization,* trans. C. T. Campion (1936; Buffalo: Prometheus, 1987), 309.
9. David Kolb, *Experiential Learning* (Englewood Cliffs, NJ: Prentice Hall, 1984), 40–43.
10. Otto Sharmer, "Presencing: Learning from the Future as it Emerges" (presented at the Conference on Knowledge and Innovation, May 25–26, 2000, Helsinki School of Economics, Finland), 2.
11. M. K. Smith, (2001) "Chris Argyris: Theories of Action, Double-Loop Learning and Organizational Learning," *The Encyclopedia of Informal Education,* March 2004, 6, online at http://, (accessed October 2004); Chris Argyris and Donald Schon, *Organizational Learning: A Theory of Action Perspective* (Reading, MA: Addison Wesley, 1978), 18–20; Chris Argyris and Donald Schon, *Theory in Practice* (San Francisco: Jossey Bass, 1974), 18–19.
12. Ibid.
13. Argyris and Schon, *Organizational Learning,* 20–29; Argyris and Schon, *Theory in Practice,* 18–19.
14. Barbara Mackoff and Gary Wenet, *The Inner Work of Leaders* (New York: AMACOM, 2001).
15. Ibid., 55, 53–56.
16. Ibid., 84.
17. Ibid., 48–50.
18. Ibid., 49, 49–53.
19. Ibid., 39–92.
20. Fred Koffman, "From Unilateral Control to Mutual Learning," *Leading Learning Communities* (Miami, FL: Boulder, 1995), 23–24.
21. Pamela Kruger, "A Leader's Journey," *Fast Company* 25, 116 (June 1999); also available online at http://
22. Ibid.
23. Ibid.
24. Ibid.
25. Ibid.

26. Ibid.

27. Ibid.

28. Argyris, *Overcoming Organizational Defenses* (Needham Heights, MA: Allyn and Bacon, 1990), 12–25; Argyris Chris and Schon, *Theory in Practice*, 63–84, 6.

29. Ibid., 104–117.

30. Charles Handy, *The Hungry Spirit* (New York: Broadway Books, 1998), 80.

31. Viktor E. Frankl, *The Unconscious God: Psychotherapy and Theology* (New York: Simon & Schuster, 1975), 113.

32. Storm, *Seven Arrows*, 11.

33. Bernard Bass, *Bass & Stogdills Handbook of Leadership*, 3d ed. (New York: Free Press, 1990), 781.

34. Robert F. Kennedy, speech to South African students, University of Capetown, June 6, 1966, available online at http://www.rfkmemorial.org/RFK/ (accessed October 2004).

35. Sam Johnson, personal conversation with the author at the Johnson School, Cornell University, Spring 2003.

36. Warren G. Bennis and Robert J. Thomas, *Geeks and Geezers* (Boston: Harvard Business School Press, 2002), 178.

37. Daniel Goleman, *Working with Emotional Intelligence* (New York: Bantam, 2000), 239–45, 258–77.

38. Peter Novak, *The Vision of Nietzsche* (Rockport: Element, 1996), 33.

39. Ibid.

40. Bennis and Thomas, *Geeks and Geezers*, 110.

41. Ken Blanchard, informal talk given to the Roy H. Park Leadership Fellows, at the Johnson School of Management, Cornell University, January 2003.

42. Stephen R. Covey, *The 7 Habits of Highly Effective People* (New York: Simon & Schuster, 1990), 287.

43. Jay Paxton, Brigadier General, U.S. Marine Corps, "Attributes of Leadership," talk given at the Johnson School of Management, Cornell University, September 2001.

44. Handy, *Hungry Spirit*, 150.

45. Taken from Ken Blanchard Companies Self-Leadership program, with permission.

46. Natalie Goldberg, *Writing Down the Bones* (Boston: Shambhala, 1986).

47. Peter Senge, *The Fifth Discipline* (New York: Doubleday Currency, 1990) 238–40.

48. Covey, *7 Habits*, 235.

CHAPTER 4

1. Wei Wu Wei, *Ask the Awakened: The Negative Way* (Boston Little Brown, 1963), 1.

2. Malidoma Patrice Some, *The Healing Wisdom of Africa* (New York: Jeremy P. Tarcher, Putnam, 1999), 32–33.

3. John Neihardt, *Black Elk Speaks* (Lincoln: University of Nebraska Press, 1988), 194.

4. Richard Hackman, *Leading Teams* (Cambridge, MA: Harvard Business School Press, 2002), 233–34.

5. Ibid.

6. Peter Senge, *The Fifth Discipline* (New York: Doubleday Currency, 1990), 233–269

7. Hackman, *Leading Teams*, 5–22.

8. Ibid.

9. Ibid.

10. Ibid., 31, 51.

11. Bertrand Russell, *The Conquest of Happiness* (1930; reprint, New York: Liveright, 1996), 18.

12. Mihaly Csikszentmihalyi, *Flow* (New York: Harper Perennial, 1991), 149.

13. Viktor Frankl, *Man's Search for Meaning* (Boston: Beacon, 1984), 94–95; Csikszentmihalyi, *Flow*, 92.

14. Chogyam Trungpa Rinpoche, *Shambhala: The Sacred Path of the Warrior* (Boston: Shambhala Publications, 1988), 34.

15. Hackman, *Leading Teams*, 177–78, referencing original work of C. Gersick, "Time and Transition in Work Teams: Toward a New Model of Group Development," *Academy of Management Journal* 31: 9–41; and Hackman, *Leading Teams*, 181–82, referencing A. Woolley's original work, "Effects of Intervention Content and Timing on Group Task Performance, *Journal of Applied Behavioral Science* 34, 30–49 (1998).

16. Robert Kaplan, "Integrating Intangible Assets into Corporate Value Creation," talk given in the Roy H. Park Leadership Speaker Series, Johnson Graduate School of Management, Cornell University, November 2003.

17. Hackman, *Leading Team*, 97.

18. Charles Handy, *The Hungry Spirit* (New York: Broadway Books, 1998), 149.

19. Thomas Jefferson, letter to P. H. Wendover, 1815 (ME 14:283); available at http://etext.virginia.edu/jefferson/quotations/jeff0750.htm (accessed October 2004).

20. Personal consulting experience with Meredith Corporation, fall-winter 2001–2002.

21. Lao Tzu, *The Way of Life According to Lao Tzu*, trans. Witter Bynner (New York: Capricorn Books, 1962), 34–35.

22. James Collins and Jerry Porras, *Built to Last* (New York: Harper Business, 1997), 91.

23. Daniel Davies, "1997 Business Leader of the Year," available at *Business Leader Online* (Research Triangle Region, NC), vol. 9, no. 7, 1–4 (January 1998) available at http:// (accessed October 2004).

24. Ibid.

25. Adapted from Arthur Beck and Ellis Hillmar, *Positive Management Practices* (San Francisco: Jossey-Bass, 1986) 26–27.

CHAPTER 5

1. Chief Seattle, speech (January 1854, verbatim transcript doesn't exist); filmscript adaptation by Ted Perry, 1971; Chief Seattle's speech versions available at http://www.synaptic.bc.ca/ejournal/seattle.htm (accessed October 2004).

2. Carole S. Napolitano and Lida J. Henderson, *The Leadership Odyssey* (San Francisco: Jossey-Bass, 1998), 111.

3. Peter F. Drucker, *Concept of the Corporation* (New York: John Day, 1972), 307–305.

4. Chogyam Trungpa Rinpoche, *Shambhala: The Sacred Path of the Warrior* (Boston: Shambhala, 1988), 125.

5. Russell Ackoff, *Creating the Corporate Future* (New York: John Wiley & Sons, 1981), 15.

6. Ibid., 63.

7. Peter Koestenbaum, *Leadership: The Inner Side of Greatness* (San Francisco: Jossey-Bass, 1991), 3.

8. Ackoff, *Creating the Corporate Future*, 33–34.

9. James Collins and Jerry Porras, *Built to Last* (New York: Harper Business, 1997); and James Collins, *Good to Great* (New York: Harper Business, 2001).

10. Collins and Porras, *Built to Last*, 55–57, 224.

11. Ben Cohen and Jerry Greenfield, *Ben & Jerry's Double-Dip* (New York: Simon & Schuster, 1997), 46.

12. John Gertner, "The Virtue in $6 Heirloom Tomatoes," *The New York Times Magazine*, June 6, 2004, 44–47.

13. Collins and Porras, *Built to Last*, 24.

14. Ibid., 28.

15. Michael Porter and Mark Kramer, "The Competitive Advantage of Corporate Philanthropy," *Harvard Business Review*, December 2002, 56–68.

16. Peter Asmus and Marjorie Kelly, "100 Best Corporate Citizens of 2003," available online at http://www.business-ethics.com (accessed October 2004) 1–5.

17. Collins and Porras, *Built to Last*, 140–68.

18. Henry Mintzberg, *The Rise and Fall of Strategic Planning* (New York: Free Press, 1994), 23–29.

19. Peter Senge, *The Fifth Discipline* (New York: Doubleday Currency, 1990) 17–26.

20. Mary Guthrie, "True North: Keeping Your Bearings in the Business World," *Cornell Enterprise Magazine*, Fall 2000, 21–22; developed from a talk given by Ori Gadiesh on September 7, 2000.

21. Mintzberg, *Rise and Fall*, 86–87, 223–24, 267–75.

22. Ibid., 86–87, 258–266.

23. Robert Kaplan and David Norton, *The Balanced Scorecard* (Boston: Harvard Business School Press, 1996).

24. John Kotter, *Leading Change* (Cambridge, MA: Harvard Business School Press, 1996), 35–51.

25. Senge, *Fifth Discipline*, 174–205.

26. Marvin Weisbord and Sandra Janoff, *Future Search* (San Francisco: Berrett-Koehler, 1995), 42–45.

27. Result of a search conference conducted by Cornell University Extension for the Seneca Nation in June 1994.

28. Collins and Porras, *Built to Last*, 58.

29. Larry Bossidy and Ram Charan, *Execution* (New York: Crown Business, 2002), 98–99.

30. Ibid., 99–101.

31. From Johnson School students working at IBM, personal communication.

32. Kevin Freiberg and Jackie Freiberg, *Nuts! Southwest Airlines' Crazy Recipe for Business and Personal Success* (New York: Broadway Books, 1998), 224.

33. Bossidy and Charan, *Execution*, 99.

34. Bossidy and Charan, *Execution*, 186.

35. Collins and Porras, *Built to Last*, 1–21, 225.

36. Ibid., 71.

37. Ibid.

38. Robert Greenleaf, "The Servant Leader" (Robert K Greenleaf Center, 1991), 9; originally published by Robert Greenleaf, 1970.

39. Collins and Porras, *Built to Last*, 9–10.

40. Ibid., 22–41.

41. Jack Welch and John Byrne, *Straight from the Gut* (New York: Warner Business Books, 2001), 107.

42. Porter and Kramer, "Competitive Advantage," 64–65.

43. Ibid.

44. Chris Argyris, *Integrating the Individual and the Organization* (New Brunswick, NJ: Transaction Publishers, 1990), 34.

45. Tom Chappell, *Managing Upside Down* (New York: William Morrow, 1999), 53.

46. Collins and Porras, *Built to Last,* 115–39.

47. Mary Guthrie, "True North," 21–22.

48. Chappell, *Managing Upside Down,* 77.

49. Collins and Porras, *Built to Last,* 141–68.

50. Ibid., 148.

51. Rudolph Giuliani, *Leadership* (New York: Miramax Books, 2002), 41–43.

52. Collins and Porras, *Built to Last,* 37–138.

53. Ibid., *Built to Last,* 163–65, 167, 68.

54. Arie Degues, "Planning as Learning," *Harvard Business Review* 66, no. 2: 70–74, 1989.

55. See, for example, Cornell University's Project 2000: available at http://www.news.cor-nell.edu/releases/March96/Project_2000.jkp.html (accessed October 2004).

56. Kotter, *Leading Change,* 51–67.

57. Daryl Conner, *Managing at the Speed of Change* (New York: Villard Books, 1995), 117–21.

58. Noel Tichy, *The Leadership Engine* (New York: Harper Business, 1997), 1, 4, 57.

59. Welch and Bryne, *Straight from the Gut,* 167–84.

60. Chappell, *Managing Upside Down,* 77.

61. Vaclav Havel, "A Joint Session of the U.S. Congress," in *Toward a Civil Society: Selected Speeches and Writings, 1990 - 1994,* 31–45; available from (accessed October, 2004).

62. Chogyam Trungpa Rinpoche, *Shambhala,* 29.

63. Daniel Davies, "Business Leader of the Decade," *Business Leader* 11, no. 5 (November 1999): 1; available online at http://www.businessleader.com (accessed October 2004).

64. Ibid., 3.

CHAPTER 8

1. Joseph Campbell. *The Hero with a Thousand Faces* (Princeton, NJ: Princeton University Press, 1973), 25.

2. David Giber, Louis Carter, and Marshall Goldsmith, *Linkage Inc.'s Best Practices in Leadership Development Handbook* (San Francisco: Jossey-Bass, Pfeiffer, 2000).

3. Cynthia D. McCauley and Ellen Van Velsor (Editors), *Center for Creative Leadership Handbook on Leadership Development* (San Francisco: Jossey-Bass, 1998).

INDEX

Abbott Laboratories, 220
Abrashoff, Michael, 18–19, 22, 107
Ackoff, Russell, 8, 173
action intelligence, 56–57, 68
    also see Warrior
action learning
    individual learning and development,
        87–105
    team learning and development, 140–46,
    organizational learning and development,
        178–202
    similarities to other models, 95
    Wheel as model of, 87–92, 140–46
    *also see Nurturer, Sage, Teacher, Visionary,
        and Warrior*
adaptive learning, *see double loop learning*
agility, 69, *also see balance*
Allied Signal, 186
Allport, Gordon, 39
American Express, 177
ancients, learning from, 4–6, 37–39, 86–87,
    93–94, 133–35
archetype, 38–39, 41–43, *also see Nurturer,
    Sage, Teacher, Visionary, and Warrior*
Argyris, Chris, 190
    dialogue, and, 102
    Model I and Model II, 100–102
    single and double loop learning, 96
Arriens, Angeles, 37
authentic presence,
    basic goodness, ground of, 105–106
    definition of, 25
    discovery of, 103
    purpose, relationship to,103–104
    Warrior, relationship to, 104–105
authenticity, 25, 67, 102, 103–107, 192–193
    also see Warrior, and authentic presence
awakening the heart, *see Nurturer*

awareness,
    dialogue, and 102, 146–148
    openness. and, 93–94, 146–148
    organizational change, 200
    Turning the Wheel, role in. 93–94
    also see openness, Sage, Teacher

Bain, 45–46
balance, 39, 42, 66, 67–69, 70, 86, 92, 135
Balanced Scorecard, 182
basic goodness
    authentic presence, ground for, 105–106
    belief in, 14
    corporate values, similarities to 105–106
    definition of 23
    discovering, 23–25, 66–67, 73, 105–106,
        187
    Maslow, similarities to notions of, 106
    spiritual traditions, similarities to, 105
    becoming, energy of
        balancing, 13, 86
        definition of, 7,11–12
        heroic journey, and, 16, 175
        hooking/harnessing, 16, 38, 106, 138, 216
        hungry spirit, as a, 7, 11, 106, 138
        purpose seeking energy, as 175
        self-interest, and, 12, 86
        *also see Nurturer, Sage, Teacher, Visionary,
            and Warrior*
Ben & Jerry's, 175
Bennis, Warren, 18, 48, 107, 108, 110
Black Elk, 135
Blanchard, Ken, 27, 110, 116
Block, Peter, 27, 62
Body Shop, 175
Bolman, Lee, 14
Bossidy, Larry, 186, 187
Boyatzis, Richard, 86